Globalization and its Terrors

Teresa Brennan

Routledge
Taylor & Francis Group

LONDON AND NEW YORK

First published 2003
by Routledge
2 Park Square, Milton Park, Abingdon, Oxon, OX14 4RN

Simultaneously published in the USA and Canada
by Routledge
270 Madison Ave, New York NY 10016

Routledge is an imprint of the Taylor & Francis Group

Transferred to Digital Printing 2005

© 2003 Teresa Brennan

Typeset in Times by
BOOK NOW Ltd

British Library Cataloguing in Publication Data
A catalogue record for this book is available from the British Library

Library of Congress Cataloging in Publication Data
Brennan, Teresa, 1952–
     Globalization and its terrors / Teresa Brennan.
        p. cm.
     Includes bibliographical references and index.
     1. Globalization–Economic aspects. 2. Globalization–Environmental aspects.
     3. Globalization–Health aspects. I. Title.

JZ1318.B74 2003
337–dc21   2002028360

ISBN 0-415-28522-4 (hbk)
ISBN 0-415-28523-2 (pbk)

Globalization and its Terrors

It has long been realized that the poorer countries of the South have paid for the unstoppable onward rush of globalization in the exploitation of their natural and human resources. Recent events have made it clear that there is a price to be paid in the West as well.

In this elegant, lucidly presented account, Teresa Brennan argues that the evidence already exists showing that globalization has for years been harming not only the poor of the Third World but also its alleged beneficiaries in the affluent West. She illustrates how the speeding up of contemporary capitalism – in which space is substituted for time – means that neither the environment nor the people who live in it are given the opportunity to regenerate; she shows, moreover, how this leads directly to pollution-induced, immune-deficient and stress-related disease. In a final chapter she suggests some alternative ways forward through a return to region-ally based production, with an emphasis on local economies.

With much talk of religious judgment on either side in the current global conflict, the author argues that global reasoned analysis combined with local action counters economic exploitation. Left to itself, such exploitation produces environmental catastrophe, turning judgment from a prophecy to a probability.

Teresa Brennan is Schmidt Distinguished Professor of Humanities at Florida Atlantic University, where she designed the first "public intellectuals" PhD program for the Dorothy F. Schmidt College of Arts and Letters.

For Columb Henry Brennan:
1913–1998,
Journalist.

This was his book.

Contents

Acknowledgments   ix
Preface: the critique of judgment   xv

1 Introduction   1
A theory of time and space 11
From socialists to localists 13

2 Daily life in the West   19
Deregulation and the theft of time 20
Human health, human stress 21
  Traveling further, migrating more 22
  Working longer, working harder 25
  Unemployment and rising living costs, lack of time,
    indebtedness 26
  Breakdown of communities, growing personal isolation
    and depression 28
  Bodily consequences 29
Reproduction as a generational factor 31

3 The war on the atmosphere   33
The pollution of air 35
Electricity 38
Transportation 40
International trade 41
The failure of a global trade agreement: policy and protest 44

4 The war on the land, sea and other conditions of life   51
Tolerable temperature and stable climate 51
Protection from ultraviolet (UV) radiation 54
Safe water 55
Adequate food 56

viii   *Contents*

Food and genetic engineering 59
Speeding up food supplies – and slowing them down 61

5 **Health cuts and corporate wealth**   66
   Health 69
   Aging, pensions and sick pay 74

6 **Education and the cost of children**   78
   Welfare reform 80
   Education 87
   Conclusion 93

7 **The third way and the feminization of poverty**   96
   Third way formation 98
   Deregulation and social policy 101
   Deregulation and labor mobility in historical context 105
   The third-way conquest of time and space 108

8 **The source of profit**   111
   The labor theory of value 114
   Profit in Marx 119
   Revising Marx 120
   The negative energy capability of substances 122
   The two axes of profit and production 129

9 **Price, inflation and energy**   133
   Speculations on price 134
   *Inflation and a new periodization of the stages of
      capitalism 137*
   Periodization 139
   Immiseration 146

10 **The prime directive**   150
   Gandhi and the advocacy of localism 152
   The real third way and prime directive 156
   Religious and reasoned judgment 161
   The prime directive 163
   *The nostalgia issue and the political standing of the
      directive 165*
   The prime directive in practice 168

   Notes   173
   Index   233

Acknowledgments

Toward the end of this book, I note that my mode of research followed a path of hypothetical deduction (and logical speculation) in the first instance. What I mean by this is that I set out from a theory and turned to the facts in the light of it. The theory as such is set out in *History after Lacan* (1993) and *Exhausting Modernity* (2000). This book is their empirical companion. The logic of the theory that pre-existed my research demanded that states committed to economic globalization would *have* to reduce that proportion of income they give to social provision (or human reproduction) as well as environmental protection (the reproduction of nature). Human reproduction includes the education and health of the next generation, as well as the daily regeneration of the current workforce and their families. If I was right in my theoretical deductions, the USA, Britain and other advanced states should be reducing the expenditure on health and education, as well as welfare. As I was working this out in theory, there was a vast array of social scientists demonstrating that it was beginning in fact, while other critical theorists (Shiva, Plumwood, Buck-Morss, Cornell, Derrida, Harvey, Giddens, Jameson, Altvater) argued, as I do, that this new global world demanded a rethinking of space and time as fundamental to modern social analysis. Consequently, the conclusions of this argument intersect frequently with those of others. Where I am aware of an overlap or indebted to a source, of course I have noted this. But where there are overlaps to authors or organizations of which I am unaware, even though my theory suggests that I should be aware, I would be glad if they could be drawn to my attention through <www.whatistobedone.org> (where additions to the Notes at the end of this book can be listed interactively provided a relevant citation is given). Routledge has the option of issuing a new edition of this book with those names and relevant organizations in five years' time.

On the one hand, the theory that follows here is really in the air. On the other hand, what is distinctive in the theory proffered in this book is the idea that environmental degradation is the *inevitable* consequence of the pursuit of profit. One can either side with Mammon, or with the living against the dead. I arrived at this conclusion through recognizing that Marx's theory was wrong in its essential premise ("labour is the source of all exchange value") but correct in insisting that without the raw materials provided by "nature", there is no profit.

This book was written with the aid of a remarkable research team. They were willing to take on counter-intuitive claims arising from my theory, such as: "Blair has to be spending less on health" – "NAFTA has to be against environmental concerns" – when the rhetoric was entirely the other way. The members of that research team were: Peter Arvantely, Sally Aulich, many Brennans, Vanessa Kaplan, Frederic Kiernan, Polly Kiernan, Sandra Hart, Michele Mattisons, Karima Ridgely, Ilaria Sernia, Tanya Soloman, Laurie Tanner, Woden Teachout, Heather Wdowin and Rosslyn Wuchinich. They were witty, intelligent, and superbly resourceful. Rosslyn Wuchinich did so much for this book that at one point I asked her to co-author it. She declined because she did not think she should take credit for my theoretical work, but as I have tried to point out, this theory is in the air. Enough that an initial version of Chapter 5 is being published as a joint article by us both. Thank you Rosslyn. Good luck with the union. Similarly, Heather Wdowin drafted much of the material on the conditions of life in Chapter 4. Thank you Heather. Good luck with the naturopathy PhD.

Heather's and Rosslyn's posts as my research assistants were paid for by the Schmidt Family Foundation bequest attached to my chair at Florida Atlantic University (FAU). Experience at this working-class school (in a rich community) struggling to become a respected university taught me two things. The first is that there really are honest conservatives who put the right to free speech before considerations of finance. The second is that few people live out the process of democratizing intelligence and all it implies. But some do, and I would like to thank my colleagues and the PhD students I advise (and who also advise me) for all their contributions, and for working through many of these issues: in particular, I thank Henry Abramson, Lynn Appleton, Tom Atkins, Jane Caputi, Fran Chelland, Rod Faulds, Paul Forage, Natalia Gianni, Suzanne Kelly and Lorraine Cobb.

To return to those honest conservatives. Outside the university, in the rich and formerly anthrax-ridden town of Boca Raton, I came to know Daphne and Gary M'aingot, Maria Sachs, Jennifer Augspurger, Scott Bedell, Sandy, Leslie and Joni, and other women and men outside the university. They and their families introduced me to a world of concerned Republican Catholics, who really are worried about the environment and the children of the future. Different as we are, we agree that the way to have people of different races and classes act on their shared concerns was to draw out the commonalities between us: we are concerned, regardless of race, class or creed, for the future of our common children and concerned that they have an environment they can inhabit. Our health, and that of those we are close to, is already affected by pollution. In our case, although we have yet to see how widespread this is, we do not believe that any human being should work in sweatshop conditions, or work for just enough to stay alive without any breaks in which to live and to educate their children or themselves. We think genetic engineering for food is human hubris at its worst: these newly manufactured organisms are only putting an already endangered ecology further at risk. Given that we agreed as well that communism had been an historical disaster, I was able to talk about the explanatory use of Marx's account of capitalism without setting up a red flag. Daphne M'aingot was able to explain why "small business" was wary of "big government", and so forth. We found our common ground, often beyond right and left. But we also emphasised something which need not be common to right and left, and that is compassion. I had been struck, when I was first at university, how the conservatives were often much kinder to women they knew than the socialists, although the socialists had more concern for women and men they did not know. It seemed as if one either had compassion in a personal context, or in a social one; was either kind to one's spouse or changed the world.

While many women especially may agree on what needs to be stopped, many will not agree with my account of the cause of what needs to be stopped (global capitalism). But unless I and others are prepared to offer such accounts, we cannot have the necessary discussion about what needs to change if we are to do away with allergies and illness contingent on environmental pollution, sweatshop labor, genetic engineering, illness, death, and so forth. But offering accounts is not easy. Simply put, it is easier to say what is wrong with an existing theory than it is to propose a theory oneself. In proposing such a theory, I see it as subject to the classical criteria by which theoretical worth is gauged: internal consistency, consistency with the known facts, explanatory force, parsimony, and refutability.

Susan Buck-Morss, who read the mss twice, and whose solidarity equals her intellect, argues that the notion that social being determines social consciousness is simply wrong. Empirically, too many revolutionaries have left their own class. Whatever it is that leads a person to reason to a conclusion not in their immediate material interests, that quality lies in many of the Republican women who go to church groups and "do good". In many cases they are starved of the information they need to direct their desire to change the world toward the good they wish to do. For this reason, I am glad I have lived in South Florida, and glad to have argued baseline Christianity with women who really believe in it, and social justice. Yet in every case where I argued about the effects of globalization (in for instance destroying small business) with a person prepared to follow an argument in Boca, where I came to grief in seeking shared premises was in discussions of sexual orientation. It may be that, if there is to be an effective resistance to globalization that does not involve more terrors, this will mean suspending discussions of sexual orientation and choice generally, and working together on the things we do agree on. For instance, small farmers in South Dakota in the US are effectively using the state legislature to ban genetic engineering. But suspicion of homosexuals has come between them and their natural allies in various environmental groups, and it works on both sides. My belief is that a diminution in the realm of sexual projections which divide the various groups opposed to globalization will or would occur as one works with them, seeking grounds for unity rather than division, finding out that gays do not eat their young. We will see.

Especial thanks to Martin Jay and Robin Blackburn for comments on the initial (1998) drafts, and Chris Wallace-Crabbe, Linda Alcoff, Chris Rowland, and Val Plumwood, for comments on the more recent ones. Donna Bentolila helped undo the Gordian knot that got in the way of completing this book. Mari Shullaw of Routledge was a great editor (Mari, good luck with the theology degree) and James Cooke of Book Now patient and skilful throughout the production process. As ever, thanks to Alice Jardine, Sue James, Quentin Skinner, and other friends for enduring this process, and just enduring.

I began writing this book when Marilyn Strathern invited me to give a paper on reproduction at Cambridge in March 1998. My father died the weekend I presented the paper, and his journalist's shade haunted its subsequent development into a book. I thank him for teaching me to attend to the empirical state of things, and I thank my daughter Sangi, for continuing where he left off, with such love. Woden Teachout was there throughout all final writing and editing, arguing, asking questions, making me think. I suppose it is possible that I could have finished this book without her, but I do not see how.

Preface
The critique of judgment

The need for a global economy is producing an ethic appropriate to a global police force (the NATO military alliance) for that economy. It is now permissible to invade another country and destroy its government. What was and is done in Afghanistan and Palestine is planned for Iraq. The question is not whether one likes the government. The issue is the assumption that one country can interfere forcibly with another country's sovereignty, especially when that country resists Northern or Western economic interests, on the grounds that that country *may* be a threat. Aggressors traditionally justify themselves this way. Now that an ongoing economic war on the South by the North is turning into a military war, the search for ideologies of justification is urgent. The war on terrorism is framed by something claiming to be Christian in the North, just as it is by Islam in the South. These are universalist ideologies appropriate to expansion, and to a pan-national resistance to that expansion. Both sides use vocabularies echoing a series of recent movies claiming that judgment is at hand; the apocalypse is now.

One side initially styled its war on terrorism "Operation Infinite Justice." The other calls its enemy the Great Satan. Both sides are supported by so-called religious leaders, drawing attention to the real incidence of the plagues and fires and weather disturbances prophesied in all major religions as the moment of judgment. The collapse of the twin towers (remembering that the biblical tower is the symbol of human hubris) has been remarked on again and again, more so outside the US than within it, although the idea that God has lifted "the veil of protection" from the US is also current here. The disagreement between proselytizers from the North (the United States, Europe, Russia) and the Islamic-identified terrorists of the South is not over the idea that this may be the moment of judgment. It is over the nature of evil and the source of it. Traditionally, the triumph of evil is followed by its destruction at the moment of the apocalypse, which is also the moment when what has been hidden is revealed. In most religious traditions, the degree of destruction depends on the resistance to evil. That is to say, there is the hope that things will be done differently.

Both sides in this war are quite sure their opponents are evil. But when it comes to saying why they are evil, what it is they do that is evil, and how it can be reversed, their stories diverge on most things. Only on questions of women and sexuality do the fundamentalists of either side begin to converge. Homosexuals and loose women are held responsible for God's turning away from the US, just as they are sometimes blamed for the woes of Islam. After this, agreement comes to an end. President Bush says Iraq, Syria and North Korea are rogue nations, and with al-Qaeda constitute an axis of evil because they destroy innocent life.[1] Al-Qaeda, and the regimes opposed to the US, say it is evil because it destroys innocent life for greed, not only because it supports the state of Israel. The numbers are on their side. When Imams in the South call the United States the Great Satan, they have the support of millions disenfranchised in body and spirit by globalization. For them, the matter is straightforward. The US and Europe exploit the South's labor and resources and in doing so destroy more lives than terrorist attacks can ever destroy. Israel is hated because it took land from the Palestinians more than for any religious reason.[2]

The common denominator, according to Islam-identified critics, is imperialism, a term which is widely used but much misunderstood. The genesis of the term in the works of Lenin and Luxemberg defined it in relation to markets and capital accumulation; the main debate concerned whether or not capital was self-reproducing (Lenin's strict reading of the labour theory of value) or whether it required new markets to sustain a necessary relation of consumption (Luxemberg). Through Frank's dependency theory, and the subsequent work of Wallerstein, the emphasis shifted toward understanding "imperialism" as unequal exchange and unfair trade practices between the first and third worlds, where the first world grew fat by forcing the South to buy dear and sell cheap. This seemed to fit with the realities of a situation where the center benefits from the periphery, but it is an explanation based in exchange, rather than a consistent theory of exploitation through production, as we will see in the Introduction. The point here is that understanding the issues in terms of imperialism obscures the extent to which some Arab countries have different stakes in globalization, in that they provide oil to fuel the global economy. By feeding oil to the West, these countries feed globalization, as we will also see in what follows. They perpetuate it though oil politics which return in the form of a depleted environment and women dispossessed of economic rights, whatever their status in Islamic law (and it varies widely, as Susan Buck-Morss shows) throughout Islam.[3] Moreover, I will show that the consistent opposition to globalization necessarily means a change in the position of women as mothers which recognizes their pivotal economic position. Of the 1.3 billion living on $US1.00 or less daily, 1 billion are women.[4] This book will draw out the structural reason for this, and show that opposing globalization means waging war on terrorism toward those living now in poverty, the great majority of whom are women with children, and all those living in the future.

Globalization, unimpeded, will destroy the climate, hence the lives of billions of humans and thousands of species in their totality. This book demonstrates that fossil fuel emissions are the direct cause not only of climatic crisis but of the increases in numerous diseases in the West (Western Europe, the US, Australasia) and the North (the West, Japan and the erstwhile Soviet world) in other ways, but the tie between fossil-fuel emissions and oil deserves immediate attention, in the context of the present war. The Kyoto Protocol was devised in relation to conservative estimates of the damage done to the future by the present rate of fossil fuel emissions. Conservative as it is, the Protocol is emblematic of an attempt to have human reason overcome human greed. Through the exercise of human judgments, it established a series of deadlines for the reduction in carbon emissions. These deadlines have not been met. *Il Corriere della Sera* puts it this way:

> Three years ago, the world gave itself a calendar to reduce carbonic anhydride and other overheating gasses. But since then, the situation has worsened. The government promised to reduce the deadly emissions by an average of 5 percent before 2010 (starting from 1990 figures). Instead, most countries are burning more oil and more fossil combustibles, and blowing out bigger quantities of greenhouse gasses. The US, Japan, Australia and Canada, which together produce two-thirds of the carbonic anhydride of the industrialized countries, have increased it by 10 percent, the EU by 3 percent.[5]

The Kyoto Protocol represents the human response to a projection forward of how far we can go before global warming accelerates so much that the seas no longer subsidize the food chain as rising heat kills the microorganisms that are the first line of ingestion, while rising sea levels destroy up to a third of the existing land on which human and other species depend for life. This is how things looked in 1997, according to the text of the Protocol:

> Global mean surface temperatures are projected to increase by 1.4–5.8°C by 2100, the fastest rate of change since the end of the last ice age. Global mean sea levels are expected to rise by 9–88 cm by 2100, flooding many low-lying coastal areas. Changes in rainfall patterns are also predicted, increasing the threat of drought or floods in many regions. Overall, the climate is expected to become more variable, with a greater threat of extreme weather events, such as intense storms and heatwaves . . . The effects of climate change are already starting to be felt, for example, in the earlier flowering of plants and egg laying in birds . . . Although some people may benefit from climate change, the IPCC warns that more will suffer, with potentially dramatic negative impacts on human health, food security, economic activity, water resources and physical infrastructure. Farming could be seriously disrupted with falling crop yields in many regions, and tropical diseases, such as malaria or dengue fever, are expected to spread into new areas. Fresh water, already in short supply in many arid and semi-arid regions, is likely to become even scarcer in those regions, while sea level rise and changing weather patterns could trigger large-scale migration from more seriously affected areas. While no one will be able to escape from climate change, it is the poorer people and countries who are most vulnerable to its negative impacts.[6]

Since then, we have had the terrible droughts in Africa, Asia and the United States, the worst storms on record, the hottest years on record, the North Pole is melting, tropical diseases are migrating to the warmer West, millions die from air pollution annually, and still the US does not sign the Kyoto Protocol. At the time of going to press, all Europe was united behind its immediate ratification. "But" as one observer sums up, "Kyoto will only become legally binding when it has been ratified by 55 percent of the signatories, representing 55 percent of developed countries' 1990 carbon dioxide emissions." As America produces one-third of all emissions, almost all other developed countries must ratify Kyoto if it is to come into legal force, which is why the EU decision was "welcomed by environmental groups, who hope that moral pressure will force America to reverse its policy. Michel Raquet of Green-peace said: 'After President Bush slammed the door on the Kyoto Protocol in March 2001, and the very bad joke of the Bush–Exxon climate plan last month, it is now time for the USA to come back to the Kyoto Protocol.'[7]

At the very moment where it should reverse course by signing the Kyoto Protocol before it ceases having a chance to be effective, the US is escalating a war over and in oil rich regions or nations such as Afghanistan with access to oil rich regions. By this escalation, it is increasing fossil fuel emissions in the present, and attempting to guarantee their continued rate of emission into the future. Here, it is worth remembering that the term, "rogue nation," was also applied to the US in the 1990s with respect to its refusal to sign the Protocol.[8]

Rapid transport from here-to-there is the condition of the global economy and of the proliferation of global pollutants. Today's news (August 15th, 2002) announced that the US President is only one procedural step away from securing fast-track authority to negotiate trade agreements. The consumption of fossil fuels is the condition of rapid transport over global distances. To use less fuel is to use less transport, or less noxious transport. To use less transport means finding raw materials and labour closer to hand. It means turning from a global to a local economy, and hence reversing the logic of the freetrade expansion of the last fifty years. I will try to show in this book that we cannot have it both ways. It is either globalization or the climate, either land use for cashcrops for the North or the subsistence foods of the South, either the decimation of species or their survival. In the West, it is either the short-term benefits of the global market, or a future for those as yet unborn.

This book suggests that, at a certain cumulative point, fossil fuel emissions really will destroy the life of the future. As they do so, aided by other aspects of Western capitalism, they bring into being the blood-red moon, the boiling seas littered with dead fish, the plagues, famine and drought, the people who have to pay for water: all listed in the apocalyptic events of the Book of Revelation.[9] Global warming, the thing responsible, is mentioned as marking the end-time in Judaism's *Ein Yaakov*, insofar as it warns of great heat. To read Revelation and similar texts as visions of this future, here and soon, is to begin removing prophecy from the sphere of the inexplicable. As Freud noted, there are visions of probable futures in dreams and involuntary conscious images. Einstein added that everyday life in space and time is in some way a fantasy.* Freud attempted to find a rational line of cause and effect in accounting for premonitions and was unsuccessful. But that does not mean these things lie forever beyond human ken, anymore than the cause and effect leading to environmental disaster is beyond the reasoning of those prepared to read. The coincidence of the Protocol and the texts of apocalypse exists, I suggest, because reason is godlike and because God also works by reason and in fact is reason, even though much of this reason has remained beyond the comprehension of human creatures.

Where rationality could not provide an anchor for faith, the followers of Moses, Christ and Mohammed have accepted that there are reasons that surpass human understanding. They have even gone to war over their faith in credos which their reason could not support. At least, Christianity and Islam have gone to war, seeking to expand their territories in the name of the supremacy of their prophets. Until recently, the followers of Moses did not persecute others of different faiths. I am one of those who believes that after the holocaust, there had to be a state of Israel, but that such a state had to conduct itself in the spirit in which it was established. The role of Freud, Einstein and other secular prophets in taking one closer to understanding the logical relation between prophecy and probability suggests to this writer that the Jews are the chosen of the intellect, not the conquerors of the territories.** Zionist assertions of historical supremacy not only mirror the claims of Aryanism in relation to Poland, and like Nazism, justify grabbing one's neighbours' lands. They also mark the divergence between Judaism as a faith which insisted on memory, reason, argument and deduction as godly things, and Judaism used to

---

* There is more on this issue in my *Exhausting Modernity*, (London: Routledge, 2000) and the *Transmission of Affect* (Ithaca, NY: Cornell University Press, 2003) and in a forthcoming brief book on social pressure, which completes this trilogy. *Globalization and its Terrors* is a maverick in that sequence intended to show that the theory developed in the trilogy is relevant to the present.

** I return to this question briefly in the last chapter (p. 162), having raised the notion that for Jesus, revelation comes through the Jews because it comes through reasoned truth as well as inspiration or spirit (John 4:21–3). In this passage as I read it, spirit (*pneúma*) is a necessary but not sufficient condition of revelation, which also requires truth (*alitheia*). In the Greek philosophical context, *alitheia* is tied to the distinction between *doxa* and *episteme*, especially to episteme as the finer, rational or logical form of knowledge. In both Plato's *Theatetus* and Aristotle's *Metaphysics* truth lies in judgment; that is to say, the joining together of concepts in relation to sense reality. (See also *De anima* 3, 430a). Alitheia in short connotes a process dependant on reason, which suggests Christ is saying that inspiration is not enough. One is also obliged to think.

justify national expansion. Aryan supremacy to this day is asserted in relation to semites, who are Arabs as well as Jews. Allah allocated land through the left-hand line of Hagar and Abraham, as surely as God gave Israel to the right.[10]

By following its deductive chain, by reaching the conclusion that the environmental disasters prophesied in various religions are our own work, this book seeks to persuade those whose reason led them from faith that the metaphysical issues of religion are in fact issues for the here and now, and that the coincidence between the prophecies of the religions of the Book (and the West) and the realities of climate change is great enough to require an explanation. This argument also seeks to persuade those whose faith leads them to acts of suicide that they are perpetuating and expanding negative emotions and affects (fear, anger, the anxiety and pain which interfere with thinking) of which they are also victims. But it has begun by drawing attention to the coincidence between the prophecies of Kyoto and those of Revelation, prophecies which are common, with different stresses, to the three religions of the Book. I take the coincidence of human-made catastrophe and revelation as indicative of the way that humans are invested with more decision-making power than customary models of religion allow. If human beings have this much agency in shaping their fate, we should assume that the deadlines we set ourselves for reversing course are judgments whose day has indeed been determined – by ourselves.

The future may invest the timing of the attacks on the US, and the fact that they coincide with the unmet passing of the Kyoto deadlines, with an understanding based on more thoroughgoing awareness of the laws of life and balance, and what happens when toxicity passes a certain limit and the preservation of the future is at stake. It may be that arguments from reason and observation will yield something now that persuades the US to reverse course, and realign its trajectory with the side of life by reducing its fossil-fuel emissions; ex-President Clinton now calls on the US to "lead the world rather than run the world in this century." Or it may be that the desire for cheap gas and profit will win out over the claims of unborn generations to come and those living in poverty now, in which case the US will continue to attract odium to itself for arrogance; it may defer but not defeat a judgment which will worsen in proportion to the degree it postpones right action. Either way, judgment comes upon us through our own hands.

Eleuthera
August 2002

1 Introduction

"An unseen hand that strikes from nowhere without accountability, destroying innocent lives." That is the incumbent US president's definition of terrorism.[1] From the perspective of the South, it is also a definition of globalization, insofar as the invisible hand of the market destroys the conditions of life for human beings, among other species. Other species are destroyed at a rate now reckoned in hours.[2] The destruction of the life conditions of human beings proceeds more slowly, although the invisible hand leads to loss of human life as abrupt as that caused by the unseen hands of terrorism. It does so directly, through industrial and nuclear accidents. It also precipitates more rapid death in other ways. In India since1998, over one thousand farmers have committed suicide since losing their livelihood to corporate agribusiness.[3] For others, including those who die of globalization's effects on ill health in the North, the market's unseen hand takes its time.

For the main part this book concentrates on the detrimental effects of economic globalization (which I will define shortly) on human life in those countries which purport to benefit from it. The new anxieties over terrorist attacks are only the latest in a series of fears generated by globalization in the West. They overlay increasing chronic ill health, longer working hours, greater debt, running hard to stay in the same place. They go hand in hand with cutbacks in welfare and education and health benefits.[4] Globalization not only generates these day-to-day anxieties, but abets terrorism, which is a self-conscious response to global economic policy.[5] The terrorist attacks on the World Trade Center were explicitly attacks on the symbol of the global economy. They were an attempt to do to the North, or the West, what the North has done to the South: destroy life without accountability.

The global economy, as a cause of terrorism, was given prominence in the Middle Eastern press response to the collapse of the twin towers.[6] But while the link between terrorism and economic globalization was forefronted in the Middle East, it has been given scant concern in the West, where the emphasis is on the Palestinian–Israeli conflict. Terrorism is portrayed solely as the work of Islam-identified extremists and fanatics hostile to Israel, a representation which leaves out the fact that recruitment by the relevant organizations depends partly on the unemployment generated by free trade. Cocooned by candy-floss news, the large majority of people in the United States are unaware of this, just as they are unaware of the damage done in the name of US economic interests. Americans are told by their president that they are hated for their freedom, not that they are hated because they use over a third of the world's nonsustainable resources for 7 percent of its population, or because the pitiful wages paid in the Third World subsidize the inexpensive cuisine and low-priced goods to which US citizens are accustomed.[7] Nor are Americans told that the same cuisine depends on cash-crop agribusiness displacing the subsistence farming at base not only of a varied diet, but often any diet in the Third World. If chat rooms and radio talk shows are an in indicator, Americans generally are convinced that they feed the South through aid programs, not that they are responsible for starvation.

In the heterogeny that is its real strength, the US does not only live in ignorance. Before September 11th, it had produced the most active and effective of the resistance movements to globalization. That same movement, at and after the demonstrations against free trade at Seattle in December 1999, generated increasing awareness of the harm done in the name of the US. It highlighted how the global economy damaged the interests and lives of the majority of those in the United States, where more people sink below the poverty line or struggle harder to stay in the middle classes each year.[8] The movement was beginning to draw out the ill effects on Western health. But attending to the ill effects of globalization in the West as well as the South has been diverted by the war on terrorism. The sanity of the opposition to globalization has been undermined by the violence of the terrorist response to it. One of the many tragedies engendered by the attacks on the World Trade Center is that they have made it harder to oppose globalization, although globalization was such a prominent factor in motivating the attacks in the first place.

Terrorism does not need to bring the consequences of globalization back home. They are already here. I will show in this book that physical illness in the West increases as global profit grows, and that there is a strong case for believing that mental illness grows as well. I will also show that there is a relationship between globalization (which in this book means economic globalization) and the destruction of the climate by pollution. Indeed, there is an observable relation between globalization and the rise of environmental, immune-deficient, stress-induced and depressive disease. We are dealing with a causal chain, in which globalization increases profit because it speeds up production and distribution. As production and distribution speed up, so do fossil fuel emissions, whose quantitative increase far outweighs the positive changes in emissions control. Hence more pollution and climate damage. Hence environmental illness. Of course profits were made by speeding up production and distribution before globalization, just as environmental sickness preceded the growth in trade that has marked the past thirty years. But globalisation makes it worse.

As defined in this book, globalization is the continuation and logical outcome of a process of extension, a process which begins with the division between household and workplace, grows through specialization in production, then through colonialism, concentrations in land use, through urbanization and suburbanization, and though other forms of spatial reach. Against the use of globalization, it has been argued that "the concept of imperialism, with its focus on the value creation of labor and the value appropriation by capital, is more to the point: it sheds logic on the different loci of exploitation (labor, dominated countries) and accumulation (capital, imperial firms and states)."[9] The reason I use the term globalization in preference to the term imperialism is that globalization encapsulates the spatio-temporal logic which imperialism, as a theory of capital accumulation and/or underconsumption, either ignores or substitutes for an understanding of value extracted at the point of production.[10] While the economic theory that follows is anchored in a theory of value, it is also a theory of how expansion is the unavoidable accompaniment of speeding up the extraction of profit in production. Speeding up production necessarily means going further afield for markets and raw materials. By globalization, then, I mean an economic dynamic whereby the increasing speed of production entails expansion as a matter of course, while expansion necessitates more rapid production and distribution to sustain itself. There will be more on this in the next section.

Traversing greater distances at increasing speeds means consuming more oil and generating more fossil fuels. Even if some businesses produce without pollution, they cannot avoid the demands of the more rapid distribution instigated by their global competition. The more global distribution becomes, the more fossil fuels are used for transportation, even if a particular production process is free of them. The fact that more fossil fuels are needed to maintain and extend the global economy is flagged by fears of oil shortages. Before this war, the US President had already declared his intention of drilling for oil in the Alaskan wilderness and off the Florida coast. In addition, the control of oil pipelines is at issue in the war against terrorism. In this, present struggles for hegemony in Central Asia repeat a pattern that has been ongoing for a century. The "Great Game" of the latter part of the free trade *belle époque* of the later nineteenth century was about moving the chess pieces (as sometime Viceroy to India Curzon put it) around the Central Asian board.[11] The "New Great Game," as Ahmed Rashid termed it, is over transportation and access to oil from the Caspian and nations surrounding it.[12] The Taliban was allied with and supported extremist organizations, but it also broke its promise, given to the US in return for aid, to support an oil pipeline proposal originally mooted by a multinational consortium evaluating construction of a Central Asia Gas (CentGas) pipeline between Turkmenistan and Pakistan. (This is known as the Unocal project, although Unocal has since withdrawn.) Part of this pipeline would have crossed western Afghanistan.[13] Bombing Afghanistan accomplished the aim of installing a government which has already signified full backing for the pipeline proposal. Whatever its other outcomes, the war on terrorism is fostering oil acquisition, which in turn feeds speedier production and more rapid transportation, and greater fossil-fuel emissions. Iraq only produces 3.9 percent of the world's oil, but control of Iraq is critical to control of the region that produces most of it.

Fossil-fuel emissions are not the only consequence of speed. Speeding up production, and global production in particular, contributes to other forms of chemical pollution, leading in turn to rapidly increasing levels of cancer, allergies and immune disorders. The "green-washing"[14] directed by corporations and governments toward the growing majority concerned with increasing ill health denies any connection between health and economic globalization. Indeed there are arguments that "natural capitalism" and "green" investment portfolios can solve the present environmental crisis . . . with a little goodwill thrown in. They can certainly help, and the following argument should not be taken as an argument against the implementation of less polluting technologies in any context. If the first priority of meeting the Kyoto Protocol is assisted – and it is – by technologies which reduce emissions without changing the basic system of production, only the perverse would argue against their introduction. Nonetheless the idea that these technologies will stop environmental degradation of themselves neglects the real barrier to their implementation. In any system of extension, from centralization to globalization, profit is made by speeding up the rate of extraction of natural, especially biological, resources (such as trees, plants, fish, animals, and so forth), as well as the "productivity" of human labor, and thus taking more from nature than one returns.

The idea that there is any necessary connection between globalization, the destruction of the climate, and mental and physical ill health is not only denied by monetarist-influenced policy. The same is true for the new center-left embodied in the US Democratic Party, the British Labour Party and a growing number of erstwhile social democratic organizations. The center-left makes more concerned environmental noises but, like the new right, it believes in globalization. This combination of the right noise and the wrong direction is what Blair made known as the "third way".[15] The "third way", as a putative solution, has also been mooted by US democrats. It supports globalization while nominally supporting the environment. But one cannot have it both ways. To support globalization and free trade is to foster climate destruction (and hence eventually the destruction of most species). As I will show in the first part of this book, there is no avoiding their link, except in the most fanciful technophile imagination. Not only this, but, as the links are followed through, it is plain that that global capitalism attacks all the conditions of life: from climate through to air, food and water. Any war, from Iraq through to Afghanistan, increases those attacks through increasing fossil fuel and other toxic emissions, and diverts attention away from the damage done to long-term survival by the global economy war protects and extends, while securing more fossil fuels for the future.

The fact is that globalization is about securing more oil to keep profits going at the expense of the young and unborn. Additionally, globalization is about cheap labor markets and forcing down wages and salaries. It is about reductions in corporate tax, increases in taxes for the employed, and cuts in social services. Most of all it is about using up the earth's resources at an increasing speed and at a massive environmental price.

The myth is that globalization is about cell-phones and little teeny microchips, rather than the heavy-duty transport of natural and biological resources.[16] This is not true. Computers have drastically increased the use of coal,[17] and in this they are typical telecommunications products, relying on electricity which in turn relies on fossil fuels. Aside from that, by 1990, over a quarter of goods traded were natural "'primary products' such as timber, fish and copper."[18] Nearly three-quarters of goods traded are manufactured products. Of these, machinery and transport constitute 35 percent of all goods traded, while chemicals, iron and steel and other semi-manufactures constitute 17 percent, and clothing and textiles 6 percent.[19] Manufactured goods are made from biological and natural resources, which means they also draw on natural reserves.[20] "With the important exceptions of minerals and petrochemical products, virtually all the raw materials used in industry are of biological origin, coming from the agricultural and forestry sectors."[21] The goods that now move more rapidly around the globe include everything from croissants to refrigerators: electrical goods made in Japan and the US go to Egypt and Nigeria; Nigeria in turn exports its trees. Or it did. Exports have now fallen drastically in response to overlogging.[22] Even the most cursory survey of the increased global traffic in commodities shows that globalization is about far more than clean, new information technologies. Any move to expand the territories covered by trade agreements, or conquer the ones that are non-compliant, results in more rapid exhaustion of natural resources, and more transportation of heavy goods and services, as well as the less noxious ones.[23]

Contemporary celebrants of globalization have claimed additionally that free trade ensures adequate commerce between the "brain" countries and "body" countries, as one book styles them.[24] The "brain" countries, of course, are the rich ones, and their riches are due to their brains. But these rich "brains" have their own bodies, bodies which are made daily weaker by their polluted environments. Meantime, the underfed and underused brains of the "body" countries are denied the time and income with which they might pursue an education. They sell – cheap – the natural resources and physical labor which might pay for that education, were it not supporting the First World "brains." They are not in a position to seek an education. Not only this, but the labor market for unskilled and semiskilled labor is far more extensive than the demand for skilled and educated labor. Unskilled and semiskilled labor is used in the production of the goods and services which meet basic human needs. These goods, in turn, constitute the bulk of the world's domestic and global trade, trade which helps human "brains" to be embodied, fed, clothed, housed and serviced.

Free trade not only increases the traffic in natural resources, thereby depleting the global environment. It not only accelerates the fossil-fuel consumption needed to transport those resources.

It also accelerates the traffic of human beings, who also use up fuel making their way to centralized workplaces. As we noted, historically, centralization is the first stage of the same dynamic that brings globalization into being. The more centralized production is, the bigger the company has to be in order to compete, and the more mergers and acquisitions take place. Jobs become fewer, and you have to go further to get them. Both the new right and the third way promote centralization and globalization at the same time as they cut back on spending for human needs, from basic education to welfare and healthcare. They cut back just as everyone gets sicker, and more depressed, and now more paranoid, for fear of more attacks.

The same global process which accelerates pollution also results in increasing inequality in income and access to healthcare. It results in cuts in social provision, otherwise known as the welfare state, throughout the OECD countries as well as increasing poverty in the South. The reason most of this book pertains to the Western world, to those who have ostensibly benefited from global capitalism to date, is twofold. First, many in the North are unaware of how negative the impact of globalization on their lives and health is and has been. They are even more oblivious now the focus is on terrorism. Second, the South or Third World, like the Second World or former Eastern bloc, is daily made an empty promise: the promise is that they, too, if they follow the global path, will be rich and prosperous. The promise is false not only because the North's prosperity, in large part, is made at the expense of the South. It is also false because life, for more and more of the North's inhabitants, is increasingly insecure, unhealthy, ill-educated, and impoverished. As there are already excellent accounts of the effects of globalization on the South, especially in the work of Martin Khor,[25] it seemed of more use to the South to expose a false promise for what it is. In addition, with the threat of terrorist attacks reiterated daily in the US, and general fears concerning them gathering in Britain and France, the West at home forgets what it was suffering before it was distracted. It was distracted of course by a threat which now justifies a war on third world countries, a war whose interests cannot be separated from US and Northern oil interests – interests which are advantaged by this war even if they did not of themselves cause it.

In health terms, all those in the West (Europe, the US), like those of the South or Third World, are negatively affected by centralization and globalization, no matter how much money they make. Yet this fact is downplayed or disowned, as popular and political thought proclaim that the globalizing path is the only path. Capitalism is not only right, we are told, but natural. Naturally, capitalism will go global wherever it can, exercising its right to produce as much wealth as possible. It is true that capitalism as a system strives to go global. But capitalism is not the only form of market economy. There are some markets which do not incline toward globalization. The existence of these markets is not advertised in a world where globalization is ruthlessly promoted, and any alternative economic vision suppressed. Islam's spectacular recruitment rates are partially affected by its opposition to Western capitalism. But the alternative vision offered by Islam-identified opponents of globalization is compromised by its attitude to women. As we will see, the position of women, economically, is critical in any effective resistance to global capital. This will emerge through a reworking of Marx's economics, which shows how the reproduction time of human labor is a drag on capital's profit. At the same time, *contra* Marx, I will show that the basis of long-term profit lies in nature as well as labor. But nature can be consumed without regard to its reproduction time, while this is harder in the case of human beings. In the short-run, however, profit is made by consuming the sources of long-run profit (nature and labor) faster than they can adequately reproduce themselves – or, to say the same thing, faster than the time it takes to meet human needs and safeguard the environment.

Like the new right, social democracy now fosters rather than challenges the way globalization uses up biological and other natural resources; how it breaks up communities, increases poverty, especially women's poverty, and how it has devastating environmental consequences, leading to an increase in chronic ill-health in the North and death in the South. These social democrats justify the damage generated by multinational corporations and global investment by the promise of the "trickle-down" effect. Eventually, they say, globalization will lead to wealth within the poorer countries, and more wealth in the richer ones. But even a weak arithmetician can gauge that this is highly unlikely, when globalization has produced massive job loss in the First World, and when most of the new wealth produced by the South's labor and natural resources is removed to the First World.

Terrorism aside, there are various responses to globalization and its consequences. Traditional conservatives stress the importance of community; the remaining actual social democrats emphasize the need for a more equitable distribution of wealth. Members of both groups speak for environmental protection and unified environmental standards in all countries. This is the condition of human health, as I will show, although human health, as such, has yet to generate its own political movement. But, as they stand, the extant responses to globalization are not integrated, and their protagonists are frequently bitterly opposed. The opposition is yet further fragmented by the onset of terrorist attacks on the large scale. An integrated response requires a new economic vision, a real third way between capitalism and socialism. The trouble is that, if one accepts the Democrat and "New Labour" third way, the search is over before it has really begun. In the words of New Labour's leading intellectual, Anthony Giddens, the "third way" assumes that "there is no alternative to capitalism."[26] Other, presumably, than that offered by some versions of Islam.

Whatever the disasters of socialism, whatever its rigidity and lack of innovation, it did at least provide an alternative vision to Islam-identified fundamentalism and to capitalism: a second way. But the costs of the second way were so great that the first way had to seem better, even if its consequences are proving worse in health terms and as bad politically. As John Gray notes, the "open" or democratic society is endangered by capitalism as well as socialism. Free trade and capital's needs can be better served by autocratic regimes, as they have been and are in East Asia and Latin America.[27] They are also served by war, when this secures access to regions which otherwise resist the blandishments of global capital. In the North, there is no real challenge to the present course of capital. The new right monetarists insist that free trade is the natural way to go. Deploying a different vocabulary, social "third way" democrats agree. To be against globalization is to be somehow provincial and definitely behind the times. It is also to be in a dubious position in the war on terrorism. "War Slows Down Globalization Crowd," headlined the *International Herald Tribune*, noting that patriotism and a desire not to be identified with terrorism had affected the energy and mobilization of a movement hitherto stronger in the US than elsewhere.[28]

The antiglobalization movement now seeks to articulate a challenge to globalization which is also an alternative to the terrorist response to it. In articulating that challenge, certain spatiotemporal facts should be salient. Capital needs rapid, unimpeded access to all global spaces, and this it secures either through trade agreements or through war. The social costs of healthcare, welfare and pensions give people time to grow up, be well, and grow old with relative stability. But they are unattractive costs, so social democracy takes them away, just as the new right did – and does. Human time is sacrificed to spatial expansion. History is here repeating itself. In the second half of the nineteenth century, the British state followed the enactment of Draconian poor laws with an extensive liberalization of free trade. As Gray argues, we find the same double move present today: the implementation of treaties extending the sphere of free trade coincides with serious cuts in social provision.[29] What Gray did not note then, but now surely will, is that the free trade policies of this era are leading to war, just as the trade expansion of the *belle époque* fed directly into the causes of the First World War conducted among European states.

The double move sacrificing time for regeneration to spatial expansion is also revealed in increasing environmental illness on the one hand and reduced healthcare on the other. The first is due to the way profit and pollution alike are increased by speedy expansion through space. The second, reduced healthcare, is one instance of the general reduction in time and money for human needs. But it is the most interesting, and telling, instance; interesting because it shows how the species in its Western variant, and increasingly so elsewhere, seems bent on the destruction of its individual members at home and that of whole countries abroad. The paradox of the present situation is that the production of greater (unevenly distributed) wealth has adverse health effects for most, even including those who benefit from the wealth. This is not to say that the rich are without privilege in the flight to filtered water and organic foods; nor is it to say that all are equally at risk from air pollution. As Plumwood has shown, they are not.[30] The point, rather, is that, in the long run, there may be a contradiction between an individual's right to live well and that same individual's right to live at all.[31] Constituting a physical danger to oneself, let alone others, is intrinsic to the legal definition of insanity, when the body is at risk from the mind. And if the well-off mind knows, however unconsciously, that it is endangering the body, this would only increase its anxiety, depression and, for that matter, paranoia. It knows it is under attack from somewhere, it knows life is at stake, but it looks for the source of its fears anywhere but in its own conduct.

That said: globalization favors (although it reduces the numbers of) the well off. The present cuts in social provision for human needs are exacerbated by cuts in corporate taxation. Soros notes that "the ability of the state to provide for the welfare of its citizens has been severely impaired by the ability of capital to escape taxation and onerous employment conditions by moving elsewhere."[32] The burden of taxation has shifted from capital to citizens.[33] The overtaxed middle classes are invited to castigate anything other than corporations, welfare recipients first among them. But in some countries cuts in corporate taxes have reduced revenues from 18 to as much as 30 per cent. Like the working classes, the middle classes are already feeling the globalizing pinch in other ways; either it impacts them directly, or their smaller businesses are negatively affected by it. Or they are sick. It is these middle-class taxpayers to whom new right and now center-left governments appeal with their talk of "no rights without responsibilities." No rights . . . except for multinational corporations, which neither stand their share of social costs, nor are much affected by shortages of minimally educated, often chronically ill, labor.

A multinational corporation can, after all, pay less in taxes somewhere else, and get labor and raw materials there as well. It does not have to wait for them to regrow (in the case of many natural raw materials) or simply grow up (in the case of people). Nor does it have to wait for them to rest and repair themselves. Waiting takes time. Crossing the globe to get labor and raw materials cuts that time. If it saves money, there is even less reason to wait. Reversing the course of globalization, as I said at the outset, means focusing on how *globalizing capital substitutes speed and space for time*. A real third way has to counter the substitution of space for time, but it can do this only if it grapples with how this substitution is the key to global capital's profit.

A theory of time and space

This failure to challenge the dynamics underpinning capitalism is due to the failure to understand how they are making life over in favor of death, both at the level of everyday life, and by business as usual. In turn, this failure is partially tied to the victory of "perfect competition economics" – and its various mainstream offshoots – over classical political economy: the theories of Smith, Ricardo, Marx and others. Mainstream economics regards the realities of natural time, the environment and healthcare as "externalities." There are attempts to recuperate these externalities; those invested in the idea of natural capitalism want nature to count as a cost in production.[34] But these attempts at recuperating nature as economically intrinsic seem ignorant of the history of classical political economy, which begins with nature. Together with capital's most trenchant critic, Karl Marx, this natural premise has been neglected by economists, although this is changing. Marx's present readership is less likely to lie with capital's critics than with its proponents, who find his diagnosis useful: even *Newsweek* proclaims "there is no better analyst of capital." My argument here is that Marx's diagnosis is even more useful if its fundamental premises are reworked, and that this reworking will take us to the core of the spatiotemporal dynamics of capital.

Marx's economic theory is commonly known as the labor theory of value. As its name implies, this theory sees labor as the source of exchange-value and profit. What is deeply radical about this theory, the thing which takes it to the underlying dynamics of how profit is made, is the notion that money and technology of themselves are not the source of wealth. Money, strictly speaking, is nothing. The value money has must be determined by something other than itself. For Marx, of course, this something was labor.[35] In my reworking of it, the labor theory of value becomes a theory of time, space and speed. Time and space only become salient, however, because nature is treated in the same way Marx treated labor. For Marx, profit is realized through the disjunction between what labor adds in production and the cost of labor's reproduction. Reproduction, in classical political economy, involves both the reproduction of the next generation and the daily repair of human beings, estimated in terms of food, shelter, clothing, healthcare and education: the sum of human needs. The reproduction costs of labor – at the daily or generational level – can be estimated. These costs determine wages. I am proposing that the reproduction costs of nature could be calculated in the same way. This would mean that the cost of nature, like labor, is what nature needs to reproduce.

In my theory, time and speed matter because of an ongoing tension between the speed of production and the way that the reproduction of natural resources, including labor-power, cannot keep pace with that speed. In the case of other natural resources apart from labor-power, this tension may be resolved by going further afield. Rather than waiting for the natural sources and resources at issue to regenerate on the local scale, one finds them somewhere else, "over there." Trade, investment, and manufacturing agreements extend the global reach of capitalists who have exhausted local resources. But this procedure does not work easily for the reproduction of national labor-power, precisely because this reproduction takes time.

This means that the cost of reproducing and educating labor at home becomes a drag on the speed with which profit could be made. So do the costs of healthcare, welfare and pensions. When Soros and Gray note that the taxation of corporations is now insufficient to subsidize welfare states,[36] they are of course right.

However, there is a deeper cause: the substitution of speed and space for time. Modern politicians are not ignorant on this. "After each crisis, it is clear that capital flows have to be connected with direct production, that is, trade flows," says President Cardoso of Brazil. France's former Premier Jospin reaches similar conclusions: "The speed of trade lags behind capital flows, but this does not mean we should speed up trade."[37] But Jospin and Cardoso overlook what "speed" does at a third level: the reproduction of people and natural resources. The gap between trade and finance is disastrous, but there is something worse: this is the gap between the speed at which natural resources and human beings are used up and the time they need to regenerate. This gap contributes to ill health not only through the pollution it generates. Rifkin has argued that the distance between natural biorhythms and the accelerated timelines of modern life affects human health through increasing stress and entropy.[38] If it is correct to say that human reproduction is out of time with the central speedy dynamic of capital, then we can predict that there will be more cuts in social provision, from pensions and welfare to healthcare and education; we can predict, too, that there will be a constant push for new resources and new markets, whether these are won through war or more multilateral agreements. In either case, pollution will proceed apace. In this all too likely event, ill health will increase as production and distribution accelerate across space, just at the point where healthcare is reduced.

From socialists to localists

A real alternative to global capitalism would have to address the realities of time and space very differently. It would have to go to the heart of the spatiotemporal profit imperative and overturn it. This would mean limiting the distance from which profits could be extracted, and allowing for the natural reproduction time of things and people. Limiting distance and allowing for time entails slowing down the speed of both production and consumption. It also guarantees the preservation of the environment, as well as the well-being of those within it. It means making production local and regional rather than global. I am of course not the first to advocate local and regional limitations. The idea that production needs to return to the local is the theme of (among other works) Mander's and Goldsmith's *The Case Against the Global Economy*, and of Lang's and Hines's *The New Protectionism*. It is also advocated by many action groups opposed to globalization, from Friends of the

Earth to Greenpeace. Proponents of a locally based economy are evident from the rise of industrialization.[39] Of these, it is perhaps Gandhi who focuses most directly on speed – and the elimination of barriers based on distance – as the heart of the problem.[40] The problem is that Gandhi had no plan for getting from A to B, from where we are now to where we might be. In the work of Schumacher, who is Gandhi's principal economic successor, there is an attempt at tracing paths beyond engrossment, but these do not have a structural basis in existing conditions, something they can grow out of, something that already exists. Here, proponents of localism turn too frequently to taxation (although there are exceptions), and redefining the role of international organizations.[41] Such proposals are found in the work of Lang and Hines, for instance. But they are also found in localism's more sympathetic and best opponents: the supporters of "natural capitalism." Shortly, I will outline a structural solution which takes us beyond the system as it stands. But my first point is that taxation is not the solution. This year's tax reforms are next year's election fodder, easily thrown over, and a constant source of resentment among the small business class as well as the multinational corporations. As a rule the taxation of business works to unite the interests of local or regional businesses with those of global corporations, although, as we shall see here, their interests are fundamentally opposed. But taxation forces them into sympathy with one another. It makes them feel their interests are one and the same. There are also fundamental oppositions among the very wealthy, who, whenever the word tax is mentioned, fall into alliances which are less natural than they appear to be. Here, too, basic oppositions are obscured by the failure to grapple with the dynamics underlying the extraction of profit.

While Gandhi did not engage with these dynamics in depth, he was aware that time and speeds were at their heart, so much so that there is a concordance between Marx and Gandhi. More accurately, there is an agreement between Gandhi and the conclusions I reach on the basis of reworking Marx. Why take this route to reach Gandhi's conclusions? First, because in India, among other Third World countries, Marxists continue to believe in centralization as a solution, and hence oppose the followers of Gandhi, whom they would do well to work with; second, for the simple reason that reaching Gandhi through Marx is a route which identifies trends and enables predictions about the turns global capital must take next. Reworking the labor theory of value enables us to identify a genuine third way between socialism and capitalism, a third way which opposes globalization and redistributes wealth, but also draws on market principles without sacrificing women and children. Under certain circumstances, local and regionally based production can accomplish this. Where natural resources and human beings are concerned, local production puts a limit on the rate at which natural resources are consumed, precisely because one cannot exhaust one's own supplies and go elsewhere. None of this means that international trade, or travel, or the education that comes with understanding cultural difference firsthand should cease. Nor does it mean technological innovations will cease.

Critics of socialism point out that, as an economic system, it discouraged entrepreneurship and technological creativity. But we should not conclude that the only alternative to uncreative socialism is a process of global exploitation. One can be just as creative, in fact more so, in a local enterprise than one can in a management-constrained multinational. The market, as we noted at the outset, is not the same thing as capitalism.[42] The principal form of market economy that predated capitalism, and might succeed it, had a different relation to space and time. It depended on the regeneration of natural resources close to home. Because of this dependence, it could not exhaust those resources entirely. It had to wait. This different relation to time is why a market anchored in local and regional production is opposed to, rather than an extension of, global capitalization in general.

An oft-repeated Marxist mistake is to assume that all local or "petty commodity production" merely paves the way for big business. But, historically, local and regional production for local and regional markets is antagonistic to capitalism, for the same reason that unchecked capital necessarily turns into globalism. The reason is this: if space and the acquisition of goods and services through space takes the place of time, production speeds up, as we have seen. As we will see, the faster production is, the more short-term profit it makes (and the sicker we and the world become). This is not the case with a business which is constrained by time, and which has to wait for its raw materials to regenerate. But if the two come into competition, the interests of a business which has to wait are opposed to the interests of a business which can discount waiting time through going elsewhere.

The point at which the earlier form of market gives way to capital is the point at which some businesses begin substituting speed and space for time. Obviously, to do this, they had to find substitute resources beyond their immediate sphere of operations. But, in addition, their holdings had to be sufficient to carry the preliminary costs of expansion. Finding a real third way means reversing this procedure. It means substituting time for space; that is to say, allowing for the reproduction time of biological resources, and limiting their acquisition across space. Necessarily, this will slow down the pace of production, although, as we will see, this reversal will increase real wealth in the long term. I will argue that the structural basis for a real third way lies in the fact that, while businesses governed by speed cannot afford to wait for nature to replenish, or pause to take a less polluting path, especially when they are at war, those enterprises which are governed by the time of natural reproduction can do so. The line between natural time and artificial acceleration through space identifies which enterprises work for, and which oppose, a process that pollutes and exploits. It shows which contribute to illness. It also shows how environmental interests are allied with those of social justice. Social justice, in this book, means giving back to human beings the time and means they need to replenish themselves. This is human reproduction time (in both the daily and generational sense) or time for human needs. As we noted earlier, the sacrifice of this time, like the sacrifice of the time nature needs to replenish, is the other side of speedy acquisition through space. By this argument, then, human and environmental needs are aligned through their common spatiotemporal exploitation.

There are many books on rethinking approaches to the environment. There are manuals – the self-help market is replete with them – on avoiding environmental hazards to health. There are also numerous books which try to rethink the issue of class and poverty. Aside from the health manuals, which are generally individually focused, many of these books are critical of the new hegemony of globalizing thought. But they do not synthesize critiques of health, environmental exploitation, and poverty into a coherent theory and an alternative for practice.[43] That said: theories of space and time are in the air, as are many of the things I advocate. Activist groups have long perceived localization as the solution. "Practice always marches ahead of theory." What is novel about my account is that it shows why environmental degradation and ill health are the *inevitable* consequences of global profit based on increasing speed. This account also carries the task of synthesis further. Synthesis is necessary, as the short-term needs of people are often pitted against environmental interests, especially now. The short-term interests of the South and countries which are not overdeveloped are pitted against their own environmental needs. Hence the controversy over the Brazilian rainforests in Brazil itself: they are a value-producing industry in a poor country. While I do not discuss this in depth, the South has to stand the cost of the North's profits in other ways. In addition to recurring financial crises, there is the process described by Harvard's president, Lawrence Summers. When he was vice-president of the World Bank, in 1991, Summers argued that the South should be the dumping ground for the North's toxic waste because pollution-induced illness would not matter so much where people die young: "the economic logic behind dumping a load of toxic waste in the lowest wage country is impeccable and we should face up to that."[44] When the memorandum became public in February 1992, Jose Lutzenburger, Brazil's then secretary of the environment, wrote to Summers: "your reasoning is perfectly logical but totally insane . . . A concrete example of the unbelievable alienation, reductionist thinking, social ruthlessness and the arrogant ignorance of many conventional 'economists' concerning the nature of the world we live in."[45]

To talk vaguely of "preserving the environment" while abetting globalization is to foster the very insanity at issue. Not signing the Kyoto Protocol, not pausing to safeguard the climate and environment, is just as insane as terrorism. Destroying the conditions under which homo sapiens can reproduce is more so. A species that attacks the conditions of its own survival is not sane, however much it tries to defer its reckoning with the conditions of its own survival by shifting the burden of ill health onto others. But the point is that that reckoning can no longer be deferred. All the conditions of human life are being undermined in the advanced countries here and now. The conditions of human life are otherwise known as human needs, or, in Marx's terms, the conditions of human (daily and generational) reproduction. Definitions of human needs are contested, but it is generally agreed that human needs are distinct from wants, and that they can be listed as: food, water, air, a livable temperature or shelter. To this minimum list, I want to add the opportunity to enjoy life, since without this opportunity the organism becomes depressed, and depression also lowers immune function, and thus the chances of physical survival.[46]

In this book we will see that every one of the minimum needs, beginning with air and extending through to a livable temperature, is being degraded to the point of disappearance in some cases. Human needs, hence human life in general, constitute the price for current profit levels. Present pollution, and stripping, of the environment denies a future to generations to come, human and animal alike. Chapter 2 gives an account of everyday life under globalization; it discusses how speed, by robbing human beings, like nature, of their reproduction time, increases their exhaustion. Chapter 3 shows how speedy production and distribution increase pollution and ill health through accelerating transportation. It also shows how speedy production, the acquisition of natural resources and human labor across space, is aided by regional and global free-trade treaties whose priorities are directly at odds with environmental legislation. The impossibility of meeting the requirements of the Kyoto Protocol unless transportation is cut back will be evident by the third chapter, together with the fact that meeting it necessitates ending globalization. Chapter 4 discusses how food and water, the other conditions of life, are not only polluted in the West but diminishing on a global scale. In Chapters 5 and 6, the issue is the other side of policies privileging speed and space: policies which limit the time (that is to say, money) given to human reproduction and regeneration through cuts in healthcare, education and social security, among other human needs. Throughout the chapters on ill health and social provision, it will be plain that policies sacrificing time to space have been common to so-called conservatives and social democrats since the 1980s. The election of George Bush's so-called Christian government and the commitment to a war with an oily corrolary has only accelerated the attack on life.[47] These issues, together with free trade, are now submerged in the rhetoric of war, but they continue to generate anxieties independently of the fear of terrorism. Chapter 7 briefly discusses the alleged third way, and how it mistakenly contributes to the very issues it seeks to redress: the cuts in human and natural time for the sake of profit based on spatial expansion. It shows as well why women as mothers are at the intersection of time and space, and impoverished by it. Chapters 8 and 9 are theoretical, drawing out how profits based on extension necessarily sacrifice time to space, undermining the basis of long-term wealth in the process. But the immediate point is that the thinking of the new right follows, just as it preceded, the third-way policies introduced to cut reproduction time and to accelerate free trade. The difference is that the new right, so far, moves with increasing urgency and in defiance of the traditional principles of conservatism, as we shall see in Chapter 10. Chapter 10 also introduces Gandhi and other localists, and considers what a real third way would mean in terms of reversing course, and how this could be accomplished. Paradoxically, such a third way would draw on genuinely conservative as well as radical traditions: a conservatism that takes the concept of responsibility to the future as well as the past seriously, a radicalism that insists on social justice for all living things; a conservatism favoring economic localization and trade restrictions, a radicalism in enjoying and protecting the cultural and biological diversity from which human beings continue to learn, even as the attempt to obliterate diversity accelerates.

2   Daily life in the West

The ruling economy requires sacrifice of human life in order to feel buoyant, and it obtains it through what I am terming "bioderegulation." Deregulation has a liberating sound to it. But its effects are precisely the reverse for human beings and other species as distinct from corporations. The deregulation of biology, bioderegulation, erodes the internal constraints protecting the body at the same time as deregulation in the legal sense steals human time in the name of market freedom. In this chapter, I examine some of the forces pressuring everyday human life, forces shaped in turn by economic globalization and other forms of deregulation. Building on the work of John Gray, Juliet Schor and others, we will see that the effects and results of deregulation (in both the usual sense and my own) are to make humans work harder conforming to the new rules of inhuman time, to restrict human interaction and personal contact, and to make us commute further (and migrate as a matter of course). The other side of deregulation in all its forms, from free trade to the privatization of phones, trains and essential services (such as healthcare and water) is the increasing pace of production, distribution, exchange and consumption. This is why I mention Juliet Schor's analysis of overwork (which is not concerned with legal deregulation as such) in the same breath as John Gray's, which is. For Gray, "The central dilemma of public policy today is how to reconcile the imperatives of deregulated markets with enduring human needs." Schor is documenting how human beings are also abandoning social customs, or tacit regulations ("no work after sundown"), because they have to. The technologies employed in setting the pace can go faster, much faster than their human adjuncts, whose presence slows things down.[2] Automation, or the replacement of human beings by machines, speeds up those aspects of production that the human presence slowed down.[3] The fewer the humans needed for production to take place, the more rapid the industry.

Among Western economies, the US is the one most governed by deregulation, but of course deregulation, globalization and the tremendous economic inequalities accompanying it are spreading. Other advanced countries are mirroring or beginning to show the same social trends. By my argument, they are forced to follow these trends because the imperatives of global capitalism affect survival (in more than the literal sense; there is "career survival" as well). Deregulation of the human body, and deregulation of trade, labor and environmental legislation, seek to remove the constraints which human time, and natural time, impose. This can be done by laws which permit corporations to go further afield, and to work their labor longer, but it can also be done by letting labor know that jobs depend now on going the extra mile, literally and figuratively. As speeding up accelerates, it impinges on more conditions of survival (as subsequent chapters on air, food and water will show). In the remainder of this chapter, we will see that, if survival means working harder, severing familial and community ties and so forth, this is done, although the willingness to do it varies from culture to culture.[4]

Deregulation and the theft of time

Let us now extend the critique of deregulation, and why it enslaves humans rather than delivering the freedom the word promises. In essence, this is my reasoning: deregulation does not mean the *absence* of all forms of regulation; it means passing regulation to the machine. The faster the machine can go, the greater the temptation to make all components of production (including human labor) perform at the same pace. Where deregulation abolishes labor standards, so labor can be regulated by the machine, labor is more likely to be pushed past reasonable limits. This is especially the case where anxiety over minimal survival motivates labor to sacrifice its health. Such sacrifices are not limited to sweatshops. The fact and threat of layoffs due to concentration or mergers on the one hand, and automation on the other, is also tied to the globalizing imperative. It means, as well, that sources of energy other than human energy are used more. As we will discuss in the next chapter, these sources are the very ones (fossil fuels) whose excessive use is the major factor forcing climate change and air pollution. The rapidity of the global economy, and the distance it commands, depends on these energy sources rather than human labor. Although human labor cannot be dispensed with, it can be and is minimized, and where it is not, it is pushed to keep pace with a rate of production that outstrips all known predecessors. Far more time is now given to work in the US, Australia and Britain.[5]

Work time increases annually from country to country, but it does not increase fast enough for globalization. Because human labor cannot perform at the same pace as other factors in production, it appears to capital that its value is less. At one level, this appearance is the exact opposite of reality. Exchange-value and all profit in the long-run, as we will see, comes from natural energies, including human energy, and from them alone. However, profit depends not only on the quantity of these energies, but on the *speed* with which they are extracted.[6] Because, as we will also see, speed rather than energy is taken for the source of profit, speed itself is a determinant of price. This has the confusing result that one of the real sources of energy, human labor, is devalued because of its slower speed.

Human health, human stress

We have already had glimpses of how human beings are affected not only by pollution, but also by adapting their bodies to a new spatiotemporal regime. This adaptation takes many forms, from the anxiety of credit card debt to more time spent in personal transportation because one cannot afford to live "closer in," or has no car. Or it can take the form of migration. A British talk show host, in conversation with a man called Bill from Exeter, heard that he travels five hours to work daily, rising at 3 am to be there at 8 am, leaving at 5 pm to be home at 10 pm for five hours' sleep. He does not move because his wife's job is in Exeter and their children are at school there. He does not stay over because they can't afford two sets of lodgings.[7] One may dismiss this story, but, on examination, it seems that there is a new form of slavery growing, an enslavement to survival in that sleeping as well as leisure time alike are lost to transportation. The time to regenerate is lost because you have to go further afield to keep pace with the distance over which goods and natural raw materials are now acquired. The length of time it takes to journey to or from work (without a car) has increased just as commercial transportation has increased. The technologies that maximize speed demand that human beings not only work harder, but that more of them travel further, covering greater distances annually. The increase in time spent in transportation counts as one of the many stresses involved in keeping up with the new spatio-temporal order, one of the many causes of ill health in the era of deregulated speed. But in the way human beings now work more for less, in the lengthening paths they take to get from A to B, there lies a microcosm of the global process of extension, where goods and raw materials travel ever-expanding distances. There lies also the other side of exploiting energy sources for rapidity: humans who are underemployed, unemployed or working too hard. In sum: in the increasing time given to work, there is an attempt to keep pace with the accelerating speed of production. But, just as that pace outstrips the ability of nature to reproduce or sustain itself, so too does it press human beings to their limits. The difference is that human beings press themselves willingly. They berate themselves for laziness or keep on when they should stop, ignorant of the price they will pay for the money they make, or anxiously aware of that price, but lacking an alternative when the cost of living steadily outstrips salaries and wages. What the human mind has devised is now at war with the human body, and this, too, is a question of regulation, in that the body's "self-regulating systems" are over-ridden by the pace and demand of production. To match that pace, the human mind demands that the body sacrifice its own good, or "deregulate." The deregulated body is one that goes without enough sleep, rest, proper food – taking prescribed drugs to silence its chronic illnesses and escalating allergies.

From here on, I focus on some illustrative details of this human-sacrificing process. The personal shortfall, between what a body can do and what it is asked to do, is not only met by travelling further or migrating or working harder and working longer. It is exacerbated by unemployment or underpayment, rising living costs and indebtedness. These are the results of an economy in which time for human regeneration becomes expensive, often because there is no time, and, because there is no time, additional costs are expended to cope with provisioning and cleaning, and household production generally. The costs of living make dual incomes a necessity, but this puts an additional strain on partnerships with or without children. Employment often takes one partner elsewhere, which may lead to the breakup of partnerships and geographical connections between parent and child. This contributes to the much touted but little remedied breakdown of communities, as does enforced as well as voluntary relocation. Personal isolation and depression accompany these changes.

Traveling further, migrating more

Increasing individual travel contributes to air pollution through the growing use of personal vehicles, and the use of personal vehicles is tied to the centralization and extension process which establishes cities and then suburbs. Extended roadways evolve. Housing construction grows in outlying areas; personal vehicles proliferate. The result is suburbanization. Both suburbanization and distance travel contribute to air pollution. While the US is the worst offender here, it is not alone. Despite declining urban populations, there are more cars on the road and there is heavier air pollution. The Italian Statistics Bureau (ISTAT) blames stagnant public transport services, which have not grown to keep pace with suburbanization, and the railway sector, because "it had canceled many suburban stops for the sake of increasing speed, which also contributed to the increase in private cars."[8] Cheaper housing costs in outlying areas are another factor. British capitalism has put a bright face on this process: you can buy a house for half the price if you move from Swansea to Carmarthenshire in Wales.[9] These points of course are linked. One is more likely to buy that house in Carmarthenshire because of the new road link which will get one to Swansea in twenty minutes.[10] Naturally, if one wants to live with or near family or friends in Carmarthenshire and does not have a car, there is a much longer commute.

From 1960 to 1990, in the US, the number of cars per household increased threefold. In addition, the US interstate highway system was virtually completed during this era, while public transportation was deliberately downgraded by illegal corporate activity.[11] These factors influenced worker commuting habits; over this thirty-year period the number of people driving alone to work increased almost without interruption. "From 1960–1990, total workers increased by 78 percent, while workers commuting by private vehicles rose to 135.5 percent" (from 43 million in 1960 to 101 million in 1990). At the same time, public transport decreased "as more and more people began to drive alone to work."[12]

The US took the process to the greatest extreme (as it has with all forms of deregulation), but the process of investment in roads was international. It resulted in most cities of the world developing surrounding rings of suburbs during the latter half of the twentieth century. From 1970 to 1990, residential and employment densities consistently increased in suburban counties,[13] while job and residence locations became increasingly decentralized. It is clear now, according to the United States Department of Transportation, that the number of workers with jobs outside of their county of residence increased 200 percent from 1960 to 1990. This thirty year period also witnessed the birth of extensive global trade and the death or depletion of the atmosphere, as will see in the next two chapters.[14] It is an arbitrary period in some respects, but it is also when the effects of deregulation on human needs become apparent.[15]

The growth of business service activities and of office functions in cities has maintained high daytime populations in central areas. Since white-collar workers are more likely to live outside the city in relatively affluent suburbs, a large population of workers commutes from suburban communities and metropolitan fringes.[16] But not all commuting takes place from suburbs to city. The significant class variable here means that jobs are not accessible to those without cars, unless they devote too much time to a distance commute by bad public transport. William Julius Wilson sums up on recent studies by labor economists:

> in addition to finding that the lack of automobile ownership among inner-city blacks contributed significantly to their lower wages and lower rate of employment . . . African-Americans "spend more time travelling to work than whites" [and] "the time cost per mile traveled is . . . significantly higher for blacks" . . . the amount of time and money spent in commuting, when compared with the actual income that accrues to inner-city blacks in low-skill jobs ion the suburbs, acts to discourage poor people from seeking employment far from their own neighbourhoods . . . it was quite rational for blacks to reject search-and-travel choices when assessing their position in the job market."[17]

One of Wilson's respondents (following the transfer of many Chicago jobs to the suburbs) puts it this way:

> You gotta go out in the suburbs, but I can't get out there. The bus go out there, but you don't wanna catch the bus out there, going two hours each ways. If you have to be at work at eight, that mean you have to leave for work at six, that mean you have to get up at five to be at work at eight. Then when wintertime come, you be in trouble.[18]

This process of commuting positions people in class terms on the basis of the speed and ease with which they get from A to B. Living in the suburbs and commuting to the city via car and freeway is stress,[19] but the stress is less than taking two to four hours for the same journey, or making it in sardine-can conditions. "Commuter trains [in Britain] are packed to overflowing" and conditions are "appalling," with rail companies carrying numbers "far in excess of their supposed limits." One consequence is that car travel into London, down since the 1980s, is increasing again.[20] That the European Union is perfectly aware of the crisis in road transportation is clear in a 1998 document, "Averting the Three Outriders of the Transport Apocalypse: Road Accidents, Air and Noise Pollution." Here the impact of transport on the environment and human health is seen "as a major political concern throughout Europe."[21]

Commuting between countries on a regular basis is an alternative for some to migration. The point to introducing migration in the context of a discussion on commuting is that, if we were to draw it, we could see how the circles of human travel in different domains have extended their compass in similar ways. Humans commute longer distances in more numbers; people migrate longer distances as well as migrating more often in search of work, and often return to their country of origin. These are all processes of extension that reflect the extension accomplished by globalization. Saskia Sassen has argued that migration is the direct result of globalization in that there is massive displacement of villagers when their agricultural economies turn from sustenance agriculture to export-oriented production. Once displaced, these people usually migrate. This, as she argues also, is a process that must spread just as globalization spreads, and as more areas are closed off to migrants and guest workers. The immiseration produced by this process is already apparent, which is not to say it will not become considerably worse.[22]

Working longer, working harder

Alexis de Tocqueville wrote that "Americans are always in a rush."[23] The rush is accelerating. In 1965, 24 percent of US citizens said that they "always feel rushed." By 1992, it was 38 percent.[24] Juliet Schor's analysis of Census Bureau data makes this plain. Between 1969 and 1987, people reported an increase in worktime averaging an extra month (or 163 hours) per year.[25] The chief cause of this increased pace is the demand for productivity. It is a demand that is being met, although the sources of that productivity increase are debated, with some attributing it to technology and others to people working harder.[26] Most rushed of the rushed are working mothers: "More than two-thirds of wives with children under age 18 are in the paid labor force, up from about one-fourth in 1960."[27] In Western Europe between 1980 and 1990, women made up 7 million out of 8 million of the new labor force entrants. In the US, female rates of participation in the paid workforce have increased exponentially: the annual growth rate for female workers is 2.9 percent; for men it is 1.6 percent.[28] These are the women (or women with the same demographic profile) who also report working longer hours than they have hitherto and, of these, more are working mothers.[29]

Internationally, says the International Labor Organization (ILO), "the bottom line is that while more and more women are working, the great majority of them are simply swelling the ranks of the working poor. [Their] economic activities remain highly concentrated in low-wage, low-productivity and precarious forms of employment."[30] As with all of the economic effects of globalization, it is women who are worst hit by unemployment. Women's unemployment rates run from 50 to 100 percent greater than for men in many industrialized countries.[31] Wherever globalization has a negative effect on human beings, whether it is increasing the time they have to work, or the time they have to spend in domestic work, or the time they have to spend in consumption, women are hit worse than men. They earn between 50 to 80 percent of male wages for the same work (outside the agricultural sector) in all countries. They hold less than 6 percent of senior management jobs. They work on average ten to twenty-five hours more per week than men, in paid as well as unpaid work. In all regions of the world, women work longer hours for less pay than their male counterparts, and there are no signs that this situation is improving.[32]

What is most interesting about the increasing numbers of women in the global workforce is that it has been tied directly to globalization. The ILO's director-general states that "Their relatively cheap labour has represented the cornerstone of export-oriented industrialization and international competitiveness for many developing countries." Which is a polite way of saying that the pitifully low wages paid to women (and children) in the Third World make their countries more attractive to global capital. The men are also paid badly, but less so. It has been clear for some time that capitalist industrialization favors the man, worsening the living standards of women vis-à-vis men in every case where it has taken hold, in the First, Second and Third Worlds.

Unemployment and rising living costs, lack of time, indebtedness

The ILO report on world employment (1998–9) notes that "the share of total wages in GDP has fallen almost everywhere," with a corresponding fall in real wages. (As elsewhere in this book, "real" means adjusted for inflation.)[33] The sharpest contrast between real wages and economic growth is in the United States. "The American culture of contentment" Galbraith remarked upon no longer exists: there is a radical and new insecurity in the American middle class, where permanency of employment is no longer the expectation. "A mid-life layoff" is now an omnipresent fear, the migration or relocation for work reasons is commonplace, and the incarceration rate is five to fourteen times higher than it is in the rest of the world.[34] There is a "Brazilification" of America taking place, in that inequality levels are rising dramatically, and race is tied to class position. But perhaps worst affected by rising living costs are the peoples of the former Second World, Central and Eastern Europe, who continue to "suffer dramatic and painful declines in living standards."[35] It is, however, difficult to ascertain the extent of real poverty and unemployment in the advanced West, where the picture is blurred by the increasing prevalence of disguised unemployment and part-time work, as well as outright and recorded unemployment.

Despite the claims for "economic growth," recorded global unemployment is escalating. At the end of 1998 1 billion workers (a third of the world's labor force) were either unemployed or under-employed (underemployed means they want to work more). Unemployment in the European Union remains basically constant, at about 10 percent. Worst hit after Asia (and the 1997 economic crisis) are Central and Eastern Europe. The so-called transitions to democracy have, according to the ILO, "been accompanied by a rapid rise (from about zero to over 9 percent) in unemployment, lower real wages and an increase in income inequality."[36] The one exception in the bleak unemployment picture is the United States, where unemployment, on the face of it, is at its lowest since the early 1970s. However, the figures in the United States have been queried on the basis that the method of counting makes many invisible, and because a substantial portion of the US population is incarcerated.[37] Moreover, the increase in employment in the US has been accompanied by the most severe real wage stagnation in the OECD countries, which suggests that an uncharacteristic form of socialism is being practiced in that country: more people get something, but everyone gets less. The results of the "third way" withdrawal of welfare support for single mothers indicate that poverty in the forms of hunger and homelessness is increasing in other ways.[38] The residual "safety net" of a minimal welfare apparatus is not picking up "all the truly needy."[39]

Aside from the record number of people holding down two or even three jobs in the West, especially the in United States, there is also a record number of women performing labor outside the home, and unpaid work within it, without assistance. When one is too rushed to cook, one eats a prepared meal, which costs more than the ingredients used in its construction. Household labor, no matter who performs it, has always offset the living costs of paid labor. But when there is no time for those household tasks, one has to spend more on living costs, and the circle closes.[40] In this respect, women's accelerated entry into the workforce over the last forty years undermines – at the same time as it provides – household resources outside the market.[41] Cutting corners with household production means spending more on food and appliances. The increased consumption of fast food is the other side of the expansion of the service industry. More and more fast-food chains flourish, supporting those who no longer have time or energy to eat at home.[42] But the takeover of the food industry by the prepackaged meal extends well beyond fast food. Most foods acquired in a form in which they are more readily consumable are more expensive: the work that would have been done in the household is now done in the factory. By the same token, the work that was until recently done in the office comes into the home. Telephones and computers complete business started elsewhere, but they cost, just as electricity costs. The acquisition of these new necessities usually means borrowing ahead of savings, and the result is the increasing indebtedness which is now most apparent for the majority in the United States, but which is also making itself felt in Europe.

Necessity is not the only cause of indebtedness in a social order in which the machine is the regulator. One is told, for instance, that one has to look financially successful in order to count. More money, then, is spent on keeping up appearances, and the relief of the financial sense of failure afforded by a little luxury. This is not to reduce credit-card debt, and indebtedness in general, to a matter of imaginary aspirations. Whether aspiration or necessity have the larger part varies, and even those who consume only for effect are not entirely wrong economically. In sum: indebtedness is a direct consequence, first, of unemployment; second, of underemployment; third, of having to spend more to make up for time spent outside paid employment, as well as in it; and fourth, in keeping up appearances.

Breakdown of communities, growing personal isolation and depression

Relocation feeds growing personal isolation, and the numbers who live alone not by choice, as well as those who choose a single existence. In fact the elements at play in unemployment, migration, commuting, housing, marital breakdown and the simultaneous need for two incomes are linked in mutually reinforcing cycles. In Britain the forecast for new homes is rising. Probably 5 million new homes will be needed by 2016 "to accommodate the increasing single people, divorcees, elderly people and immigrants."[43] The single (whether by choice, divorce, death or immigration) are by far the biggest component. We have already seen that road links and cheaper housing are connected. The entry of women into the workforce means that there are now, on average, two commuters driving alone per household.[44] The rising cost of living also reinforces the cycle. The rising cost of living is reflected in moves to find cheaper housing, but such housing is purchased at the polluting price of the commute. Not only this, but community breakdown plays a part here too. In the US, "Driving alone to work has consistently increased at each census point from 1960 to 1990 while carpooling has consistently decreased."[45] Time alone has increased in general, together with tiredness, depression, paranoia and violence. These are linked, insofar as aggression and depression are two sides of the same process.[46]

Bodily consequences

A new form of immiseration, or something like it, is making itself felt at emotional and bodily levels. This new form of immiseration is stress, and it is due not only to anxiety but to environmental pollutants. But perhaps what is most interesting about how globalization causes stress is that the temporal disjunctions it generates are endemic to the very definition of stress as such. Stress means "effort, demand upon physical or mental energy." It is caused especially by tugging on one system in an integrated organism while blocking another. The notion of systems, like that of cycles, permits us to think in terms of internal bodily regulations. At the cyclical level, the simplest system of bodily regulation involves regular rhythms of sleep, concentrated activity or work, and relaxation.[47] When these rhythms are forcibly overridden by will and necessity too often, human beings become tired, if not exhausted. Before they become really tired, they simply live with stress. "Stress" is the name for the state we live in most of the time, between exhaustion and the biological rhythms of the naturally formed body. What happens to a human organism when it rushes to keep up, to complete a series of assignments by deadlines, is that its sympathetic nervous system is working at a pace which forces organs to carry loads such as intestinal adrenaline, which in turn affect the gastro-intestinal system.[48] Gastrointestinal diseases are one of the drastically escalating chronic diseases in the West, afflicting some of those who argue for deregulation in public and many who practice it in private.

Deregulation has gone further in the United States than anywhere else, and health is worse in the United States than it is in any of the advanced countries. The fact that Britain is now seventeenth, and the United States is twenty-fourth, on the global "longevity with good health" list indicates to the rest of the world what to expect from the deregulation of the body.[49] Countries where alimentation is respected fare better: France is fourth. In the United Kingdom, the "Indicators of the Nation's Health" show worsening trends in adults' general health, longstanding illness and acute sickness.[50] The related increase in stress-related illness in the US (higher than in the UK) suggests that US citizens are more fearful of unemployment, and prepared to push their bodies and their minds beyond acceptable stress levels to avoid it. If one discounts the matters of death and disease, they are not wrong: unemployment benefits in the United States are good for six months only, and healthcare is often dependent on employment.[51] This is worth stressing. Proponents of monetarism, globalization and so forth claim that anyone who wishes to find work can do so, but they neglect to add that, when people *have* to find work, and will do anything to get it, they are more likely to die before their time.

We have seen that the body "deregulates" when it ignores the *regular* and rhythmic relation necessary to the harmonious interplay of its cycles. What disrupts this interplay most is anxiety over real or imaginary survival. The function of anxiety is to signal alertness, to react and anticipate as necessary, not as a matter of course. But where keeping track of a myriad things that need to be anticipated and reacted to in order to survive (literally as well as socioeconomically) anxiety can become a habitual state.[52] There is cause for congratulation in just staying on the edge.

Those who advocate globalization have access to knowledge about the shortfall between what a body can do and what it wills itself to do. Pushing themselves, they also read about health. They are well informed about alternative health practices, and have access to medical information.[53] They respond by attentiveness to the "technology of the body," or what the body needs to compensate for overwork (such as working-out, a process which means the body releases its tensions and toxins at an accelerated pace, matching that of the mind). What is being done to the human body in terms of using resources at a pace that exceeds their regeneration parallels what is being done to the planet. Global deregulation is rooted in the realities of production, in service industries and professional trades as well as manufacture. It is rooted in the squeezing of nature, as well as human beings, and it is reflected in those trends we have discussed so far – chief among them, asking longer or more intense hours for less pay.

Reproduction as a generational factor

In the introduction, I referred to how Marx saw reproduction as both a daily and a generational matter. In this chapter, the focus has been on daily reproduction, on what is needed to be able to report for work, or find work, the next day. Later, this book will show that reproduction on a generational basis (the cost of children, education, healthcare) is becoming costly to the point where fewer people are undertaking it or are able to avoid poverty or anxiety when they do undertake it. Not only this, but infertility is rising, as it does automatically in all species under stress. Human infertility, as we will discover below, is attributed to a variety of chemicals in food and water as well. We can see now why Marx was right to treat both daily and generational reproduction under the same heading. The inability to regenerate on a daily basis affects the ability to reproduce the next generation. "In 1960, the US had a birth rate of 23.8 per thousand, but by 1990, the birth rate had dropped to 16.7."[54] The ideological counterpart of this drop is the active and growing "child-free" movement in the United States, resentful of the tax breaks given to people with children. Three-quarters of all murders of children take place in the United States.[55] It is quite clear where this is going. The number of children in the comparatively affluent West will continue to decline. There will be a backlash holding women responsible for not being real women, and glossing over the fact that women are suffering more and more. Such reactions have been evident at each stage of capitalist expansion; hence, at critical periods, women are held responsible for taking men's jobs. The Taliban of Afghanistan, in getting women out of the workforce, were also responding to unemployment. That they did so with more Draconian measures than are used in the West should not blind us to the structural similarities in the various historical campaigns to return women to the home. Nor should it lead us to overlook the fact that the economic situation of women as mothers is worse than it was when they were supported by men.[56] As Ehrenreich has shown, the right-wing women's movements were often entirely sensible in responding to the economic changes in the relation between the sexes in the playboy fifties, changes that encouraged "men to get sex for free without having to commit to marriage."[57] I would add that the second women's movement, or "feminism," also had roots in the 1950s, insofar as the divorce of older women with children in favor of younger ones escalated, while the objectification of women intensified. The young students and other intellectuals who gave the movement its initial public voice may not themselves have been suffering economically (in terms of class), but the campaign for equal pay for work of equal value gained its impetus from those who had. What has become clear, in the course of the last forty years, is that those who perceive the struggle against globalization as a women's war are not wrong. We will explore the reasons for this in later chapters, showing how the splitting of home and locality from workplace is the other side of globalization. The same dynamic that consistently impoverishes women wherever it takes hold is the dynamic leading to the deregulation of human biological life. Humans are already straining to keep up because the pace of production outstrips that of reproduction and regeneration. If one cannot sustain oneself, one can sustain the other only with difficulty, especially if one is going to the limit to survive.[58]

3 The war on the atmosphere

To project forwards on the basis of current trends, assuming business as usual, is to foresee a planet denuded of most of its species through global warming, whose natural resources of good air, fresh water and rich earth have been spoilt and worn out, whose storms are too violent and whose sun is too harsh, and which has lost a third of its habitable surface to a dying sea. In the face of this colossal harm to other species, the earth and its future inhabitants (in many polluted cities, the average inhabitant is under sixteen), making a fuss about human health may seem to concede too much to the self-interest that caused the problem in the first place. But insofar as government policy – which is pro-globalization, privatization, deregulation and free trade – justifies itself in the name of economic freedom for those living today, that justification is stretched when it affects their freedom to live at all. The top percentage (somewhat less than 1 percent) of the global population – those who are the beneficiaries of economic freedom in that they do not have to worry about money – can offset the pollution damage to their health with relative ease, but they are nonetheless affected. Whatever the dictates of their conscious selves, their bodies are allied with the interests of those who suffer from trying to keep up with rising living costs and growing inequality, while suffering as well from pollution, like all living things. As I have argued, overriding the regenerative needs of the body and of nature itself is a form of deregulation: bioderegulation. Bioderegulation involves dismantling the natural "rules" which govern living things, rules which allow for replenishment both in humans and in nature. Like economic deregulation, it privileges immediate profits over long-term sustainability. This will be plain if we turn to how all of the conditions of life – air, water, food, temperature and shelter – are imperiled or degraded through globalization and other forms of speeding up production and consumption. I will review each of the life conditions in turn. We begin with air, leaving climate, water and food to the next chapter. The lines of causality in relation to air and climate are similar (although not identical) so there is a twofold purpose in drawing these lines: one is to draw out the damage done to the health of those living now; the other is to show how the future will be unlivable unless the atmosphere, together with the climate, is preserved. Climate, like air, is degraded by globalization because globalization increases fossil-fuel based transportation.

Globalization, by definition, depends on increased transportation and telecommunications. The last chapter pointed to the escalation in personal commuting; after discussing air pollution, this chapter will discuss increases in commercial transportation and telecommunications, which together consume more than two-thirds of the fossil fuels used annually. As we saw in the Preface, while the US and other countries draw back from the minimal Kyoto Protocol, they abet fossil fuel consumption through free-trade treaties. Fossil-fuel consumption is also assisted by the present war against terrorism, insofar as this has safeguarded an oil route through Afghanistan. A future conquest of Iraq would also increase the likelihood that oil can be secured from and through that region. By trade or conquest, fossil-fuel emissions increase; they also expand through the surge in electricity use demanded by the communications networks accompanying and facilitating transportation. Electricity, insofar as it depends primarily on fossil fuels, is not clean.

I turn first to the extent of air pollution and the illness it causes, followed by a discussion of the constituents of air pollution and their origin in fossil-fuel emissions. The next section discusses fossil-fuel dependent electricity. It notes how the production of electricity is necessary for technology's setting a pace – in the service of profit – which outstrips the biological rhythms of human beings as well as other natural entities, leading to stresses on biorhythms and biospheres. The section on transportation demonstrates how the increase in fossil fuels is tied directly to globalization by this means. In the following section, I will show how the deregulation of the human body is paralleled by the deregulation of trade restrictions. Just as the human body can make itself go faster in the short term but pay a price in the long-run, so deregulated trade speeds up production, but at the cost of the exhaustion of the earth's biological resources. Free trade extends the access to raw materials, so that, if the pace of production and consumption exhausts the raw materials that are close to hand, the corporation moves on. In concluding this chapter I will return to how spatial or territorial barriers are not only overcome by free trade but can also be dealt with by conquest. The impetus to expand (and find the fuel to maintain) transportation and telecommunications networks was a common cause of twentieth-century war. Afghanistan indicates that it will also feature in the twenty-first century.

The pollution of air

Air is not the only victim of the new economy, but it is the most immediate of the conditions of life. One survives without food for months, without water for a few days, without air for two minutes. In the introduction, I said that human needs can be defined, first, in terms of the conditions for staying alive; second, as the conditions for enjoying that life. The only thing that detracts more from enjoyment than poverty is ill health. Traditionally, human needs for staying alive, and well, have been defined in terms of food, water and shelter. That is the standard, minimum definition, adopted throughout the world. No one thought that the need for oxygen and clean air, or tolerable climate, would have to be spelled out. Now it does.

In 1999 an estimated 1.4 billion urban residents (a quarter of the global population) were breathing air that contained more pollution than the World Health Organization deems safe.[1] In the United States alone, over 90 million people live in areas that do not meet national air quality standards.[2] In Britain, one-third of the population is also at risk from polluted air.[3] These concerns are shared throughout the West, the North and most of the South.[4] Asthma deaths among people between five and thirty-four years of age increased more than 40 percent between the mid-1970s and mid-1980s in many affluent regions, beginning with Europe and North America. Asthma overall increased by 40 percent in the same period, and by 50 percent in the subsequent decade. There is evidence too that asthma is emerging in urban areas of both Africa and Asia.[5] At the current air-pollution levels, asthmatic children are the most effected group in the population. Air pollution is also contributing to rapidly growing increases in allergies and other lung diseases. Yet existing regulations governing air emissions are more likely to talk of "clean air" than they are to mention the diseases resulting from its opposite. The official position of the Environment Agency of England and Wales is that "we have set our long-term sights on a future where everyone will be able to enjoy the benefits of a clean, safe and healthy environment. . . . From 'greening' business and reducing human impact on the environment, to safeguarding the landscapes and reducing flood risk, the vision's ultimate aim is to improve the quality of life for both people and the wildlife." This sunny projection makes no mention of illness.[6]

While some researchers hesitate over the obvious correlation between increasingly degraded air and dramatic increases in respiratory diseases, the combined weight of the diverse studies on air-related diseases is conclusive. Moreover, the health effects of air pollution have been gauged, from the outset, through human rather than animal studies. But we live with only limited and very partial recognition of the health threat. The vigorous campaign and vigilance against lung pollution through tobacco is absent in campaigns against other forms of air pollution. Yet in some cities of the world merely breathing the air is equivalent to smoking two packets of cigarettes a day. As in the case of smoking, it is difficult to isolate one single factor causing cancer in this case, or lung disease in that one. It is the combined effects of biological and environmental insults which work on a human body, playing on an old injury, a psychosomatic or genetic weakpoint. Those treating poor health, and many of those suffering from it, would rather there was a single ingredient whose removal or neutralization would cure all. But the quest for this is as futile as the quest of those who astonish the French nation by searching in French wine and/or red meat for the ingredient that gives French people better health than their American counterparts. In what follows, I will not be blaming benzene alone, or pointing the finger only at nitrous oxide, or even at carbon monoxide. Rather I will be saying that the combined effects of these and other pollutants stress the normal respiratory system beyond its capacity for resistance. For good and ill, the human organism reacts to stress as if its diverse causes operated as a totality in their effects. As a Harvard Working Group has it, "all social and environmental changes are potentially reflected epidemiologically, since conditions can affect the opposing processes of contagion and recovery, acquisition and loss of immunity."[7] Increased illness overall, not only disease linked directly to environmental degradation, would be the indirect result of pollution. Quantity is also significant. Enough nitrous oxide, like enough carbon monoxide, will finish anyone. One of the key points in this chapter is that globalization is dangerous because it generates far greater *quantities* of known air pollutants, due to its increasing demand for more transportation as well as greater speed in all forms of production.

Air pollution – as smog – consists of ground-level ozone,[8] particulate matter[9], carbon monoxide,[10] benzene,[11] nitrogen dioxide[12] and sulfur dioxide.[13] All of these exhibit negative effects on the cardiorespiratory system.[14] All of them, as single let alone combined factors, have contributed to lung diseases and resulted in the asthma increase, together with the increase in bronchitis, pneumonia, and other common ailments of the lung. Although the chemicals in smog are especially damaging in concert, individual traces and lines of causality connect these chemicals with the increased incidence of certain illnesses, including not only asthma, bronchitis, and general inflammation of the lung, but numerous pulmonary and other allergies, leukemia[15] and, of course, lung cancer. Benzene has been linked to leukemia, non-Hodgkin's lymphoma and lung cancer,[16] carbon monoxide to mortality and impaired cardiovascular function.[17] Nitrogen dioxide increases the risk of lower-respiratory difficulty in children especially.[18] To take one example: the LA smog layer is responsible for a whole generation of young people growing up with decreased lung capacity. In 1990, Sherwin and other researchers at the University of Southern California did an autopsy of one hundred 15- to 25-year-olds who died of nonmedical causes and found that 80 percent had "notable lung abnormalities" and 27 percent had "severe lesions on their lungs." Sherwin noted that these youths were "running out of lung," and that these lung abnormalities were "above and beyond what we've seen with smoking or even respiratory viruses . . . [These youths] would have had a very high probability of clinical disease within 15 to 20 years – by the time they got to be 40."[19] LA's story of automobile-driven pollution is being replicated in Amsterdam, Athens, Barcelona, Cologne, Helsinki, London, Lyons, Milan and even Paris, where acid rain is held accountable for a 3 percent increase in daily mortality.[20] According to the latest estimates provided by the WHO European Office, about 80,000 deaths a year in Europe can be attributed to long-term exposure to road-traffic air pollution. Research suggests that, apart from professional drivers and road workers, the elderly and the very young are most at risk of adverse health impacts.[21]

It can of course be claimed that the increase in lung diseases is due to something other than growing air pollution – consequent on increased transportation and other forms of fossil-fuel consumption. It has been suggested, for instance, that the increase in asthma was genetic, and/or that there has been only an observed rather than a real increase.[22] With the 50 percent growth in asthma in the affluent countries, this position has become untenable. The World Bank itself attributes the increase in asthma to increased air pollution.[23] Moreover, the researchers, who estimate that 20 to 75 percent of asthma cases are genetically based, are the first to point out that this remarkably wide estimate means that an equally wide range of asthma cases is unaccounted for, genetically speaking.[24]

There has been progress in the control of air pollutants. Some legislation has been effective in improving technological controls on emissions, and work on finding and improving these controls continues, as does the labor of enforcing the often-violated existing regulations.[25] But this war for the air will be lost unless emissions and other technological controls are supplemented by a decline in quantities of emissions. Increasing the speed of production and deregulating trade and labor conditions means that the overall quantity of emissions must increase, together with the use of electricity and transportation.

Electricity

Most of the polluting byproducts of electricity result from the combustion of fossil fuels used in converting thermal energy into electrical energy.[26] The use of conventional fossil fuels (coal, oil and gas) dominates most of the world's electricity production, providing about 62 percent of the total net generation of electricity. Hydro-electric power follows, yielding about 19 percent, with nuclear power providing approximately 17 percent.[27] Fossil fuels were used to produce 64 percent of the electricity in North America, 88 percent in the Middle East, 73 percent in the Far East and Oceania, 48 percent in Western Europe and 67 percent in Eastern Europe.[28]

From mechanized production to electric lights to electrically charged cell-phones, electricity saves time and the expenditure of human energy, while providing the conditions under which humans deregulate their bodies. In addition to its contribution to lung diseases, labor-saving electricity creates a hostile environment for the labor it is supposed to save through radiation and possible electromagnetic pollution. Electromagnetic effects accompany any form of electricity. The fact that that electricity was generated in a benign way does not affect this. I note this here because, while many of the illnesses and environmental issues we confront could be solved by the institution of solar and wind power in place of fossil-fuel combustion, the fact is that we do not know and are only beginning to uncover the full effects and extent of electromagnetic pollution. It seems these may generate tumors, or, as Elaine Scarry has shown brilliantly, bring down planes.[29] But while electro-magnetic pollution is a new field of investigation, the damage done by fossil-fuel emissions to health has been established.

The increase in fossil-fuel emissions from electricity arises from domestic and corporate use. In France and Italy, an observed increase in household energy demand is attributed to "widespread penetration of household appliances," as the household has to keep pace with production outside it.[30] British and American households since 1980 tell the same story.[31] Residential energy consumption is projected to continue increasing by more than 22 percent overall between 1998 and 2020; 74 percent of the growth is attributed to increased electricity use.

Corporate increases in electricity also escalate with the number of corporations. The number of corporations has grown from 7,000 in 1970 to roughly 35,000 in 1990.[32] The growth in the size of national corporations, as well as the number of multinationals, means corporations have to produce more to justify their megalithic existence, and producing more means consuming more raw materials. Their larger output in turn requires new markets, and new markets mean more transportation, more communication and more production of electricity. More electricity is used as globalization expands, regardless of whether production is domestic or transnational. In part, this is because globalization is not only about free trade. It is about speeding up all aspects of production, especially transportation and communication, which are involved in an endless loop with distribution, consumption and exchange. Accordingly, in the last thirty years electricity use overall has doubled.[33]

Before globalization, electricity use expanded more or as much through the mechanization and automation of production. Mechanization was, still is, celebrated for the increase in human output it occasioned, meaning the reduction in the number of human beings required to produce the same amount. But through electricity, it substitutes the energy of other natural resources for human labor. As it did so, it generated technologies to which human beings were adjuncts. But these technologies, hypothetically and in fact, could perform at a more rapid pace than the human beings who tended them. Increasing productivity subsequently entails trying to get human beings to move faster, to move at the pace of the machines. Production transportation and communication, which rely on electricity generated by fossil fuels, simultaneously set a pace which is stressful in itself. In many occupations, mechanization has flowered (if that is the word) into automation, the further displacement of human energy by fossil-fuel consuming electricity, as well as the deregulation of human bodies and other organisms entailed by the new pace of electrified communication and transport, to which we come next.

Transportation

Since 1970, the "global fleet" – the cars, trucks, buses and scooters on the world's roads – has been growing at a rate of about 16 million vehicles per year.[34] Significantly, road transportation increased steadily in this time period while fleet transportation of oil tankers and ore decreased. Globalization, far from decreasing heavy transportation, increases the capillary transportation within countries.[35] Despite the efforts of North American and European governments to reduce the pollutants emitted by these vehicles, emissions of nitrogen oxides have remained constant since 1980. An estimate from 1993 claims that air pollution from the increasing number of motor vehicles threatened the health of at least one third of the world's urban population.[36] Others cite "mobile sources" as the major contributors to urban air pollution: emissions of nitrogen oxides are actually increasing now in much of Europe, mostly due to increased vehicle numbers and usage.[37] Meanwhile, the South is being turned to as a new market with great "growth potential" for motor vehicles, which can only lead to increased emissions of nitrogen oxides, as well as other air pollutants.[38]

While cars – used in commuting – are responsible for a significant percentage of the increasing combustion of fossil fuels,[39] commercial transportation is growing faster.[40] The more transportation, the more fuel consumption. Already transportation consumes approximately one half of the world's oil production, mostly as motor fuel, and accounts for more than one quarter of the world's commercial energy use.[41] According to the International Energy Outlook, 1999, report, energy use will increase markedly over the next twenty years, and every energy source except nuclear power is expected to grow. Transportation oil will reportedly remain the dominant source of energy because it does not have any competition in the transportation sector. Currently, 48 percent of world oil demand is for transportation energy.[42]

For the affluent countries in general, the transportation sector is the only area of the economy that consumes significantly more petroleum today than it did in 1973. But in the next ten years, the strongest growth in energy use is expected to occur in the South. Over the next two decades the developing world will experience fast-paced growth in the transportation infrastructure; energy use for transportation among the developing countries is projected to grow at double the rate of that in the advanced countries. Developing Asia and South America are expected to account for 52 percent of the increase in the world's motor vehicle population, and this increase is tied directly to their participation in an increasingly global economy. It may be assumed that other countries will also exhibit strong increases in freight transportation, if only because of the large number of multinational corporations now based in them.

The parties to the Kyoto Protocol are also parties to international trade agreements that conflict with this and other environmental protocols, or legally override them. I will show shortly that environmental regulations and international trade agreements are coming more and more into conflict, and that, when they do, the trade agreements win out.[43] Not only this, but the new trade agreements guarantee that the increase in the quantity of emissions will escalate. They guarantee this in that they lead to yet more commercial transportation.

International trade

Given that lung diseases, especially asthma, increased by nearly half in the last thirty years, we should note that international trade and transportation began their great leap forward in the same period. Between 1948 and 1993 there was a fourfold increase in world trade, concentrated especially in the last twenty to twenty-five years.[44] A paean to the first fifty years of existence of the trading system GATT-WTO remarks on this impressive growth:

> Growth trends in trade and foreign investment are reflected in the growth of international transport. In 1948, merchandise shipped internationally is estimated to have amounted to 490 million metric tons. In 1997, 4,491 metric tons, or 10 times as much, was shipped. As for air transport, the number of kilometers flown grew almost 23 percent per year between 1958 and 1997. Measured in freight tons per kilometer, the estimated annual average growth rate over this period was 13 percent. Growth in "transport" of information over telecommunication networks has been even faster.[45]

It was calculated that the creation of the single market in Europe in 1993 would increase air pollution by 30 percent,[46] and it has. Instead of making use of rail or water connections, the transportation of goods in Europe after 1993 relied more on roads. In 1999 the Committee of the (European) Regions extended the calculations backwards, working out that European freight transport has grown by 70 percent since 1970.[47] Transportation is still growing due to to the increase in international trade, the extension of the

European Union to Central and Western European countries, and the enhanced cooperation with Mediterranean countries. There is a parallel process in North America. A US government environmental review predicted that NAFTA would lead to the annual 1.8 million truck crossings in 1991 reaching 12 million by 2000, and a minimum 32 percent increase in air pollution was also predicted.[48] This too has transpired: transportation using fossil fuels between Canada, the United States and Mexico has increased by 34 percent since the NAFTA was introduced in 1994. As we have also seen, preliminary figures show that the incidence of asthma in the United States has accelerated. It will be interesting to see how Mexican lungs are faring.[49]

It would be reassuring (especially for liberal and social democratic governments) if globalization, environmental preservation and healthcare were compatible. But they are not, because "opening new trade markets" is synonymous with "transporting more goods further afield," and transportation is the main consumer of fossil fuels. The US Department of Energy holds "*long-term growth in international trade*" (emphasis added) responsible for the fact that "ocean transport energy use" is now rising "at about twice the rate seen in recent years."[50] An increase in rail transport is also projected. The situation on planes is unclear. Plane transportation has increased most of all, but, in line with the wishful thinking about microchips, this is attributed to more far-away vacations being taken by members of the industrialized world, and only incidentally to an increase in travel for business.[51] This vision is contradicted by the realities of air transportation use in the South.[52] But, whichever use pattern prevails, air transportation uses forty-seven times as much energy as sea transportation.[53]

In sum, it is clear that air transportation, together with sea, road and rail transportation, has increased with the growth in free trade, and fossil-fuel consumption has risen accordingly.[54] Moreover, the full impact of international trade as such can only be worse than the picture painted here. I have restricted myself to available international agency and government statistical information, and this is very uneven. For instance, we have information about the dramatic increase in ocean transport in the last ten years (based on shipped tonnage), but we cannot compare it with land freight tonnage. Why? Because none of the British, European or US figures allow us to do so.[55] Nonetheless, there are strong indicators of how transportation for free trade has grown. For instance, if we analyze the US Department of Transportation figures on waterborne commerce, we find that there has been a 58 percent increase in foreign commerce between 1975 and 1996,[56] while the domestic increase is only 16 percent.[57] The Department of Transportation does not provide comparative domestic and international figures for other forms of transport, but we can infer some increase even from its figures. Goods for international trade do not just arrive at the docks by themselves. An increase in ocean transportation necessarily means an increase in road and rail transport. While, in the United States and throughout Europe, imports and, especially, exports increased and national production declined, internal freight transport still grew 2 percent per year in the US from 1970 to 1996,[58] while Europe experienced a 3.3 percent per year increase between 1980 and 1992 – and that increase was almost completely met by road transport. Goods may go half-way round the world by sea, but when they arrive at their destination they have to be distributed domestically. This means that a significant proportion of transportation used in international trade can bury itself in domestic statistics. The situation is similar for transnational road and rail transport. It is difficult to sort the domestic from the international, when figures are given on a country to country basis. To repeat: the picture can only be worse than the one that can be drawn with certainty.[59]

The price paid for increasing productivity in the short term, aside from the increase in electricity, is the depletion of resources close to hand. Bioderegulation of the natural cycles necessary for food reproduction has led to the exhaustion of soils, foodstuffs and water at home, which means seeking them abroad, and deregulating trade accordingly. Capital seeks to match the bioderegulation it has imposed upon its own citizens and resources with deregulation policy whose most acute challenge today is providing itself with unimpeded market access beyond national borders, and fuel to get there.

Here, as elsewhere, policy that once restrained this push now facilitates it. The overthrow of numerous trade restrictions damages health and nature directly and indirectly. Directly, the new trade freedoms override sovereign environmental and labor legislation. Indirectly, as I have argued, they facilitate climate damage and air pollution by facilitating global transport. The principle underlying this push for mobility and access can be understood in terms of either mainstream economics or political economy. In the case of mainstream economics, the economies of scale contingent on consolidation and larger production plants result in more output for input in less time. In terms of political economy, and my revised value theory, they also result in extracting the substance which is the key to profit: human and natural energy. In either frame of reference, profit is meant to accrue because the technology speeds up production by producing more at a more rapid pace. But producing more means using more . . . more energy, more natural materials, more of human time. It means owning or controlling more: frequent mergers are rationalized in terms of the economies of scale they permit. Increasing speed, distance, centralization and consolidation go together because they result in "more output for input" and a bigger share of the market, as well as the extraction of more value or profit.[60]

Crucially, most mergers mean lay-offs, rationalized either by relocation, or in terms of ending duplication of function. Free trade exacerbates these effects. NAFTA, famously, has harmed US manufacturing. Because of its "most favored nation" and other clauses which mandate that "all North American companies regardless of national origin be treated the same way," each signatory competes with the others for foreign investment by striving to offer the best regulation waivers, the most available natural resources, and the most docile – and cheap – labor-power to multinationals. Free-trade agreements are, in this respect, another trend contributing to the sacrifice of time to the interests of spatial conquest. They lead directly to unemployment.

The failure of a global trade agreement: policy and protest

The economic and political treaties governing regional groups such as the European Union and, to a lesser extent, the NAFTA, represent a midway step between nationalization for expansionist economic ends, and unrestricted global economic access, in which no trade or government regulations inhibit the antics of the market. The existing global agreement is the 1947 General Agreement on Tariffs and Trade (GATT), enforced by its "court," the World Trade Organization (WTO). The GATT was designed to encourage free trade between its member states, which now number at least 111 countries, by regulating and reducing tariffs. It does not have the power to override national sovereignty on labor standards. But the NAFTA is less innocuous. The NAFTA has benefited multinational companies, but has led to reduced real wages in the United States and Canada and a marked decline in Mexican labor standards. It has had severe environmental consequences in the border regions especially.

The last seven years witnessed a concerted attempt to extend the NAFTA situation globally, going beyond the powers of the GATT.

In 1995 the OECD inaugurated a proposed Multilateral Agreement on Investment (MAI).[61] The prime mover behind the MAI in the OECD was the US.[62] From the inception of the idea, the advocates of a multilateral investment agreement debated whether the OECD or the WTO was the more appropriate forum. The *Financial Times* said as much in a leader,[63] while *The Economist* suggested that the way to view the MAI was as a prototype for a future WTO agreement.[64] When the MAI failed after the French left the negotiating table in October 1998, plans were launched immediately for a similar agreement in the WTO. The preliminary plans for a new roundtable on trade and investment – leading to a MAI – failed in Seattle. Delegates were unable to agree on an agenda.[65]

The agreement which the OECD hoped for, and which the WTO still has in mind, will be the most far-reaching in a series of trade and antiregulatory agreements extending the global reach of corporations. Under MAI-type legislation, corporations may be able to indict national governments which mandate labor conditions and environmental safeguards, among other things, on the grounds that such regulations are anticompetitive.[66] As we have seen, such legislation is now in place with the NAFTA. It also features in a series of over 1,600 bilateral agreements which made it easy for labor and environmental standards to be bypassed. The pressure for more such agreements, with an extended international range, is mounting.[67]

Existing WTO agreements do not do the job for capital adequately. *The Economist* spells it out: "there are many countries where foreign investors cannot be reasonably sure of being treated fairly. In most, foreign investment policy tends to yo-yo. The benefits of rules that prevent backsliding, and encourage countries to become more user-friendly, are therefore obvious."[68] Moreover, while the existing WTO trades agreements protect multinationals, they are not entirely "user-friendly." The present European, especially French, resistance to US hormone-beef imports has taken advantage of the loopholes in the WTO, although formally Europe has been told to pay compensation to the US. But under the GATT, national labor and environmental standards, whether they were implemented before or after the agreement, still have considerable legal sovereignty.

What makes a MAI-type agreement attractive to multinational capitals is that, under the guise of investment legislation, it makes it illegal for signatories to institute environmental or labor legislation that undermines their profits.[69] And this can be extended from pure investment to natural resources, making it legal to extract natural resources without penalty or restriction.[70] The right regulations might restrict capital. The prototype MAIs will enhance its profit.

The OECD negotiations failed in October of 1998. As *The Economist* has it, the real problem with the MAI was not its content, but the fact that it was initially negotiated in the OECD. This was a problem because it was not intended for the rich OECD member states alone. The MAI "Preamble" stressed that all countries can accede to its terms. This meant that the natural resources and labor-power of signatory B (let us say it is Brazil) would be available to signatory A (America?) without restriction. Not surprisingly, this led to accusations, says *The Economist*, of imperialism: "the governments of developing countries increasingly see MAI as an exercise in neo-colonialism, designed to give rich world investors the upper hand. This unease has been handled badly." Much better to handle it in the WTO, to which "developing countries" also belong.[71] Six weeks after the OECD negotiations ended, a leaked discussion paper for the EU Council outlined an initial strategy for including a multilateral investment agreement "as one of the new issues" in the WTO's millennial round of negotiations.[72]

Had this magna carta for multinationals gone through the OECD, or if it goes through the WTO or another international agency, its Southern signatories will stand witness to an accelerating circulation of resources which exhausts their habitats and their labor in the name of progress. Its Northern signatories will, by increasing the speed of production and global distribution, further degrade the environment of their peoples. Under existing GATT and WTO agreements, the production of any given commodity which uses up the resources of one country need not be slowed down because labor becomes expensive or raw materials are depleted. A company can simply shift its operations elsewhere. Under MAI-like terms, it can indict labor conditions and environmental standards as "noncompetitive" (just as it has successfully done under the NAFTA).

There were gestures to labor and the environment and even to local manufacturing standards in the MAI text. Similar environmentally concerned statements were made before the GATT and the NAFTA. Writing before the GATT, French notes that, "Under international law, if both parties to the dispute are members of both agreements, the most recent treaty generally holds sway." He adds that this "would tend to protect most environmental treaties." The protection of environmental treaties here presupposes that they are the most recent. But when NAFTA clauses conflict with existing environmental legislation, NAFTA wins; in every case, the environmental issue has come second to the trade issue.[73]

If the NAFTA's effects become global, if the GATT's effects are intensified by more global free-trade legislation, the consequences already evident in capital historically and in moves to globalization thus far will also be intensified. Among these effects is the increase in transport, the resulting increase in pollution, and the consequent decline in human health. Just as most banned chemicals in the US are nonprofitable, so do environmental factors come second to profit in the policy war between governmental agencies, a war which is generally resolved at the executive level in favor of the entirely unfounded idea that, left to themselves, free markets lead to wealth trickling down.[74] The environmental concerns of OECD officials are genuine; what is missing is the factual analysis of how free trade and globalization policy necessarily degrade the environment.

Here the reflections by some environmentalists on the NAFTA before its introduction are salutary, as is the (better) history of environmentalism in the European Union. As well as condemnation and caution before NAFTA's introduction, there was optimism. NAFTA might be a vehicle for products and technologies that help environmental clean-ups and ecological health. It may regulate environmental excesses rather than lead to them. The three governments who signed the treaty were to establish an environmental commission charged with raising environmental awareness and encouraging stronger environmental policies, although, as one commentator said at the time, "It remains to be seen if it will be granted the powers it needs to do this effectively."[75] There was also caution concerning how far NAFTA would be used to challenge or overturn existing environmental regulations, as well as prevent new ones. In order to stop environmental concerns "masking protectionism," both NAFTA and GATT (after the Uruguay round) require a "science test." But because scientists disagree, "the domestic environmental laws in some countries could be subject to challenge."[76] All you need is the right scientist.

Historically, caution was fully justified in both respects. NAFTA was supposed to invest billions of dollars to try and remedy the pollution problems plaguing the border area. Seven years after its inception, there is not a single environmental project financed by NAFTA in operation.[77] The same seven years of NAFTA have provided ample illustration of how easily corporations may use the agreement to attack environmental laws. Canada repealed a national ban on a gasoline additive and known human neurotoxin after its producer sued the Canadian government under NAFTA's provisions.[78] Other successful challenges in Canada have been over the right to dump toxic waste.[79] Meanwhile, in Mexico, the US-based Metalclad Corporation sued the government in 1997 when it prevented the company from opening a hazardous-waste disposal facility on a site over an underground stream. The governor of the state of San Luis Potosi had declared the site, where a previous disposal facility had contaminated groundwater, an ecologically protected zone. Metalclad, citing NAFTA's strong provision on expropriation, is seeking $90 million in damages, a figure higher than the combined annual income of every family in Mexico.[80] In addition to these cases, there may be others which have remained unknown to the public: NAFTA permits investors to sue governments using rules of the United Nations Center for International Trade Law (UNCITRAL), which is neither an agreement nor an institution, and which thus has no secretariat to maintain publicly accessible records.[81]

The significant thing about the known disputes brought under NAFTA so far is that they concern the right to dump toxic waste (four known suits) and the right to pollute (two suits). By contrast, the suits brought by Third World countries under the existing global provision, the GATT, concern their rights to exploit their biological resources and eliminate certain species. In other words, in tracing out the patterns of legal action, one can trace out two lines of environmental assault. The first is concerned with waste and pollution (from the North), the second with the disruption and depletion of living organisms and biospheres. The fact that legal actions in this respect have originated from the South makes them an easy target for the projected environmental concerns of the North. Clinton never tired of telling Third World countries to stop polluting and to protect their environmental reserves, such as rainforests, for the sake of the climate. However, what matters here is that the South sells its life conditions together with the energy of its labor to the North in order to survive in a global economy, while the North, especially the West, lives abundantly from Southern as well as Northern biological resouces, while sending its waste to the South.

Presently, the West is limited in relation to the speed with which it can extract Southern resources in areas where free trade does not hold sway with sufficient scope. The difficulty with the GATT, as with its labor provisions, is that it conveys no right to override national sovereignty in relation to environmental restrictions. The main effect of this, an effect reflected in the lawsuits, is to slow down the pace at which goods can be produced and circulated. In other words, what is at stake here is not only the resources, which are being bought and sold under the GATT as it stands, but the right to use them up rapidly. It is not only a question of access to labor and biological resources as such, but faster access. As established in the previous section, rapid production, like rapid transportation, is more likely to pollute and produce waste because it consumes more fossil fuels. It doing so it obviously consumes more raw materials, and at a speed that generates other waste aside from pollutant emissions. As we will see, both the speed and the raw materials consumed in production have to increase if profits are to remain at their present levels. This increases the expenditure on the fuel for production, transportation and communications, as well as expenditure on the other raw materials used in the production process. With the pressure on for greater access to raw materials and cheap labor, this is no time for an increase in the cost of fuel, or for regular fuel supplies, such as those guaranteed by Iraq, to be cut off.

Hence expansion by free trade and expansion by conquest are linked, and they are linked by the need to safeguard the conditions of their own expansion. Before the first war of the last century, the "Great Game" or "the real battle" in Central Asia was about communication and transportation links, "as it is today."[82] In the late nineteenth century, "the Russians built railway lines across Central Asia to their borders with Afghanistan, Persia, and China, while the British built railway lines across India to their border with Afghanistan. . . . Today's Great Game is also between expanding and contracting empires."[83] We have seen that whoever controls Afghanistan can bypass Russia, as well as Iran, Iraq and Syria, in access to Caspian oil. The struggle is and has been between Russia, attempting to control access to Caspian oil by building pipelines through its own territory, and the US. "Geologists estimate that sitting beneath the wind-blown steppes of Kazakhstan are 50 billion barrels of oil – by far the biggest untapped reserves in the world."[84] The problem for Kazakhstan is getting its oil beyond its landlocked borders. "The longer the pipeline, the more expensive and vulnerable to sabotage it is."[85] Kazakhstan is closely allied with the US, and so cannot take the shortest route, which is through Iran. Control of Iran demands a compliant Iraq, or an alternative route through Western Afghanistan (as noted above).

Many of those who hitherto opposed globalization support the war on terrorism, despite the global fuel issues which are refracted in that war. The expansion of the "war on terrorism" beyond Afghanistan to Iraq (imminent at the time of going to press) only makes those fuel issues more salient. What this book makes plain is that the opposition to globalization is also opposition to the damage done to the atmosphere and the climate through fossil-fuel pollution, which produces illness in the West now. It is also opposition to the conditions that foster terrorism. It is opposition to the exploitation of labor, unemployment and the loss of a living through the land. Globalization, in short, visits terrors on the South and on the future, directly through war, starvation and exploitation, and indirectly through the destruction of the atmosphere.

4   The war on the land, sea and other conditions of life

I began this book with the idea that globalization is the outcome and continuation of a process of extension, which entails speeding up production, distribution, exchange and consumption. While air pollution and the climate are directly tied to the increase in trade, insofar as half of fossil-fuel combustion goes to transportation, other forms of speeding up production, nationally and internationally, imperil the other conditions of life (protection from solar ultraviolet radiation, adequate food, safe water, biodiversity). In this chapter, we will be discussing these other conditions of life. The first section focuses on the specifics of global warming, with its rising temperatures and climatic instability. We will see that this generation is not only accountable to the future for the climatic instability it is producing; it is also damaging itself. Following this discussion, the chapter turns to water and food pollution as well as shortages in food and water. Genetic engineering will be discussed as well: it affects both food supply and biodiversity. As we progress through the list of life conditions and their antagonists, we will see that, in all cases, life is damaged by speeding up production for profit. This leads to severe cancer increases, birth defects and drastic rises in chronic illnesses, ranging from the commonplace, such as gastroenteritis, to (in the case of genetic engineering) consequences as yet unclear.

Tolerable temperature and stable climate

As I stressed at the outset, climate and temperature are on the urgent global agenda. As with air quality, they are affected by fossil-fuel emissions (together with cement and steel production), and hence affected by globalization. While the Kyoto protocol has been blocked so far by the US, explicit concern is something of an advance. It is no longer realistic to hope, as Mrs. Thatcher did, that global warming is part of a natural cycle: most scientists agree the warming of the earth is occurring at a "rate over and above natural variability." Global warming is clearly the consequence of carbon gases and other products of engines and motor exhausts (especially carbon dioxide, nitrous oxide and methane) trapping heat in the atmosphere, causing the famous "greenhouse" effect which melts the ice and warms the seas. In August 2000, the North Pole was liquid for the first time.[1]

According to the Intergovernmental Panel on Climate Change, if we do not immediately cut greenhouse-gas emissions dramatically, average temperatures on earth will increase from 1.6 to 6.3°F within the next century; "this is no longer in doubt."[2] Not only will this increase in temperature affect ocean levels and disease-carrying vectors, it will be the biggest temperature increase in 10,000 years and will be too fast and drastic for most species to survive. It will also reclaim a third of habitable land. Coral reefs are already dying from the warming of seas. This is especially important because coral reefs are anchors for much of marine biodiversity. As the coral dies, the small fish and other organisms that live in and feed on it die. As the smaller animals become scarce, the larger fish that feed upon them are also affected, and the effects move on. The inevitable chain reaction (inevitable given the ecological inter-dependence of all things) will have more unpredictable effects, but species extinction is certain. So is their migration (for those that can migrate) as they seek to survive. The last twenty-five years have seen a resurgence in infectious diseases,[3] linked both to general breakdowns in immunity and the increase in the mobility of disease vectors, such as mosquitoes. An outbreak of West Nile virus encephalitis in New York City in 1999 killed seven people and hospitalized fifty-five others.[4] The West Nile virus strain had not been previously documented in the Western hemisphere. The encephalitis problem in New York was brought under control as the temperature cooled and allergy-provoking pesticides were sprayed.[5] For the first time, epidemics of dengue fever, a mosquito-carried viral infection, have occurred in Australia, as well as in Venezuela, Brazil and India. The disease has decreased by nearly 100 percent and WHO officials warn that it is affecting tens of millions.[6] Yellow fever, another mosquito-borne disease, is also on the increase.[7] In addition to mosquito-borne diseases, killer bees and fire ants are moving their range northward.

Given that I have already discussed how and why fossil-fuel consumption has increased over the last thirty years in particular, and – by implication – how other gases from motor vehicle exhausts have also increased, discussion of the causes of global warming can be abbreviated. While fossil-fuel corporations still deny the link between the emissions of greenhouse gases and the rise in the earth's temperature, asserting that the rise in the earth's temperature is a natural phenomenon, the evidence is there. "The global surface temperature has increased by about 0.5°C since 1975, a burst of warming that has taken the global temperature to its highest level in the past millennium."[8] Heat storage in the ocean provides direct empirical verification for global warming, tying its extent with considerable precision to the increase in carbon emissions and the decrease in forest cover. That is to say: it is not possible to measure heat storage on land, but it can be measured in the sea, which is its first victim.

The increase in global and domestic transportation, and the related speeding up of other aspects of production, is accelerating the emission of greenhouse gases at exactly the point where they most need to be cut. The information compiled by the World Resources Institute and the US Department of Energy's Carbon Dioxide Information Analysis Centre (CDIAC) on atmospheric levels from 1755 to 1995, and emissions from human activities in the same time frame, make this plain. The tables show, first, that world CO_2 emissions from fossil-fuel consumption and cement manufacturing (remembering that cement and steel manufacture are the other minor sources of CO_2 emissions) have increased from the nineteenth century onward, and especially in the last thirty years. Second, the tables show how atmospheric levels also increase from the nineteenth century onward, and that the levels accelerate even more rapidly in the period of free trade expansion. CO_2 emissions were over half a billion metric tons in 1975. By 1995, they had doubled.[9] Except for nitrous oxide (N_2O), which shows a steady increase, the other greenhouse gases, such as methane, have either decreased or remained constant since 1992; only the primarily ozone-depleting gases, the CFCs, have decreased somewhat, confirming that regulations and controls are having some effect.[10]

But the escalation of fossil-fuel consumption is unabated. Significantly, one NASA scientist now says that the rate of carbon dioxide emissions "shrank slightly in 1998 and 1999, even as the global economy grew."[11] The remark is significant because it shows, however obliquely, awareness of the link between globalization and the rate of emissions. But it does not appear to be accurate. This scientist, James Hansen, who was responsible for political interest in global warming in the first place,[12] relied on an article with the optimistic title "Carbon Emissions Fall Again."[13] The article maintained that emissions from human activities dropped slightly in 1999 and 1998. Unfortunately, the reference given for the 1998 "drop" was to a CDIAC study of emissions that went only to 1996 (incidentally, a record year for carbon emissions), while the substantial reference for the 1999 drop is an estimate, whose sole supporting source (among many apparent sources) lies in BP Amoco's projections.[14]

Protection from ultraviolet (UV) radiation

Global warming is not the only climatic threat. The thinning of the ozone layer has also accelerated in the period of rapid expansion in global trade. As with global warming, the repercussions of ozone depletion were predicted long before they were evident. Increased transportation is also one (though not the principal) cause of the depletion of the ozone layer standing between the earth and ultra-violet radiation from the sun. In 1985 a large hole in the ozone was discovered over Antarctica, and other significant amounts of thinning were reported over more populated areas.[15] Ozone is destroyed predominantly by chlorine ions that are released from CFCs. These gaseous molecules were used as propellants in, for example, aerosol spray cans, and are also employed in air-conditioning and refrigeration systems in cars, trucks and (mainly) home appliances.[16] In addition, they are used in the manufacturing of closed-cell and open-cell foams.[17] Such foams are utilized widely in shipping; they ensure that a product arrives at its destination safely, unbroken, unmarred. Refrigerator trucks used for shipping frozen goods also use CFCs for coolant. For instance, as the shipment of frozen fish from fish farms increases (due to decreasing local stocks in the North) so will the CFCs released into the environment. To this extent then, the release of CFCs is one outcome of increasing centralization and the resultant need for increased transportation. Mobile refrigeration accounts for 1 out of every 8 pounds of refrigeration CFCs produced in the US. But domestic refrigeration accounts for the remainder.[18] In this respect, CFCs are linked to the speeding up of household production and consumption. They are linked to the pace of personal consumption in other ways: CFC-releasing foams are employed to trap heat in "fast foods" to go. Styrofoam is the preferred packaging: it helps insulate the hot food. It is also cheap. Despite extensive publicity concerning the effects of CFCs, their atmospheric concentrations increased in the 1990s, and has only just begun to decrease. Their use in aerosols in some Western countries has been banned; some companies, including McDonald's, in the UK and the United States no longer utilize styrofoam packaging; Greenpeace has developed an alternative (non-CFC) refrigerator. But, in general, the use of CFCs for refrigeration and transportation continues, although utraviolet radiation has been proven long since to cause skin carcinomas and melanomas.[19] Moreover, skin cancer is only one of the health effects of increased exposure to ultraviolet radiation. Increased exposure can also cause premature skin aging and cataracts. Most seriously, it decreases immunity.[20] Leprosy, among other maladies, is more likely to occur because of the decreased ability of the body to protect itself: ultraviolet radiation increases the effects of many diseases that start on, or affect, the skin,[21] including smallpox, skin ulcers, anthrax.[22]

Safe water

Water, the second condition of life after air, has suffered from chemical plants and household consumption, and from the agricultural and petroleum industries. That fossil fuel *par excellence*, petroleum, leads not only to air pollution. The storage of the ever larger amounts of it needed for transportation affects water, as does toxic waste. In the United States, oil storage tanks have a history of losing millions of gallons of oil into the ground water, which is the source of about half the nation's drinking water. The petroleum products that have been leaking into the water supply since the 1940s are toxic as well as explosive. This is a serious matter: depending on the state involved, up to 90 percent of drinking water was drawn from underground sources.[23] Petroleum products include chemicals that are known to cause cancer as well as other health problems such as liver and kidney failure, neurological disorders, and chromosome damage.[26]

The agricultural industry's animal waste, in particular, and its pesticides have damaged the earth's limited supply of clean water. Take pig farms, one of the main water-polluting industries in the US: they constitute an excellent example of how current agricultural practices pollute drinking water. The pathogens which enter US waterways *via* these capitalist pigs can cause hepatitis, gastroenteritis, cholera, typhoid fever, eye and ear infections, giardiasis, dysentery, skin rashes, and pink eye in humans.[25] There is considerable public outcry in the United States concerning the degradation of waterways near the large hog farms, but the response to this outcry by the hog industry gives us a taste, so to speak, of what is to come. In the US and Europe, regulations are sidestepped by turning to countries with lower standards. Following the outcry, hog producers started raising pigs in Canada and are considering doing the same in Mexico; "the industry is going to go where it feels welcome."[28]

Forty years ago, when Rachel Carson wrote *Silent Spring*, her conclusion that the human species was in peril from an unprecedented influx of chemical pesticides in food and water was, of course, disputed. Her numerous detractors argued that she relied too heavily on animal studies. Mice, they said, are not little people.[27] Even allowing for the mice variable, the cumulative results of four decades of research shows that Carson was basically right. Today human beings are still, and more, at risk from toxic chemicals. Traces of hundreds of chemicals can be found in water supplies all over the world, and a report in the UK has warned that male fertility may be threatened by drinking water contaminated with hormones,[28] DDT and other organophosphates which are potential reproductive-system hormone mimickers. Hormones, DDT and other organophosphates enable more plants and animals to be produced within a shorter time frame. In other words, these chemicals speed up production. They speed it up within localities as well as nations, and could do so even in a fiercely protectionist economy.

But in a global economy, the use of chemicals spreads by the importation of Western methods. Not only this, but water as such is becoming scarce:

> the threefold growth in world water use since mid-century is pushing demand beyond the amount that the hydrological cycle can supply. Water scarcity and falling water tables are now commonplace in the former Soviet Asian republics and Central Asia, especially Afghanistan, the Middle East, North China, parts of India, North Africa, parts of sub-Saharan Africa and the southwestern United States.[29]

Adequate food

For those who survive the destruction of the sea, the climate, breathing and drinking, eating remains to be negotiatied. The food supply of the North, like that of the South, has become a source of illness and poor health. The authors of *Our Stolen Future*, a successor to Carson's work on the effects of chemical pesticides in food and water, have shown (I think definitively) that the cumulative effect of ingested chemicals is affecting our reproductive capacities, particularly those of men. Pesticide residues are also linked to decreasing intelligence, insofar as they affect thyroid function.[30] The main chemical offenders acting as food pesticides are, or have been, dichlorodiphenyltrichloroethane (DDT), poly-chlorinated biphenyls (PCB), and methyl parathion, among others. Even while some of these are subject to full and partial bans in Europe and other advanced countries, their effects live on: it is impossible to eliminate them from fatty tissue. They are also passed on through breastmilk. This is not to downplay the significance of the existing bans. Every one represents a victory; all time spent towards those bans, however partial or inconclusive the results, is time well spent. But, as with air, as with climate, as with water, the search for substitute chemicals that will hasten production continues, and the ill effects of the substitutes are known only after the fact.

The best-known offender here, DDT, was banned in the United States in 1972, barring a public health emergency,[31] because of the effects that it had on the reproductive systems of animals, especially birds. But DDT is still a global issue. The United Nations has been drafting a worldwide ban on this pesticide, but is encountering resistance because DDT is purportedly necessary for keeping malaria under control in many countries in the South. The World Health Organization has listed "control of disease vectors" as the only official use of DDT.[32] But it is apparently still employed in agriculture in many Southern countries, who do not admit to its use, and so circumvent the ban on importing DDT-affected foods to the North.[33] In addition, these countries rationalize their continued production and application of DDT with arguments extolling its effectiveness and relatively low production cost.[34] Moreover, multilateral, international organizations frequently allow high-level exposure to the chemicals used to speed the production process. For example, the Codex Alimentarius is the United Nations guide to food safety standards. Forty-two percent of its standards set are lower than the US Food and Drug Administration (FDA) and EPA standards for the United States. Fifty times more DDT may be applied on peaches and bananas grown in other countries than those grown in the United States, and thirty-three times more can be used on broccoli.[35] Finally, despite the copious evidence found in animals that DDT causes tumors and interferes with animal life cycles, there is still contention concerning the effects it has upon humans. But the contention is increasingly vague, and the consensus on its harmful effects is close to unilateral.

Given that DDT and its toxic companion, PCB, are fat-soluble and are not purged by the body, it follows that, as more of these pesticides are ingested, personal levels will continue to rise. DDT, as we mentioned, is a hormone-mimicking chemical: it mimics the action of estrogen. Like other estrogen mimickers in the environment, it has been linked to breast cancer and reproductive failure.[36] In the early 1990s, DDT was cited as a risk factor for breast cancer in the United States, Finland, Mexico and Canada.[37] Fat-solubility also retains those chemicals which reduce intelligence, and impair male reproductive function and potency.[38]

The immune system, again, is under systematic assault. The latest essential supplement in the alternative health market is a capsule of necessary bacteria which the human body once obtained through food. The reason given in the literature on the supplement as to why these necessary bacteria have deserted food is this. Needed bacteria, basically, are soil organisms ingested with food. But they have not survived chemical farming, which uses soil sterilization techniques together with pesticides. Hypothetically, this affects the immune system because these bacteria are needed to keep the "bad" bacteria at root of ulcers and other diseases of the gastro-intestinal (GI) tract in check. "Just as [these soil organisms] destroy molds, yeast, fungus, and viruses in the soil of the organic garden, they perform the same with pathological organisms in the gut, greatly augmenting the body's immune system."[39] The same product attributes part of the problem to the separation common for most between where they were born (with bacteria they became friendly with if they were allowed to play in the dirt) and where they now live (with new bacteria). This may be a metaphor for the effects on immunity of relocation, or maybe not. But, even as a metaphor, it raises the effects of continued dislocation on immune function.

The negative effects of pesticide are like a witchcraft trial by drowning: one discovers the truth of the matter after the fact. In the chemical case, one discovers by illness, not before. And there has to be a lot of illness before the effects of chemicals in food are acknowledged. Take that other common pesticide, methyl parathion, used to kill bugs on fruit trees. While the US Environmental Protection Agency issued a ban on methyl parathion in 1999, this was only after the pesticide directly caused illness (farm workers were sprayed with it), and well after animal tests indicated that it put children at risk. Many other instances of its negative human health effects, such as spontaneous abortion, lung cancer and death, have been uncovered.

Approximately 80 percent of the commodities produced in the US and Europe are manufactured using a type of chemical process,[40] which, as we will see shortly, is due to the need to speed up production, otherwise known as "increasing productivity." Repeated chemical assaults may be exacerbated by the modern demand that one run twice as fast to stay in the same place, but chemical insults, in themselves, do damage. This is in no sense to downplay the harm done the human organism by pacing it according to production processes that are too speedy to take account of human needs.[41] Indeed, the paradox is that, while human beings are running to keep up, they are eating food whose growth has been artificially accelerated, both by chemicals and, dramatically, by genetic engineering.

Food and genetic engineering

Genetically modified food is leaving the realms of the exception and attempting to become the rule. In 1998 and 1999, the debate over genetically modified (GM) organisms landing unadvertised on supermarket shelves in Britain reached the point where the Prince of Wales intervened.[42] The advocates of foodstuffs produced by this means claim that it will help feed the Third World, but it is doubtful that the companies involved would find a sufficient return for their investment in the Third World markets.[43] They are geared towards rapid production for rapid consumption, which means they are geared to the North. In no other area is the speeding-up imperative so apparent in the food industry as it is in genetic engineering. Rifkin says it most concisely: "Engineer the genetic blueprint of a tree so it will grow to maturity quicker. Manipulate the genetic instructions of domestic breeds to produce faster-growing 'super-animals.' Redesign the genetic information of cereal plants to increase their yield."[44] Genetic engineering for food is about speeding up the growth or "production time" of plants, trees and animals. As such, it is part of an economy which depends on speed to enhance its profits, as we will see, and which genetic engineering also serves in other ways. We learn from Rifkin that "scientists are now using microbial agents to degrade the minerals in which gold is trapped prior to chemical extraction to increase the recovery rate of the gold."[45]

Biotech companies claim that genetic-engineering technology will help feed the world.[46] The old *canard* about feeding the Third World is trotted out each time a risky technique needs ethical justification for its implementation. (There are variations on the theme, such as the drug companies' tune about preventing illness in the Third World.)[47] There are food shortages, but they derive from overpopulation in relation to the earth's resources, as well as the degradation of those resources resulting from disturbed eco-systems. Interfering further with those ecosystems will only exacer-bate the problem it is meant to solve. But the immediate point is that genetic engineering may have, in some instances already does have, toxic effects; it can cause severe allergic reactions because of the new gene or genes hidden in food,[48] and it damages quality and nutrition.[49] One study found that GM soybeans contained smaller concentrations of phyto-estrogens, which may protect against heart disease and cancer.[50] The nutritional effects are only beginning to emerge, but the animal studies are ominous. Rats who were fed GM potatoes suffered stunted growth and weakened immune systems.[51]

The difficulty with genetic engineering stems from the fact that DNA regulates all the functions of an organism at the most basic level; it is the blueprint for life. When foreign genes are inserted into an animal, there is no way to predict the results that will occur due to the little understood, and vastly complex, cascade of hormones and other biological chemicals all regulated by DNA. Also, once genetically engineered organisms are released into the environment, there is no way to contain or recall them. The bio-technology industry and the United States government maintain that the exchange of genetic material between unrelated species (from bacteria to tomatoes, viruses to squash, insect to tobacco, and human to fish) is no different from selective cross-breeding techniques employed between single or closely related species which enhance desirable traits.[52] Therefore, pre-market testing is not required in the US. On the other hand, "it is virtually impos-sible to even conceive of a testing procedure to assess health effects when genetically engineering is released into the food chain."[53]

The immediate health threat from genetic engineering is through food. But there are other threats. GM crops were first produced on a large scale in North America in 1996. Many of the GM crops are staple crops such as corn and soybeans. The health conscious will be disconcerted to learn that over half of the soybean crop in the US is grown from genetically engineered seeds. (Up to half is also laced with virulent pesticides. I have been unable to establish if it is the same half, but suspect that it is not.)[54] The point about genetically engineered seeds and crops is that they are modified to resist insects, to kill weeds and parasites and so forth. It is clear in some cases that they kill more than they are meant to do.[55] Apparently "the greatest threat from genetically altered crops is the insertion of modified virus and insect virus genes into crops. It has been shown in the laboratory that genetic recombination will create highly virulent new viruses from such constructions."[56] But, while the viruses increase, the resistance to the infection decreases through genetic engineering as well. Antibiotic resistant marker (ARM) genes are used in many genetic-engineering experiments. If these ARM genes recombine with disease causing bacteria, they may release a strain of dangerous, virulent bacteria unresponsive to conventional antibiotics. Increased antibiotic resistance is another possible health effect of genetic engineering. ARM genes recombine with bacteria or viruses in the environment or in the body and confer antibiotic resistance to the bacteria. This occurrence could bring about a disease epidemic with the pathogens resistant to traditional antibiotics. In short, genetic pollution from genetically engineered organisms released into the environment may breed new animal and plant diseases, contribute new sources of cancer, and develop novel disease epidemics.[57] There is no way to determine if unforeseen combinations of chemicals in the new organism will have a negative impact on the consumers of it, be they humans or other organisms in the food chain.

Speeding up food supplies – and slowing them down

At this point we should backtrack a little. Chemicals and genetic engineering both increase "productivity," to use the conventional term. This means they increase output within a given time in relation to input. In turn, this means getting more from the "input": the raw materials and labor. On the face of it, this can be done in one of two ways: either technology increases the yield, or the raw materials and labor have to "work" faster, by sheer sweat of their brow, or by growing faster, or by growing more. Growing faster and growing more come to the same thing in the end. For the sake of argument, let us say I am a tomato plant. If I produce ten tomatoes in a day, where once I produced five, I am either managing to salvage another five tomatoes which would otherwise have failed to materialize, or my rate of producing tomatoes has accelerated.

The need to increase productivity is responsible for the continued use of pesticides and fertilizers. As we have seen, a pesticide is defined as "any substance or mixture of substances intended for preventing, controlling or destroying any pest." Applications of pesticides and chemical fertilizers increase the efficiency of production by providing crop protection. Those five tomatoes which might otherwise have failed to materialize would probably have been destroyed by pests. Chemicals are an integral part of food production because they repel pests that would lessen the crop yield; more is produced within the same time frame. Furthermore, other growth constraints associated with nature are removed; not only are pest infestations removed, but so are weed infestations, clearing more space and nutrients for plants, while fertilizer speeds plant growth. More tomatoes materialize.

From 1986 to 1991 there was a 63 percent increase in the amount of fertilizer employed in the European Union.[58] Agriculture now accounts for about 80 percent of all pesticide use in the United States. Pesticide use has been calculated in terms of quantity. It is gauged in terms of a measure of the aggregate weight of applied active (chemical) ingredients. Recent years have seen a shift to chemicals that are much more concentrated and can be applied at very low rates (although total quantity is not necessarily a good indicator of environmental or health risk because of the diverse characteristics of pesticide ingredients – toxicity, persistence, solubility, etc.). But total pesticide use has now edged back up and equals the previous peak.[59] This means that quantities of even the concentrated pesticides have increased. It also means, obviously, that there is a need for more pesticides.

In part, this is due to the use of high-yield seeds – another tool employed to speed up agricultural production. These seeds produce more than conventional seeds within the same time. But they also require more pesticide than normal plants and therefore introduce more chemicals into the soil and water table. In addition, growth of such seeds helps increase resistance to pesticides, due to more use of and exposure to them. This takes us to the key reason for the increase in (concentrated) pesticides. High-yield seeds develop that resistance faster, but plants from normal seeds do so as well. When pests develop resistance to certain pesticides, the amount of the chemical has to be increased to have an effect, or more powerful chemicals have to be found. Either way, there are more chemical residues in food, and more seep into water and the soil.

Moreover, the techniques to increase productivity also degrade soil. The tomato plant that accelerates its rate of production with the application of pesticides and fertilizer does so at the expense of the soil in which it is grown. Putting the matter in physical terms: in order to "work" harder, that plant draws on more energy than it otherwise would. In the vernacular, there is no free lunch. Nothing exemplifies this more than the "Green Revolution." The Green Revolution is a form of agriculture marketed by chemical corporations consisting of high-yielding seeds and high doses of chemical fertilizers and pesticides, which allow more than one crop per year to be grown on the same plot of land. Beginning from 1970 to 1980, it impacted many Third World countries, including India. The "revolution" meant the Third World could grow more exportable produce in an attempt to compete in the global economy with industrial nations. As such, it reflected IMF globalization policy. In practice, the "revolution" is a powerful illustration of the detrimental environmental effects resulting from attempts to increase agricultural productivity. At first, production did increase, then the imported chemicals became more expensive and only richer farmers could afford them. Without the aid of chemicals, poor farmers' productivity plummeted and many lost their farms. In India especially, soil became severely degraded, and in 1998 (as noted at the outset) over 500 Indian farmers committed suicide because of the loss of their livelihood. Others have killed themselves since.[60]

Nor is the South the only victim of the new farming methods, anymore than Southern peoples are the only ones who suffer from pesticide residues in food and water. Farm numbers have declined in the West by two-thirds from 1935. Farms have been consolidated in order to achieve lower per unit production costs and to increase the efficiency and speed of processing. From the point of view of processing companies, it is more productive to process products from a small number of large providers than from a large number of small-scale providers.[61] Farm numbers are expected to decline by up to 2 percent annually for the rest of decade.[62] But since land use for agriculture has remained constant, fewer farms mean larger farms rather than less farming overall.[63] Consolidation concentrates *types* of production as much as places of production: cash cropping and the so-called green revolution have demonstrated how largely self-sustaining economies can be turned into single-crop machines. The number of Third World countries which are now banana and single-crop machines, while hitherto they had been self-sustaining in terms of food production, keeps increasing.

Agricultural practices follow human beings in stretching themselves further in space and speeding themselves up in time. Progressively, in the West, global corporations take over small farms and establish production contracts with farmers, making them subject to similar regulation by speedy production requirements over larger distances. These corporations are not tied to any one area of production; if productivity is disrupted in one area, they turn to another. Farmers, of course, know this, and that to stay in the game they have to produce and produce fast. Otherwise the corporation moves on and their livelihood is lost.

In some instances, the need for heightened productivity leads to a number of practices which ultimately result in increased pollution and degraded human health: specifically, (1) it leads to a reduction in the number of small farms; (2) it increases the amount of pesticides and fertilizers used by farmers; and (3) it encourages the use of genetically engineered crops. Consolidation has also led to a situation in which a few corporations are controlling the world's food supply and consumption patterns. Large corporations currently manage virtually all the different stages of food production. Seed fertilizer, pesticide, transportation and processing plants are closely tied, and sometimes are owned by the same corporation. In an effort to increase profit, global corporations used American hegemony within the global economic order to facilitate the worldwide expansion of US production and consumption patterns.[64] Where independent farmers once flourished, corporate agribusiness now manufactures and markets over 95 percent of the food in the United States and over 80 percent of that in Western Europe.[65] The once self-sufficient producers have lost control of the world's food supply to multinational corporations because of the pressures of a global economy. Corporations have also become involved in the production of raw food stuffs, and have changed farming considerably: "as a consequence of integration within the wider Fordist economy, agricultural production has experienced significant restructuring and changes in production."[66] Contracts with agribusiness are the key to many farmers' livelihoods because the large corporations more or less control the food industry. They are also the key to the industrialization of farm labor, and the attempt to overcome the biological uncertainties associated with reproducing life. Part of free-trade policy, and IMF dogma, is abolishing subsidies, together with tariffs. Cutting subsidies may be of benefit to agricultural corporations, but it will put small and medium-sized farmers out of business.[67] This is the most typical and perhaps the most serious pattern (after climate) in how the moves from a local economy to an extended one play out.

Just as water supplies are dwindling, so are agricultural supplies. While production and consumption speed up, the supply of food, and of the biological resources used industrially, is slowing down: "the production of grain, which dominates human diets, expanded at 3 percent a year from 1950 until 1984 . . . from then until 1992, it grew less than 1 percent annually, scarcely half the rate of population."[68] There appear to be two principal causes of this. First, growth in cropland, irrigation, and yield from fertilizer input, have all slowed down: "today, using more fertilizer in agriculturally advanced countries has little effect on crop yields."[69] This fact suggests of itself that the exhaustion of natural reserves, in this case, soil, is the price paid for earlier speeding up of agricultural production. As with genetic engineering, there is a limit to how far we squeeze before we deplete. (Marx in fact discussed the significance of the "metabololic imbalance" capitalist haste produced in the soil, and in doing so came as close as he ever did to locating natural energies other than labor as sources of surplus value.)[70] The second reason for slower food and general biological production is that "the many forms of environmental degradation – soil erosion, aquifer depletion, air pollution, ozone depletion and hotter summers – are taking a toll on agricultural output."[71] We have already seen that fish and wood supplies are dwindling. Overall, given the number of Third World countries depending on primary products, it is not surprising that, between 1980 and 1990, incomes (measured in terms of GNP) in nearly fifty of those countries fell. These are World Bank figures. For some observers, this fall in income is not an accident but a direct result of environmental degradation, especially of "forests, grasslands and croplands."[72]

The genetically engineered tomato is our modern-day apple from the tree of knowledge. Bioderegulation may seem like the Garden of Eden, but in fact it signals the Fall. One can speed up the rate of production of a tomato plant by the use of pesticides and fertilizer. The failed fruits which once fell to the ground, and enhanced the soil, fall no more. But fertilizer also becomes less effective, while pesticides leave toxic residues and, over time, their effectiveness is diminished. Topsoil is eroded by general environmental conditions, from acid rain to climate change. The threat of food poisoned by pesticides then competes with the threat of no food at all. At the point where chemical means of increasing the rate of production are becoming exhausted, genetic engineering steps in. By borrowing genes from other species, one can give a lift to that fading tomato. Fish genes will make it shine; pork genes will make it plump. No matter if there is no taste there or no nutrients or physical pleasure in their taste. It looks like a tomato, and it sells. No one would know to look at them like this that natural resources suffer from their overuse in the same way that human beings do. But just as we humans pay endosomatically if we overextend ourselves, so do they.

5 Health cuts and corporate wealth

Auto-immune diseases are increasing. Cancer and other chronic illnesses are escalating.[1] In the US, over 100 million people suffer from them. When the US administration, or the Blair government, appear to recognize this by talking earnestly about health, one is led to believe that they are making it a financial priority. This is not so. In real terms, they are spending less.[2] Together with the increase in illness goes a reduction in treatment and medication. These used to be reimbursed in full, or at least in large part. This is no longer the case. In this chapter, we will see that almost all governments are cutting social provision, beginning with spending on health.[3] These reductions are the other side of bioderegulation. Humans have to go faster to keep pace with the machine, cutting their reproduction or regeneration time voluntarily. Cuts in social provision represent the involuntary component in bioderegulation. One has less money as well as less time to repair the damage of staying in the race.

Spending on health in particular and social provision for human needs in general – the daily and generational reproduction and regeneration of people – has been cut across the board. Throughout the advanced welfare states, from the United States to Europe, Australia and New Zealand, governments have enacted cuts and alterations in social spending on healthcare, pensions, education and unemployment insurance, as well as financial aid to poor families, usually headed by single mothers. Cuts in these benefits have been the most publicized, so much so that "welfare" has come to mean direct cash payments to unemployed lone parents. At one level, the changes in welfare legislation affecting mothers and families illustrate the logic and direction of third way policy most concisely. Such changes are presented as the new version of social democracy, something that does not abandon the needy but helps them overcome "dependency."[4] But in the end, welfare reform is just another way of cutting spending. As such, welfare reform is part of a series of reductions in state spending for health, pensions and overall social provision that began before the third way was mooted.

In the US and the UK, cutbacks in health, education and pensions were first implemented by new right governments in the 1980s; in Australia and New Zealand, reductions were introduced by social democratic or labor governments. The so-called third way merely gives this process a new name and a vocabulary of fuzzy concern. It also focuses attention on one group – welfare mothers – affected by the overall cuts in social provision at the expense of others: the old, the young and the ill (which is most of us). The disproportionate attention given to the issue of welfare reform is tied to the population served by welfare programs. Cash assistance to families in the US and the UK is understood as spending targeted at a specific and relatively poor, powerless and marginalized group. As such, cuts in these programs are not as politically disadvantageous as cuts in programs which benefit an entire nation's population. That is to say: when making cuts in healthcare, pensions, and other social spending programs, governments tread softly. Yet overall, there has been an ideological shift within OECD welfare states, which began in the 1980s and was consolidated during the 1990s.[5] It is a shift away from the sense that citizens, as part of their rights, are entitled to government programs (and therefore that such programs should be available to all regardless of income) and toward a sense of obligation (you must give to get) and the idea that these programs should be available only to the truly needy. More and more, governments are asserting that citizens should take individual responsibility for the provision of their daily and generational reproduction, meaning their human needs. "Individual responsibility" here means seeking out appropriate services in the private sector. At the very least, individual responsibility means paying more of "one's share" to the government when using nationally funded social-welfare programs.

The general rhetoric of these cuts has been that of efficiency and better quality. Governments assert that, through cutting costs by involving the private sector, services are actually improved. Or they explain that cost cutting and cost sharing are necessary because of difficult times – that the government must reduce its social spending programs and everyone will need to sacrifice to some extent. The monetarist argument here is that high social spending hurts national economies, creating high unemployment, low savings and poor productivity, which drag down economic performance. Citing all of these problems with social-welfare spending, *The Economist* has advocated that services such as childcare, savings for old age, and unemployment and sickness insurance "should all be candidates for at least partial privatization."[6] Others have claimed that corporations are oppressed by welfare states. "The cost of maintaining these subsidy states has become oppressively burdensome to European business," writes *Newsweek*, concerned because German businesses must pay half the cost of retirement, health, unemployment and nursing-care insurance.[7]

As we will see, criticism of a policy which is burdensome to corporations and the language of efficiency are saying much the same thing. For if we ask why high state spending on social provision "drags down economic performance," we find that it does so because it requires corporate taxation.[8] Today, national productivity is linked to the corporate investment a nation attracts; hence nations compete with one another to lower corporate taxes. Investment can, after all, move elsewhere in a global economy. As economies become more export oriented and as domestic industries invest more abroad, as they go elsewhere to invest in their labor and natural resources, capital wields ever more power over nation-states, making corporate needs equivalent to the national good. The competition for corporate investment has led even the formerly most advanced social democracy to stand on its head. Greg Olsen notes how the journal of the Swedish business association (SAF)

> enthusiastically remarked . . . that most of the goals set out in their plan, including an end to centralized bargaining . . . deregulation in the capital and financial markets, the privatization of several state companies, a reduction of corporate taxes (now the lowest in Europe), impending membership in the EU, the elimination of the wage-earner funds, and a beginning of the break up of the "public-sector monopoly" on social programs through the introduction of private alternatives, had been achieved far ahead of schedule.[9]

Nor is Sweden alone. Corporate taxes have been reduced while taxes on the middle and working classes have increased in the bid for transnational investment.[10] Gray explains that the corporations with jobs in their gift offer them only because the host country offers tax incentives and docile labor forces. The investors are meant to generate jobs, and so, yes, the wealth is meant to trickle down. In reality, the jobs (where they exist) come with a high price: increased taxation for those employed, taxation which compensates somewhat for the reduction in corporate tax. In sum: to get the jobs, the state sacrifices its income from corporate tax – the very tax that used to pay for comprehensive health, education, and welfare coverage. It then shifts the burden onto its citizens, who then blame one another for their higher taxes. Reductions in corporate taxation, together with the breakup of social provision, are not easily reconciled with the justification for government as such – namely, the protection of citizens. Presumably, this is why such governments refer to cuts in health, education and pensions in the nonspecific language of efficiency and productivity, rather than their effects on human well-being, or in saving corporate taxes. But cost is plain in the case of health.

Health

As a rule, comparative government expenditures on healthcare are discussed only in terms of gross domestic product. This obscures the recent reductions in healthcare provision: when the focus is on GDP, we see steady increases in spending resulting in a total 1 percent increase between 1985 and 1991 for the OECD countries overall.[11] Even this minimal increase is not the result of more generous healthcare programs, although this is widely claimed. The OECD says, for instance, that the increases result, in part, from a move toward universal coverage in many countries.[12] However, as the OECD itself shows in its 1998 report entitled *Social and Health Policies in OECD Countries*, and as discussed below, for the most part, government provision of and payment for health services is becoming more and more restricted.

On analysis, the OECD report in fact attributes the small increase in state spending on healthcare to a "slow down in economic growth" and a "continued increase in health care costs" related to "the aging population, . . . medical technology growth, . . . [and] a shift towards chronic and multi-faceted diseases." It adds that "People no longer die from their diseases, but live with them."[13] The first reason does not stand up to close examination. "Slow economic growth" means that healthcare spending appears to have increased because the rate of GDP growth has slowed in many countries. This means that the amount of money spent on healthcare, even if it is the same or less than it was in previous years, might appear as a larger percentage of GDP than in previous years. In this sense, then, looking at healthcare spending as a proportion of GDP can be misleading when we are trying to see whether or not governments are actually reducing their total spending. The second reason, "medical technology growth," is also problematic. Spending on, and spending related to, medical technology may be linked to subsidies for corporate research on medical technology, or university studies carried out in collaboration with corporations.[14] That leaves "the aging population" and our new acquaintance, "chronic diseases," as reasons to be considered. We will take these in reverse order.

A study published in the *Journal of the American Medical Association* (*JAMA*) in 1996 estimated that 100 million Americans (over one third of the US population) have one or more chronic conditions, where part of the definition of a chronic condition is having "persistent and recurring health consequences, lasting for periods of years (not days or months)."[15] And 100 million is a conservative estimate. These high rates of chronic illness are often loosely attributed to the growth of the aging population. In fact, as the study's researchers were at pains to emphasize, "the elderly . . . accounted for only about a quarter of all persons living in the community with chronic conditions. Working-age adults 18 to 64 years old accounted for 60 percent of all noninstitutionalized persons with chronic conditions."[16]

Other recent research on chronic illness gives us further grounds for questioning the automatic linkage between high rates of chronic illness and an aging population. A study examining chronic disability trends in US elderly populations between 1982 and 1994 found a declining rate of chronic disability among the elderly. In those twelve years, the percentage of the elderly with chronic disabilities decreased by 3.6 percent.[17] These findings prompted the OECD to study the effects of the improving health of the elderly on future healthcare expenditures. In France, Japan, the United States and the former West Germany, there was a significant decrease in the rates of severe disability among the elderly population between the late 1970s or early 1980s and the early to mid-1990s.[18] The OECD's projections show long-term care spending (the care needed for chronic disabilities) stabilizing as a percentage of GDP in the United States, despite the demographic increase in the elderly population. Their projections also show a moderation in the trend of increased costs for long-term care in many OECD countries, such as Canada, Germany, Sweden, Australia and the UK.[19] Furthermore, a juxtaposition of OECD data on healthcare spending with the elderly populations of OECD countries shows no clear relationship between the elderly population of a country and healthcare spending. While health spending as a percentage of GDP is highest in the United States, countries such as Sweden, Germany, Italy and France (among others) have larger elderly populations but less healthcare spending as a percentage of GDP.[20]

Chronic illness is now becoming the core health issue in the advanced Western states. In the US, *JAMA* reports that "almost all (96%) of home care visits, 83% of prescription drug use, 66 percent of physician visits and 55% of emergency department visits were made by persons with chronic conditions."[21] Per capita healthcare costs for persons with chronic conditions are three times higher than for those without such conditions. Such people are at greatest risk of facing unaffordable high (given their family income) out-of-pocket costs.[22] The situation in Canada and Western Europe is similar.[23] I established in Chapters 2 and 3 that chronic illness increases with environmental degradation. Fossil fuel and other air and water pollutants, pesticides and, in the US, 100 million chemicals contribute to asthma and other lung diseases, to diabetes and to autoimmune chronic diseases such as allergies, as well as to cancer. Treatment and care corresponding to the increase in chronic illness, throughout Western welfare states, let alone in the South, would demand far more than a 1 percent increase in healthcare spending. But, in reality, the costs of chronic illness are carried increasingly by those who suffer from them through increases in personal taxation. As I have indicated, these increased taxes, in turn, are due to the reduction in corporate taxation, a reduction for the same people who brought you increased chronic illness by pursuing profit based on ever speedier reproduction. The same three-way move – less corporate tax, more pollution, more cost to individuals – is found in other advanced states with growing frequency.

The fact that the 1 percent increase in healthcare spending is in no way commensurate with the increased cost of chronic illness shows, of itself, that we are not moving toward increased health coverage. But the situation is more serious. As the OECD *Social and Health Policies* report reveals on analysis, countries which did not have universal healthcare are in fact paring back, moving closer to a US model of healthcare (public coverage only for a few population groups and private insurance for everyone else).[24] Sixteen of the OECD countries now expect citizens to pay for part of their pharmaceutical coverage, have increased co-insurance payments and/or have eliminated certain components of their coverage.[25] In Germany in 1997, co-payments increased and were increased further if a citizen's contributions to the insurance fund increased. The logic here seemed to be that, if one could manage to pay something for oneself, one could pay still more for oneself. After all, citizens who are unhappy with these increased co-payments are not bereft of options. They may opt out of the insurance agreement with the government and choose another plan, presumably within the private sector.[26]

In Australia, pharmaceutical co-payments were increased for Australians and pharmaceutical coverage was eliminated for non-Australians,[27] while a variety of limitations were introduced on Medicare coverage and on dental benefits for low-income citizens.[28] In Italy, changes were made to pharmaceutical coverage so that patients now cover more of their costs, and the overall contribution rate of the patient to health-coverage costs was increased. Throughout the 1990s, similar changes to either pharmaceutical coverage, co-insurance or overall coverage, or all of the above, were made in Japan, Greece, France, Finland, Belgium, Canada, Denmark, Mexico, the Netherlands, Portugal, Spain, Sweden and Turkey.[29] The move to limit pharmaceutical costs is particularly noteworthy because we are shifting toward medical care based primarily on the use of pharmaceuticals.[30] *It is precisely this form of care – pharmaceutical care – which is used most in the treatment of chronic diseases, and it is precisely this form of care whose cost for citizens is increasing most in the advanced economies. The Lancet* reported that people with chronic illnesses such as asthma and diabetes (frequently low-income people) would be the hardest hit by the introduction of prescription charges in Australia.[31] In New Zealand, the general medical services (GMS) benefit has been eliminated for most adults and reduced for children, welfare beneficiaries and the elderly. *The Lancet* wrote of the drastic changes in New Zealand: "New Zealand seems to be moving inexorably towards an American-style medical system, where the rich pay for themselves, the poor rely on State insurance cover, and the mass of people in the middle struggle."[32]

In 1995 a "social democratic" Australian government introduced tax penalties on higher-income earners who do not take out private insurance and established rebates on premiums paid for private insurance.[33] The government enacted these reforms on account of concern about public healthcare spending. The concern? Too many Australians opted for public over private insurance, due to the better quality of public healthcare.[34] Such changes decrease government spending but do nothing to improve the quality of private care. In addition, the 1995 healthcare reforms in Australia increased competition among healthcare practitioners to lower their fees and costs by allowing private insurance companies to negotiate contracts with different practitioners: business goes, once again, where labor is cheapest.[35]

Healthcare practitioners have been forced to cut costs by other means (costs which the state spares itself, but which are then passed on to patients). In both the United States and Australia, changes have been made that either reduce the rate at which the government will reimburse doctors or change what the government will reimburse doctors for. In 1993, the US lowered its price limits on Medicare payments for nursing homes and home health agencies. It also lowered its capital-cost reimbursements to hospitals.[36] In 1997, payments to doctors, hospitals and nursing homes were cut once again.[37] Australia has frozen its Medicare reimbursements at current prices, meaning that payments will not increase as inflation increases; it has also reduced coverage for some benefits.[38]

Canada has limited the total amount physicians can be reimbursed for particular services. In some cases, it has even introduced salaries in place of reimbursement.[39] Since 1997, UK physicians and primary-care nurses have been grouped into Primary Care Groups which "control" a flat-rate budget given to them by the state. One of the nation's leading physicians and a Labor supporter, Lord Robert Winston, publicly criticized the changes to the National Health Service (NHS), arguing that the primary care groups are putting "specialist services . . . increasingly under pressure," precisely the services needed by those who are most seriously ill.[40] Winston argued that this "internal market" structure is responsible for many of the problems with the NHS. "Our reorganization of the health service was . . . very bad. We have made medical care deeply unsatisfactory for a lot of people."[41]

Italy and Austria have abandoned their previous reimbursement system and introduced the US's Medicare reimbursement model; this means that practitioners are no longer reimbursed on a per day payment for each patient, but according to a fee determined by diagnosis and standardized treatment costs. The OECD report on the social and health policies of member states explained the effects of this change as "facilitating competitive contracting for treatments and constraining suppliers' incentives to increase service volumes. They provide incentives on [sic] hospitals to increase turnover (i.e., reducing length of stay)."[42] Korea, Denmark and Norway are testing this system or have introduced a slightly altered version of it. Italy and Canada are also working to decrease the length of stay in hospitals. In addition, they are shifting treatment to outpatient and community care.[43] Once more, this shifts the burden onto relatives and families, who pay the supposedly incidental but cumulative expenses which the state no longer picks up. OECD nations are also taking a closer look at new technologies and developing new criteria for what they will and will not fund.[44] In the UK, medical technology is judged today not only by the old criteria of "safety, efficacy and quality," but also by a new, systematic criterion of "cost-effectiveness."[45]

Overall, countries which once operated universal public health-care programs are moving away from generous public provision and toward higher citizen contributions, tightly budgeted medical care, and encouragement of private sector health coverage. As we noted, the once exemplary welfare states of Europe are striving for health-care systems more and more like that of the United States. And if you started out low, as the US did, that does not mean you cannot go lower. Despite Clinton's commitments to universal healthcare, his administration moved further away from it in real terms.[46]

Aging, pensions and sick pay

There are two other areas of underreported cuts with necessary effects on health: the first is old-age pensions or social security; the second is disability and sick pay. The cuts in these areas deserve separate study in their own right as, once again, the fact that there are cuts is disguised by presidential and prime ministerial expressions of concern for the future of the elderly, or talk of the rights of the disabled. Cuts in pensions, sick pay and disability benefits have been underway for some time. However, media attention and public anxiety about old-age pensions or social security has focused so far on a Malthusian argument, which goes like this: birthrates are declining, so the proportion of the working-age population to the retired will be smaller. Accordingly, there will be less revenue from the working population, and so less support for the elderly. Thus *Newsweek* in a recent issue argues that in a future "world of Floridas," there will be only two working adults for each pensioner.[47] The taken-for-granted assumption here is that all relevant state revenue comes from income tax. What goes unnoticed is that income tax will be the source of support because corporate tax has already been cut.

The existing cuts in old-age pensions have been justified by a hypothetical state of affairs which does not yet exist. What is true is that "old-age pensions are the single largest social security benefit in OECD countries, even in those countries with significant labor market difficulties which have high unemployment benefit expenditures."[48] Thus to make cuts in pensions is to reduce government spending in the most significant way, and governments relieved of corporate dues have already pursued this opportunity. This is true of both "left" social democrat states and new right governments. The difference between a social democratic government and a neo-liberal monetarist government in this respect comes down to the following. The new social democrats say, "you are going to have to pay for yourselves now and we are really worried about you." The neo-liberals say, "you are going to have to pay for yourselves now. High time."

In the last decade, OECD governments have undertaken reforms limiting expenditures on old-age pensions, decreasing benefit payments, promoting private pensions, and raising the age at which people can receive benefits. Eleven OECD countries have reduced the benefit that citizens receive after the usual number of years of work and/or contribution. Germany, Italy, Canada and the United Kingdom have all implemented such changes, along with Norway, Greece, Finland, New Zealand, Sweden and Portugal. Germany and Japan have changed their pension programs so that the programs no longer adjust adequately for inflation, thereby reducing the amount of money the government must disperse in pensions.[49] Ultimately, then, the elderly will have to be living on less, will have to turn more and more toward private pension plans and/or will have to work longer than they might otherwise have chosen to do.

Unsurprisingly, the relevant OECD countries are now encouraging greater reliance on private pensions, as well as trying to raise the retirement age. In the case of Australia, the UK, Canada and Ireland, private pensions are already a critical part of many citizens' retirement income, rather than simply a supplement to their public pension. Now these countries, together with Germany, the United States, Japan, New Zealand, Denmark, Mexico and Korea, have implemented reforms to get more people to invest more of their money in private pension schemes.[50] Gösta Esping-Anderson, in a paper for the United Nations Research Institute for Social Development, writes that, in this move toward privatization, the financial burden will likely fall on individuals rather than on employers: moving from public- to employer-funded pensions, "does not solve employers' labor cost problems. Privatization will more likely imply individual insurance plans and thus very unequal coverage."[51] To assume that employers' labor costs are a "problem" is to assume that the percentage of profit currently reduced by labor costs should be smaller. As the new social democratic governments, like their new right predecessors and successors, hold this assumption as axiomatic, they are also making efforts to raise retirement age.

New Zealand (1997), Australia (1997), Belgium (1997), the Czech Republic (1996), Germany (1992 and 1996), Greece (1993), Hungary (1997), Japan (1994), Korea and Portugal (1993), Spain and Switzerland (1997), the UK (1988) and the US (1983) have raised or have implemented legislation which will raise the pensionable age of their social-security programs.[52]

As we have seen, the elderly are comparatively modest in their health requirements, either reducing or keeping the percentage of their overall illness constant. It is the working population who suffer more from chronic illness, an increase due largely, by this argument, to corporate pollution. The same working age population will now shoulder the costs for the pharmaceuticals and general care a chronic illness demands when working. They will also carry the costs if chronic illness leads them to a life on disability or sick pay, just as they will now pay more and receive less for disability and sick pay in general.

Disability and sick pay insurance have been reduced together with unemployment.[53] In many cases, eligibility criteria, particularly for disability insurance, have been tightened.[54] With both sick-pay and disability insurance programs, many countries have begun to specify the kinds of medical conditions which will be considered "sickness" or "disability." The UK introduced an All Work Test in 1995 for recipients of disability insurance, meant to test their ability to perform various work-related tasks.[55] The All Work Test is now law. Blair's Labour government did not rescind it. New Zealand tightened the administration of their sickness benefits program, requiring more information about and assurance of the extent of the particular medical condition.[56] In some cases, the amount paid to workers on sick leave has been lowered. In Germany, for example, employers are now obliged to pay only 80 percent (as opposed to the previous 100 percent) of their workers' wages when providing sickness benefits.[57]

The cumulative effect of cuts in healthcare and pharmaceutical spending in general, in old-age pensions, and in disability and sick pay is to make it harder to live well and sometimes to live at all. Western medical technologies claim their greatest success in the indisputable prolongation of Western life. But the quality of the life prolonged by technology is another question. If it is to be lived in chronic illness, pain and misery, crowned by poverty in old age, it is probably a life which is giving far more of its own vital nature to the GDP than it has received from an economy's overall profits. In terms of the economic theory outlined in later chapters, it is not a life paid for at its real cost, the cost of its daily and generational reproduction. A working life that is over gives no more to corporate profit, although it suffers from how that profit is made. But because it gives no more to profit, it is, in the language of efficiency, of no use. Is it coincidental, then, that the last millennium ended with the debate on whether suicide should be legally assisted?

As opponents of physician-assisted suicide have pointed out, its primary impact may be a justification for disposing neatly of those without the means to pay for themselves or to recover adequately from their chronic and other illnesses, no matter how long they have worked or for whom. Of course the efficiency argument is not used in relation to assisted suicide – at least, not yet. Rather, the protagonists' arguments here appear liberal, an extension of human free will. This is true of many liberal arguments: one heard something similar at the time of the sexual revolution, which justified trading in one partner for another at the expense of women's economic security, a liberal innovation which had to produce feminism, or the assertion of the equal right to economic security, as its antithesis. But the process of discerning that the liberal right to assisted suicide is also a profit-making business has barely begun. Presenting itself as the solution to the prolongation of life-as-pain,[58] legislation favoring assisted suicide changes little about living with suffering.[59] What it does is make it easier to ask to die even when pain matters less than the pleasures of living.[60] Those who experience those pleasures have often found them in giving to the generations that follow, and if their individual and collective children, or their institutional care-givers, turn to them and say, with varying degrees of subtlety, "Wouldn't it be easier to live in less pain (and incidentally cost us less money)," may the old not say, "Yes, I'll do it"? We have yet to see how their children bear the burden of the costs shifted from the state's social provision to the "community," that is to say, family. But we do know that assisted suicide may be a disproportionately attractive option to the poor.[61] The aging poor, and the aging who become poor, include increasing proportions of those who have lived their lives in continuous employment. But those lives have been turned into someone else's money, often at the expense of health.

6   Education and the cost of children

We are familiar enough with the idea of child poverty and illiteracy in the South. Child poverty in the North should not, if the trickle-downers are right, be spreading. Nor should illiteracy be increasing, and educational standards be declining. But, as we will see in this chapter, they are. By 1994 or 1995, the bottom 70 percent of Australia, Canada, Sweden and the United States were earning less than they were in 1974 or 1975. Meanwhile, the top 30 percent were earning more. Furthermore, the disposable income of that bottom 70 percent in both Australia and the United States declined, while that of the top 30 percent increased. Similarly, the bottom 70 percent of Denmark, Finland, Germany and Norway were earning less in 1994 or 1995 than they were in the mid-1980s, while the top 30 percent were all earning more. And, during the same time period, the disposable income of the bottom 70 percent of Finland, Germany, Italy, Japan and Norway declined while that of the top 30 percent also increased.[1] When anxiety and stress about meeting basic needs prevail, one has less to give the other in care, either emotionally or economically, and more reason to look after oneself. The reduction in concern for the disadvantaged, apparent in the extent to which direct contributions to charities have been reduced as well as in the popularity of new right ideologies,[2] and the so-called third way, reflects the rise of pure self-interest as the factor determining outlook on behavior. But this self-interest in turn results from an economic climate in which one can take nothing for granted: one's survival is one's own concern. No one else, not even the state to whom one pays protection money, is going to do much about it. As we will now show, the real casualty of the new and often necessary self-interest is the reproduction of the next generation: that is to say, children and their mothers. In this chapter, we will be dealing with the rearing of children in two ways. First, by focusing on welfare reform and second, by discussing education. Welfare reform and education are linked at another level. The third-way advocates of "welfare reform" justify themselves and their cuts by claiming that they believe in education and retraining to help single mothers and the unemployed back to work. Yet, as we will see, they are also decreasing spending on education in real terms, and their financial commitments to retraining programs are unlikely to meet any real needs.

Stress on education and retraining highlights the importance of knowledge about and training in the new information technologies (NITS). But man and woman cannot live by NITS alone. There are only so many NITS jobs in an economy where subjects have a material existence – eating, sleeping under shelter and so forth. The production of goods designed to meet these needs and related services constitutes the bulk of employment possibilities and will continue to do so. Information and communications technology occupations account for only a small percentage of employment in both goods and services in OECD countries. In 1993, employment in office, computing, radio, TV and communication equipment represented between 0.2 and 2.5 percent of all employment in goods production, while employment in communications services represented between 1 and 2.6 percent of all employment in services production.[3] These figures may grow, although many of them have been declining since 1980,[4] but limits on NITS employment potential will still be set by production to meet other needs. So when the unemployed are exhorted to retrain in the growing field of NITS, they should know that they will probably have to scratch out a living elsewhere. Some have to stay uneducated and unable to pursue less skilled occupations because the service industry alone demands vast numbers of minimally skilled workers. The general withdrawal of welfare benefits hence serves a double purpose. It saves the state money, and it provides a larger pool of unskilled and semiskilled labor. Hence welfare reforms have to be understood in the context of reductions in unemployment insurance overall. We will consider these reductions first, before turning to the "welfare mothers" reforms. As noted above, controversy over these reforms has diverted attention from the issue of general unemployment, which has been high in continental Europe. According to the OECD's studies and surveys of member countries, it is "the major social policy problem faced by most OECD countries."[5]

Predictably enough, the relevant countries express their concerns here in terms of the language of efficiency rather than of human needs. It will be remembered that the language of efficiency is used when governments are unable to justify cuts by blaming or exhorting the victims. In the climate of corporate downsizing, it takes skill to blame the recently unemployed, so that unemployment constitutes a gray area when the language of responsibility is invoked. Concerns about unemployment insurance are thus expressed in terms not of the burden on the state budget but of harm to the national economy. The primary concern articulated by governments revising their unemployment programs has been that benefit levels may be too high, or last too long, and are therefore creating disincentives to work. Basing themselves on this assumption, eighteen OECD countries have introduced a variety of cost-saving unemployment reductions.[6] First, the duration of employment or total contribution necessary to receive full benefits has increased.[7] Second, the job search requirements for recipients of unemployment insurance have been tightened in many countries, including Germany and the UK.[8] Third, there have been direct reductions in unemployment benefits as such.

New Zealand reduced unemployment benefits in 1991 by as much as 25 percent for young single adults. Canada has reduced benefit levels as well, first in 1993 and then even more in 1996.[9] Germany reduced its benefits by 3 percent for single people and 1 percent for couples. Sweden reduced the amount of a person's previous income that it will replace from 90 percent to 80 percent.[10] Another tactic has been reducing the amount of time for which an individual can collect unemployment benefits. While retaining a right of appeal, the UK reduced maximum benefit duration from one year to six months.[11] In this, the great welfare states are moving, as they are in the case of healthcare, toward a US-style model. In the US, there has been no category for long-term unemployment benefits distinct from "aid to families with dependent children." If one is unemployed and without a family in the US, then, hypothetically, one is on the streets after six months. The UK, Germany and the US claim they want to train and educate young workers, rather than have them the passive recipients of an income from the state. This claim presupposes that the appropriate training and education can or will be funded, but, as we will see, education cuts make this problematic. Meantime, attention is focused on easy-to-blame welfare mothers, to whom we now turn.

Welfare reform

Amid much cant about family values, Clinton and the 1996, Republican-dominated US Congress introduced what is now known as the Workfare Bill. Basically, workfare means getting single mothers off welfare: in essence, it does this by placing a time limit on how long one can receive benefits. The US welfare bill's real effects are now making themselves felt. For the first time since the 1935 New Deal, substantial numbers of people have no visible means of support. This registered in a significant increase in reported moderate and severe hunger among immigrant families removed from welfare in the first year of the program.[12] More recently, there have been welfare-related increases in crime, in the number of homeless who are exceeding available shelters in some states, and in eviction rates.[13]

The US welfare legislation heralds a trend. Several countries are now following suit. Norway has introduced a three year time limit on receipt of lone-parent benefits, while New Zealand (since 1997) and the Netherlands (since 1996), as a condition of continued receipt of payments, now require lone parents to look for paid work once their children have reached a specified age. Ireland (since 1997), Germany and Australia have started programs aimed at encouraging lone parents to perform paid work.[14] New Zealand attempted to commence a "community work scheme" for sole-parent beneficiaries in 1998, but backed down.[15] Blair, right behind Clinton and the so-called third way, passed the Welfare Reform and Pensions Act. Blair's intent was spelled out in the UK government budget introduced in March 1998, which included provisions aimed at encouraging women to move off welfare and into "work," as well as public/private pension planning.[16] In what follows I will compare the US, as the most serious case, with the UK, one of the mildest.

Clinton's welfare reform bill HR3734 is entitled the Personal Responsibility and Work Opportunity Reconciliation Act, 1996. It was passed by a substantial (406 to 122) majority of the US Rebublican-dominated Congress in August 1996, and first implemented on October 1, 1996. Gathering statistics on the effects of the legislation is difficult partly because information is still being compiled, partly because the act gives substantial autonomy to the states in terms of how they respond to the demand that welfare be cut.[17] This means that there are now fifty ways to leave your welfare benefits. The one thing you can be sure about is that you will leave them after five years, and leave them for life.[18] In real terms, this means that welfare entitlements are also being reduced in the short term. "Welfare as we know it" is indeed over.[19]

The effects of Clinton's legislation on those who now lack any visible means of support have been downplayed, obscured first by bombing Iraq, then by bombing Kosovo, now by Afghanistan. But so far (August 1996–June 1999), over 9 million people have been taken off the welfare rolls. One state has decreased its welfare caseloads by a staggering 86 percent.[20] The legislation is hailed as a success, but of course its success depends on how many of those hitherto on welfare are now able to work at above subsistence wages. On this score, state studies show that only 50 to 70 percent of those leaving welfare since the reforms have found jobs, and those they have found are mainly in the service and retail industries, at wages ranging between $5.50 and $7.00 an hour, "higher than minimum wage but not enough to raise a family out of poverty."[21] This is especially noteworthy, given that unemployment in the US in the year 2000 was at its lowest in twenty-nine years. There is no sense in which workfare has been subjected to serious test. As I noted at the outset, there is also a significant increase in hunger among immigrants. Immigrants have been doubly affected, both by the five year provision, and because Clinton's original bill also reduced welfare aid to legal immigrants – both internationally and interstate. To some extent, these provisions have been reinstated, but any gains have been offset by the removal of basic legal rights for non-citizens following September 11.[22] Overall, the introduction of the Workfare Bill coincided with new legislation aimed at restricting US migration.[23] As we will see, immigrants are critical in attempts to have the reproduction of labor keep pace with production. But where immigrants are not encouraged, it should follow that the social cost of reproducing the next generation of labor-power will be forced down.

Welfare entitlements are prohibited altogether in the more common case of interstate migration, where the legislation anticipates those who might flee a harsh state for a kinder one. This legislative move is also consistent with the thinly veiled racism surrounding the bill. There is stress on the fact that those who migrate are black. There is even more stress on the disproportionate number of black single mothers on welfare.[24] The implication in much of the rhetoric accompanying the bill's passage is that the disproportionate number of blacks and Latinos is due not only to some vague sexual profligacy on the part of these women but also irresponsibility on the part of the men, who somehow just wander off. In fact they may have wandered off in search of work, or maybe to prison. While information on interstate migration for black and Latino men is difficult to find, we do know that a lack of jobs is a serious problem for many black men, at least, in the US. At one of the highest unemployment points in the last decade, over 45 percent of black men of working age in the US were not employed, compared with approximately 22 percent of white men of working age.[25] Those actively looking for work may need to be more mobile, in the hopes of finding some source of income. Many others find the informal economy one of the few potential means of livelihood and have become the target of the US's "war on drugs." In 1996 (the most recent year for which figures were available at the time of going to press), the percentage of young black men in jail was 6.6.[26] In fact, 14 percent of African-American men in the US cannot vote because of a felony conviction.[27] The US incarcerates at four to sixteen times the rate of other industrial nations.[28] Its prison population, in sum, is mainly male and disproportionately black.[29] It stands now at over 1.8 million in jail, with 3.9 million on parole or probation.[30] Of those in state correctional facilities, the number in for drug offenses increased fifteenfold between 1980 and 1996.[31]

The percentage of women in the prison population has increased since workfare was introduced, and other consequences in terms of severe deprivation are also emerging.[32] In addition to hunger and homelessness, these include a remarkable shifting of the burden of childcare onto the pension generation. The number of children in their grandparents" care has increased by 50 percent in the last decade. Half of these grandparents are single women, over half are black, over half are below the poverty line. The grandmothers are paid $215 a month – which, they suggest, is not worth the exhaustion of full-time childcare.[33]

In Britain, Blair's government in its initial stipulations about welfare reform insisted that those who really need a safety net would have it.[34] This was basic to the Green Paper on welfare reform, co-authored by Frank Field, then a Minister in Blair's cabinet. The stress on a safety net may – in part – have been tacit recognition of the negative effects of Clinton's enactment: it was certainly meant as a consolation to those who wonder if there is any point in voting Labour. On the other hand, any legislation bringing in "Workfare" will have negative effects on women and many men if it pushes them to work regardless of their childcare options. At this point, the UK reforms require lone parents to go to a work-focused interview where they must justify lack of paid employment and discuss the possibility of finding it. It does not require them to work, or prevent a lone parent from receiving benefits, as the comparable legislation does in the US, nor do benefits cease if a lone parent is unable to work. Here again, it is unemployment benefits that are the real issue. No member of a two-parent household would be forced into paid work unless he or she was already collecting unemployment insurance. That said, the final Welfare Reform and Pensions Bill moves away from any sense of a "right" to welfare benefits,[35] and makes further "reforms" straightforward.

Both Clinton's and Blair's proposals assumed public/private partnerships.[36] This applied not only to pension proposals. It also meant giving subsidies to employers for taking on former welfare recipients. Again, the rationale is different in the two countries: beliefs in the inherent laziness of unwed mothers and their reluctance to "better themselves" and the moral superiority of the wedlocked family govern the US legislation, as its other clauses make clear.[37] At least Blair recognizes that the "male breadwinner model" is no longer apposite.[38] In the British case, the rhetorical emphasis was on "a woman's right to choose." British women were hitherto unable to work, it was claimed, because the financial incentive was not there in real terms: paid childcare cost them more than staying on benefits. Furthermore, they could if they wished (and if they had mothers or other kin available) keep childcare in the family. Blair, like Clinton, made a place for grandmothers to take over childcare – for a fee. This looks good, but if the US experience is any indication, it underestimates what it means for granny to do childcare ten hours a day, five days a week. If this direction is maintained, British women will have less "choice" about using paid childcare, which can be bad for some women, who believe it is bad for their children. American women are upbraided more directly, as somehow both lazy and sexually overactive,[39] while British women are promised the chance to "choose," but in both countries women will now be producing surplus-value for capital as well as reproducing the next generation of labor-power more cheaply.[40]

Unlike the US Republican-dominated Congress, which presented its patriarchal dish undressed, the British stress on choice seems to have taken a leaf from some advertising book, some manual of manipulation which advises those who wish to institute change to do so in language which resonates attractively for the constituency they wish to persuade.[41] But in both the US and the British cases, one is left with the worst aspect of the old patriarchal bargain, with none of the financial compensation. Yet the British Labor government has shown itself receptive to criticism. There is a genuine attempt in the new Working Families' Tax Credit (WFTC) to redistribute wealth.[42] The trouble is that the tax credit does not redistribute from men to women; quite the reverse. British Chancellor Brown's initial proposal for reforming childcare and family tax credits would have led to a direct "purse to wallet" transfer, in that in many cases the husband would have received the tax credit.[43] The final tax credit, launched in October 1999, supplements the wage-earner's income directly through his or her paycheck. Therefore, in families where the father performs paid work and the mother stays at home with the children, the benefits go directly to the father.[44] Furthermore, the new WFTC sets up a double standard regarding the importance of care for children and a woman's right to "choose" whether or not to perform paid work. Two studies have shown that the WFTC provides incentives for lone parents (disproportionately women) to choose paid childcare and work over staying at home, while it does not encourage and may even discourage married women from doing so.[45] A single mother, it seems, does not have the same right as a married one to "choose" how to care for her children, and a married one who cares for children no longer receives the tax credit associated with raising them. Under the rhetoric of choice, the moralism remains the same. But it is the peculiar moralism of liberal individualism, where sexism takes a new and entirely selfish form, in which a man's children are his and his benefit by right, regardless of whether he does the same labor in caring for them as the mother. Herein, the grounds of labor on which Hobbes stood when he founded individualism are undermined. Labor once led to the right to property, or benefit. Now rights are defined without reference to labor.

As we noted, the rhetoric behind the welfare reforms is that of "rights and responsibilities,"[46] as it was in Clinton's third-way talk and remains under Republicanism. Rights and responsibilities, in the case of dual-income families, or families where the man works and the woman does not, are allied with an individual claim ("The child is as much the father's right and responsibility as the mother's" or "The needs of the child should be the basis of support".[47]) Rights and needs are not allied with the labor expended. To overlook this is to assume that men do the same work, and expend the same energy and energetic attention, in raising children as women do, and they do not.[48]

The British government has shown itself more sensitive to the issues, and is certainly less judgmental; for the main part the third way cuts in Britain are directed toward pensions, unemployment and education. Nonetheless, the move is underway in Britain as well as in the US to make women do both their domestic labor of rearing children and a job that gives them nothing in terms of satisfaction, and little in terms of income. The discrepancy between the manipulative British and the moralistic US rhetoric, even though it accompanies moves to a similar end, suggests that some other imperative is driving the US and the UK to cut women off welfare.

That some other imperative is at stake is clear if we consider just how widespread these cuts are becoming. In addition to the welfare cuts made since 1996 in Norway, New Zealand, the Netherlands, Ireland, Germany and Australia, universal family benefits are being targeted in various countries. In 1997 Greece began means-testing some of their family-allowance benefits. Italy has restricted the formerly universal family allowance since 1988 and Austria has reduced its payment levels. France tried in both 1995 and 1997 to means-test benefits, but met too much resistance to keep such changes in place.[49] The widespread nature of the cuts elsewhere means they are not the third-way novelty they are claimed to be. Opposition to welfare "dependency" has helped define the third way's identity, but the third way merely extends cuts initiated under monetarist policies by new right and other social democratic governments. It gives them a new and more appealing name.

It seems that human reproduction, in all its forms, is becoming too expensive. This is true both for human health (adequate air, food and water) and for the reproduction of the next generation. It also applies to shelter. It is not a good time to be on the streets, as a brief detour into the sphere of public housing will show. As the OECD's *Social and Health Policies* report puts it, "Just like many areas of social protection have been subject to change by governments . . . over the last ten or so years . . . the housing sector has been no exception."[50] Public housing policies have seen trends toward greater means-testing in countries where housing assistance is currently available to all or most of the population, and toward decreased construction of government housing in favor of subsidizing individuals' rents in the private sector housing market. The United Kingdom, Germany, Poland (since 1994) and Norway have shifted their housing programs toward a focus on needs-based assistance. Finland has been moving away from construction of government housing to direct subsidies to low-income individuals. The United States and Norway have also been moving away from government construction and toward direct rent subsidies to individuals.[51] As in the other component parts of the welfare state, public housing witnesses a move away from entitlement-based programs toward means-tested assistance, as well as greater cooperation with the private sector via increased subsidies. Help is being targeted more and more to the "truly needy" alone, and the operative assumption is that the private sector provides for this group better than the government can.

As I am arguing throughout, in an economy based on the speedy consumption of nature and human labor-power, meeting human needs becomes too time consuming and too costly by comparison with the other elements entering production. The prohibitive cost of life in this new economy is at its starkest if we consider the increase in child poverty in three of the countries at the forefront of third-way politics. In a paper for the United Nations, Esping-Anderson, an expert on welfare state policy, calculates that child poverty in two-parent families in the US almost doubled (from 12 to 22 percent) in the 1980s; at the same time it tripled in the UK (from 5 to 15 percent) and rose more modestly in Canada (from 11 to 14 percent). Poverty in single-parent families rose even more dramatically in both the US and Canada.[53]

To state the obvious: provision for children necessarily entails provision for single mothers or fathers because children need childcare. If children have less quality childcare, either because the institutional care a working mother can afford is of low standard, or because she herself is exhausted at the end of a working day outside the home and unable to expend the energy needed to care well herself, then the historic commitment to the idea that the innocent do not suffer has been broken. It has been broken, on the face of it, because a life without social protection breeds self-interest. I have suggested that the current intensification of self-interest is a product of the dynamics of latter-day capital. These dynamics demand not only a reduction in corporate taxes, and hence in state funding for social provision. They also demand unimpeded access to labor and natural resources, access across national borders without tariffs or other restrictions. As we will see below, to keep pace with this fast-moving production, these dynamics demand mobile individuals and the speedier reproduction of the next generation of workers, or, at the least, minimal expenditure in the overall social cost of human reproduction. Time spent on human reproduction is time spent away from the speedy pursuit of profit across space. Like capital, an individual moves faster when unencumbered.

Education

The education of children is also suffering from cutbacks, despite the concerned noises of the new "social democrats," who, once again, follow monetarism. Contrary to those concerned noises, spending on education is decreasing. In this respect, too, the North's gift to its next generation is determined by the priorities of global capitalism. As these priorities privilege profit over life, the attention given to the life-enhancing business of education declines in the "model" third-way countries – in the US overall, and to a large extent in the UK. The United States has cut its expenditures on elementary and secondary education, forcing schools to seek out alternative means of support. A recent study by the National Education Association found that, over the past two academic years, US average expenditure per elementary and secondary school student has actually declined, when adjusted for inflation. Furthermore, per pupil education spending and teacher salaries have remained stagnant over the past decade.[53] Despite the rhetoric of the importance of the educational system to national well-being, even the youngest children make do with fewer resources, larger classes, less individual attention and, therefore, a poorer education. If we look outside of the United States, we see that per student spending on primary and secondary schooling declined by 15 percent in Finland and by 9 percent in Italy between 1990 and 1996. However, many other countries saw increased spending during this time period: Australia (10 percent), the UK (6 percent), Canada (7 percent), France (14 percent), the Netherlands (10 percent) and Switzerland (1 percent).[54]

Cuts in state education spending in the US mean that schools are now seeking out other sources of income. According to the *New York Times* on one side of the Atlantic and *Le Figaro* on the other, schools are turning to parents: "educators say they have had to rely increasingly on parents in recent years, as state aid has not kept pace with rising costs and enrollments."[55] As Heather-Jane Robertson points out, education is being understood more and more as a private good, rather than a public service. The implicit message is that parents should pick up more of the tab for their children's education:

> Those who have no children in school get the message that what happens there is of no consequence to them, since they are no longer shareholders. Surely it is only a matter of time until this substantial majority of nonparents concludes that it no longer wishes to pay taxes to support an institution it neither uses nor influences. Then the other shoe drops. If parents are the school's only customers, let parents be the only ones who foot the bill.[56]

Robertson is referring to the number of people of voting age with children in school. As a percentage of people of voting age, people with children in primary or secondary school are most definitely a minority. Even if we assume that every child in school in Europe and North America can represent two parents (which is obviously an overestimation as, in the many cases of school-age siblings, two, three, four or more children represent only two parents), parents with children in school would represent only 35 percent of the electorate. With fertility rates declining, this percentage will only decrease further.[57]

Apparently compensating somewhat for the taxes they no longer pay, corporations are also paying some small part of the bill for public education. The result is more corporate influence and control over education, hence more corporate benefits from education. These take two forms, geared to direct and indirect profit. Directly, there are initiatives such as the Edison Project, a private corporation which now manages an estimated forty-eight for-profit public schools.[58] Local school districts give Edison the same funding that a regular public school would get per pupil. Edison then hires its own principals and teachers, manages the budget and teaches its own curriculum. If it can do all of this for less than what the school district gives it, Edison keeps the difference as profit.[59] Similarly, Boston University (which is privately owned) is now running the Massachusetts city of Chelsea's public school system, which serves a largely poor and minority community. A corporation called Alternative Public Schools, Inc. is running a public elementary school within a similarly disadvantaged community in Pennsylvania.[60]

Market principles of competition and entrepreneurship are also applied in the United Kingdom, in the form of "charter" or grant-maintained schools. These schools are "characterised by parental preference, open enrolment, and resources allocated mainly according to the successful attraction of pupils. This form of privatisation is completed by removing the regulations of LEAs [local education authorities], transferring public assets, and encouraging contracting out."[61] Similarly, US charter schools are publicly funded but are not controlled by local school boards; rather, they are overseen by state governments, which allow a greater degree of flexibility in their management, teaching and curriculum.

Some corporations are especially innovative in how they make their profits from schools. Channel One, an advertiser sponsored service which provides a twelve- to fifteen-minute newscast and review of current events for students, is viewed by 8 million US students in exchange for "feedback . . . as to what designer labels they prefer and what advertising they enjoy seeing on TV." The information is sold as marketing data.

It is difficult to secure comparative sources on corporate influence on education. The one comparative source that I could find on this issue pointed to the US and the UK as the most market-oriented nations, and, as with welfare reform, the "models" that other countries are watching. Throughout the Western world, however, the curricula are focusing more on job skills. In addition, the World Bank encourages countries which receive its education loans to adopt school choice programs, softened-down versions of what the US and UK are adopting. Such programs take us to the question of indirect profit. In a market-oriented approach to learning, an early training serves later corporate ends. This market-oriented approach is spreading rapidly in the erstwhile welfare states. It is an orientation which makes the tie between educational provision and the global economy explicit:

> If you ask governments . . . they answer that "globalization," the all-purpose excuse to absolve decision makers of responsibility, is shaping the education agenda. Globalization has replaced debt and deficit as the justification for dismantling the public sphere, for cutting welfare, for rolling back human rights legislation, and for ignoring environmental regulations. And, of course, for reforming schools.[62]

For example, the EU, concerned with the "upheaval" caused by the "internationalization of the economy," writes in a recent White Paper on education that it must determine "how best to use education and training to commit European countries to a process of job creation, whilst taking control of the internationalization of the economy and the arrival of new technologies."[63] Clearly globalization is a, if not the, chief concern guiding educational policy in Europe, at least. In short, as states cut back in their educational expenditures, schools become more and more integrated into the global economy.

In the frameworks of classical political economy, the reproduction costs of preparing another human being for work were determined by the costs of raising a child to the point where it could begin work. Where child labor is legal, these costs are obviously less. But so are the range of tasks child labor can perform. A minimum education extends that range at more cost. A tertiary education extends the range of tasks still further, but at even more cost. Hence the incentives to make tertiary education more profitable are considerable.

In colleges and universities, we find the same double move evident in primary and secondary education. There are cuts in state funding and there is more corporate influence over content. But the cuts and the influence are even more extensive. Between 1990 and

1996, the UK reduced its spending per student in tertiary education by 24 percent. Italy reduced it by 31 percent, the Netherlands and Ireland by 10 percent, and Canada and Switzerland by 2 percent, although France kept its spending constant, or stagnant.[64] In Britain, universities are now charging up to $1,600 per year, where formerly higher education was free. Students are no longer eligible for grants for room and board (which means they stay at home with mother, father, or both, again shifting more costs for generational reproduction back to parents). Many graduate with debts of more than $16,000 in a country which previously insured that they entered the workforce with none.[65] As the *New York Times* reports, "In a nation where free education is considered a basic right, the announcement [of these changes] was taken as a further sign that Prime Minister Tony Blair's new Government is intent on dismantling many of the most sacred vestiges of Britain's welfare state."[66]

In Canada, tuition rose by 134 percent while funding for post-secondary education has been cut by $3.1 billion in seven years. University of Toronto President Richard Prichard spelled out the effects of the budget cuts: larger classes, less personalized evaluation, and deteriorating physical resources.[67] By 2003, funding for German higher education will be one third of what it was in 1993. Berlin's three public universities are already cutting their teaching staffs by about a third.[68] In 1998, thousands of Australian academics and students walked out to protest planned cuts of $900 million to higher education by the year 2001.[69] Like Britain, Australia and New Zealand have introduced tuition fees for historically free public higher education.[70]

To compensate for the lack of federal funding, public universities have been engaging in "a hustle for private donations".[71] They have sought out corporate sponsorship. The results of this trend are making themselves apparent, especially in Canada, where the privatization of public higher education is well developed. They are reflected in changes in university curricula. As corporations are interested in investing in technology, and other market-oriented curricula and projects, it "has been remarkably hard to find commitment to the arts and humanities . . . That is the counterpoint to the new corporate generosity towards commerce and engineering".[73]

The more universities become directly dependent upon corporations for their funding, the more likely their curricula are to cater to the needs and desires of a global economy. After all, there is no profit in an education in the humanities and not much in the social sciences. Such an education only enables one to make links between disparate bodies of evidence, to draw out the logical implications of economic and historical trends, and hence gives one more chance of understanding what is going on. Another factor diminishing the chance of such understanding is the manner in which university and higher education teachers are now subject to the productivity demand. What do they produce? How much do they produce within a given time? What is the wages to output ratio?

The pressures within institutions of higher education to administer more and think less parallel the stress globalization imposes on reluctant human bodies overall, as well as on the natural world. This operates at two levels. First, there is the pressure to increase output and lower real wage costs because of cuts. This has affected all levels of education, as we have seen. Second, there is the pressure to increase the rate of publications, for a reason related to the economic demand for more output, although this is not always evident. That reason comes out clearly in Strathern's anthropology of the university research audit (an external assessment exercise) in Britain.

Strathern writes of how the time scale of the audit (every four years) and its method only make certain features of auditing visible, partly because publications and public appearance are valued, but also because research and writing have their own rhythm. Strathern, in short, is describing the difference between their time as distinct from our time, about the time of the external auditor and the time of university life. But their time also comes to act as a regulator of our time rather than a measure of how we spend our time, although their audit is meant to measure how we spend our time. Instead, argues Strathern, auditing measures a response to its own existence as an audit. Because the audit measures "number of publications" there is a rush to publish anything, leaving "book publishers racing against time with grotesquely swollen and underprepared lists."[74] Strathern argues that lack of trust underpins the audit: one could extend this and say that the lack of trust underpins bureaucracy in general. They (the bureaucracy in one of its manifestations) do not trust that the job will be done honestly. But they may also want more from the enterprise under scrutiny than it is currently evincing. This is the case when salaries and "funds" are cut. Here, the demands of productivity and the lack of trust coincide in their aim: both want to see evidence that work is being done.

It may be that the audit forces people to publish who otherwise would not have done so. But the consequences of forcing the offerings are, first and worst, that academics are publishing for the sake of publishing. Second, they are publishing the initial intuition rather than the fruit of that intuition. To publish the full fruit means living with the intuition and following it through in research and presentations seeking a real exchange. This can take years. There is a difference between presentations which are done as perform- ances ("number of conference papers" is another audit measure) and presentations offered so that one may learn and teach. The real time of "academic production" cannot be speeded up, especially in the humanities. Or, rather, when it is speeded up, it is impaired. Of course a shared tacit assumption is not subject to the test of communication and debate until it is published. But publications which foster communication and debate are precisely those that, in many cases, take time to gestate. They are unsuited to times in which no gestation period is allowed, in thought as well as in nature.

To sum up thus far: there have been three immediate results of cuts in education. First, an increased financial stress on parents; second, an increase in administrative and other workloads for people whose elected vocation is to teach; third, the growing influence of corporations on education. In many cases corporations are contributing to schools on the condition that their education policy meets corporate needs. In other words, to the extent that corporate profit is now used for educational purposes, those pur- poses must suit corporate needs. Corporations do not need people versed in the history of humanity, its philosophies of the good, or its arts. They need people who are either unskilled or trained to perform specialized labors as fast as possible. The Asia-Pacific Economic Corporation, a global trade body similar to the World Trade Organization, has a Human Resources Development Work- ing Group which addresses issues of education as they relate to economic development.[74] In 1997, South Korea drafted a pro- visional ministerial statement for the group which stated that, "The emphasis on education for itself or on education for good members of a community without a large emphasis on preparations for the future work are no longer appropriate," and that, "curricula have been traditionally developed by intellectual élites with emphasis on learning for the sake of learning without much emphasis on outcomes."[75] Explicit anti-intellectualism was cut from the final declaration, which nonetheless urged "member economies to place a strong emphasis on vocational education and training."[76]

Conclusion

I have tried so far to sketch how some OECD welfare states are moving closer to the US model in education and most are following the US in welfare cuts, while the US is eliminating even more of its already low social provision. We know now that many countries have stabilized their social expenditure budgets, which used to grow steadily each year.[77] We also know that, in all the countries leading the trend to cut social spending – the United States, the United Kingdom, Australia and Canada – there is deepening inequality and the rates of poverty are rising.[78] And we know, too, that there has been an alarming rise in child poverty in all four countries.[79]

We also know that chronic illness is increasing. Speedier production and distribution produce more pollution; pollution leads to more ill health; and globalization makes this cycle worse. This is plain wherever pollution-induced illness is high or higher, but health benefits are less. We have seen that the official reasons given for the widespread cuts in social spending studied in the last two chapters include "an unmanageable burden placed on state budgets." We have also seen that, in reality, the state burdens become unmanageable because of reductions in corporate tax, reductions designed to persuade corporations to invest here and not there in the new global economy. Yet the underlying reasons for these recent changes go deeper: corporations want their taxes reduced to maintain their profit levels. As we will see, their profit levels are affected negatively by the technological expense of speeding up production, especially global production and distribution. I will show in Chapters 9 and 10 that declining profit levels, like environmental degradation, are an inevitable consequence of the laws of profit based on speed. Some corporate consciousness of these laws is evident already, in arguments that labor costs have to be reduced to meet the higher costs of new technologies. Not coincidentally, these "new technologies" speed up production and distribution across the globe. But while corporations spend more to speed up in a global economy, in general they have *not* reduced their profit margins. Instead, those profit margins have been maintained and often increased through defraying the costs of human daily and generational reproduction.

Here it is plain why what began as an enquiry into environmental illness has extended into a discussion of health at the most basic level – the protection of one's own life and the reproduction of the species. If the reproduction of the next generation becomes too expensive for states who placate corporations, its burden falls on families. When more families are singly headed by women, in most cases not by choice, it falls directly on mothers – those concerned with reproducing life in the first place. The centralization needed for the initial acceleration of production not only produces more pollution; in all cases, it also increases the poverty of women. The most serious cost of welfare and education cuts also falls on mothers. For the rest of us, we are beginning to see the effects of spending less on our daily reproduction, our health, pensions and education. We need to decide if these are the kinds of consequences with which we can, literally, live.

7   The third way and the feminization of poverty

In the last century, the modern state was not always firm-minded about exploiting its people and its resources. With the one hand it gave environmental legislation and protection, health and welfare benefits, food and drug regulation. With the other, the state has been party to treaties such as the North American Free Trade Agreement (NAFTA) and the General Agreement of Tariffs and Trade (GATT), which take away from the environment, increase poverty and undermine the general health its protective legislation is meant to maintain. The last two chapters have shown that policy across the world is dictated increasingly by monetarism and trickle-down economics. This is as true today for the social democrats as it was for the new right governments of the 1980s. In fact, in the 1980s, social democratic parties in New Zealand and Australia were among the first practitioners of the dual craft of cutting social provision and accelerating the extraction of corporate profit. This social democratic retrenchment has only recently received its new name, "the third way," which would have us believe that it is the best of right and left, rather than the worst of both (which it may yet prove to be).

Hitherto, while the social democratic versions of Western government may have favored capital, they have also been committed to social provision: welfare for mothers and the unemployed, pensions for the retired, healthcare, often universal healthcare. Even conservative states have picked up the tab for the needy, conceding something to human requirements. But where trickle-down thinking reigns undisputed, and when it is rationalized as "the third way," this ceases to be the case. Let us be quite clear that, from the perspective of capital, securing human needs to any extent was always a concession. Favoring the time-consuming business of meeting such needs reduces the profits made by speedy acquisition through space. It was the task of social democratic politics and policy to secure concessions to human needs in spite of capital's opposition, while maintaining the infrastructure of capitalism as such. Social democracy, buttressed by a strong union movement, pulled one way, liberalism and conservatism another. The result was that state policy, in turn, was tugged in two directions: between, on the one hand, fostering profits through free trade and the like, not putting the brakes on pollution and so forth, and, on the other, making sure people stay moderately healthy, relatively literate, and alive. The compromise between these opposing forces was termed the welfare state. Whether its lineage lay in Keynes and Bevan, or in Roosevelt's "New Deal," this compromise guaranteed a lower level of inequality and wealth, as well as human services.

But now the trickle-down ideology seeps into all policy sectors and bureaucracies, from the World Bank and the IMF to the OECD and the policy makers of the different parties. The personnel of these organizations are often good people. They genuinely believe that their endeavors will lead to more wealth – for all – eventually. One of the things that needs to be reiterated here is that an ideology is at work. The essence of an ideology (in Marx's now neglected sense of the term) is that one takes a set of beliefs as a self-evident *description* of nature and reality, rather than what it is: a *prescription*, based on a view of reality which serves some interests and not others. The "development set" believe that their policies are a description of reality (and that "reality" is a situation where wealth trickles down "naturally"). The prevailing view in the West is that "greed is good."[1] But there have been historical periods in which greed was anathema and money, as such, a debatably necessary evil.

Members of international and government agencies frequently describe themselves as neither right nor left. Or they say (as does Blair for instance) that politics is not about ideology but about pragmatic "real" choices. Believing this, they "choose" exactly what capital requires them to do: they cut spending on human needs, lower corporate taxes, and facilitate corporate trade. They believe in trickle-downdom even though their ideology is unproven, and in fact proven false.[2] In every instance, trickle-down policies have increased economic inequality and environmental degradation. Again in every instance, free trade, the conduit of trickle-down practice, has done the same. In addition to the negative effects on health and healthcare, the increase in inequality and the general disregard for the next generation, free trade and globalization make it possible to dump the toxic wastes of the First World on the South, often in parts of the globe which were hitherto untouched by industrialization.[3] Globalization is the impetus behind investment and trade agreements which override the environmental laws of sovereign states.[4] I will return to the South below. Yet, as I stressed at the beginning, this book's focus is on the rich nations, and how most people in the First World suffer through globalization. Apart from the effects on general health, pensions and education, three specific constituencies lose. Farmers lose. Small regionally based businesses lose precisely because globalization enhances the concentration of wealth in fewer and fewer hands. These businesses might dream about the "big buy-out," but they are more likely to be forced out of business by larger corporations.[5] The global reach of multinationals gives them access to less expensive natural resources and cheaper labor; hence they are able to undercut smaller, local competitors.[6] The third Northern constituency affected by globalization is labor. Labor loses when production relocates to countries where labor-power is cheaper.

However, the main point here is that, while new right governments have espoused the ideology of trickle-downdom for some time, the capitulation of the social democratic parties to the new wisdom of globalization means that any semblance of the state's maintaining a balance between reproduction and profit, time and space, is lost. The deregulation of the body, like the environment, proceeds unimpeded under its auspices. Under the third way in the UK and the US, space for the expansion of corporations is doing well; time for the generational reproduction of people is faring badly. After some discussion of this, the remainder of this chapter draws out how third-way policy aids dynamics which are inherent in capital's substitution of space for time.

Third way formation

A week before the World Trade Organization met in Seattle on November 30, 1999, accompanied by a minimum of 50,000 on-site protesters, six social democratic heads of state met in Florence to discuss the so-called third way. Clinton (USA), Blair (UK), Schröder (Germany), D'Alema (Italy), Jospin (France) and Cardoso (Brazil) gathered on November 20 and 21. The official title of their conference was "Progressive Governance for the 21st Century," but its main topics were globalization, the idea of a third way, and third way policy (as defined by Clinton and Blair). The third way, although its origins rest in the US, has spread in Europe. Support for the third way was by no means unilateral at the Florence conference, but it was broad enough to suggest that social democratic governments will continue to default on their historic task of mitigating the damage, of speaking truth to power and money, and of securing for their peoples the time to be human. This is not always obvious. The social democratic withdrawal from the business of correcting the balance is covered over by the third way-speak mentioned in the introduction. It is obscured as well because many of the third way's followers, in between their moments of cosmopolitan exhilaration in the new global power they share, are actually concerned for their fellow citizens. But their concern is evident precisely in language; it is not evident in the fruits of third-way policy.

Language was integral to the third way's inception, which took shape shortly before Clinton's candidacy for the US presidency was conceived by the Democratic Leadership Council (DLC) in 1989.[7] Its founding manifesto ("The Politics of Evasion") says that "Above all, the next democratic nominee must convey a clear understanding of, and identification with, the social values and moral sentiments of average Americans . . . The consistent use of middle-class values – individual responsibility, hard work, equal opportunity – rather than the language of compensation would also help."[8] Clinton adhered to this vocabulary. Nor is he alone. Tony Blair's endorsement of the third way uses similar language.

Followers of the third-way yellow-brick road are treading a path (they say) between the two principal political forms of modern capitalism, "old-style social democracy and neoliberalism [or monetarism]."[9] Let us rather say that their vocabulary integrates left, center, and, for that matter, conservative descriptors. As we have seen, third way proselytizers are worried about the environment. Naturally they are not ignorant of the environmental perils to health. Yet, on examination, the third way is no more than the first way with cosmopolitan, liberal adjectives. It is about appearing radical while "standing still and emoting fuzzily."[10] Its proponents have been criticized for a policy that is no more than "opportunism with a human face,"[11] for blurring "the distinction between virtue and expediency" and for their belief that, if principles have a political cost, the principles must be wrong.[12] The political cost of articulating a middle path between, or an alternative to, capitalism as well as socialism was presumably too great to be borne. So the third way does not mean that, not at all. Prime Minister Jospin of France drew attention to exactly this at the 1999 Florence conference. "If the Third Way means a path between capitalism and socialism," he said, "I am for it. If it means a path between social democracy and neo-liberalism, I am opposed to it." But for the New Democrats and New Labour, the third way is precisely the middle ground between these two main political forms of modern capitalism, "old-style social democracy and neoliberalism."[13] They accept that multinational capitalism is the only game in town.[14] Brazil's Cardoso, among other Third World leaders, seems to concur, albeit with reluctance. He is regarded by his compatriots as too accommodating to globalization, but at the Florence third-way conference he spoke eloquently against Northern financial markets, detailing the havoc they have wreaked. Yet, in general, the fact that national interests conflict, especially between North and South, was left tactfully unsaid. Cardoso and other leaders of the South, under pressure from the IMF, have pursued a globalizing policy in practice.

Globalization and third way policy coincide. Neither incorporates any principle for redistributing income, other than taxes; rather than a commitment to universal healthcare, there are cuts, as there are in welfare and education. Nor is there action (only words) directed toward repairing communities. There are words again but few actions where the environment is concerned.[15] They talk of care for the really needy and of regulating globalization, but the care is elusive and the "regulations" implemented so far help globalization rather than restrict it.[16] While various items on the initial US third-way agenda fell through, items which might have led to a real alternative, those items which directly reflected the present needs of capital, did better. When the New Democrats drafted their platform during the DLC's 1990 and 1991 conventions, they listed the need for policy innovation in the following areas: universal healthcare, welfare reform, equity in the tax code, national education standards and preschool for all children, national service, more police officers, a free-trade pact with Mexico, the Family Leave Act, an expanded Earned Income Tax Credit (EITC), government capital for microenterprises, and more spending on physical infrastructure. The list is remarkably similar to New Labour's priorities, which is not surprising if Blair, as some commentators claim, imported the essence of the third way from the DLC.[17] Some of the policy fields, such as support for microenterprises, are admirable. However, what is significant here is that, of this list, welfare reform or workfare and that "trade pact with Mexico" (NAFTA) did much better in the US than proposals for microenterprises, let alone universal healthcare and education.

The third way may reflect a genuine desire to go beyond the present world in which the first way rules and the second failed. But there is a mélange of rhetoric and rationalization in third way speak, a mélange symptomatic of any attempt to move beyond the current impasse without really understanding it, or the third way's own role in abetting the very triumph of death over life which social democracy is meant to restrain. As I will now show, it is folly for the DLC, Labour, and other social democrats to claim they have found a third way. In fact their third-way policies smooth the path for the global direction capital is taking anyway, a direction which leads to increased ill health (among other things) as well as increased profits.

Deregulation and social policy

If the speed of acquisition is critical to profit, if its imperatives strive to override the day-to-day and generational reproduction of natural substances and sources of energy, and to push down the cost of labor and human reproduction where it cannot be speeded up, we can gauge political positions in terms of how far they abet or countermand this process. Most third-way thinking assists it. For instance, Blair and Blair's intellectual advisor, Tony Giddens, are evidently concerned for the environment: their critique of social democracy is based not only on social democracy's language of "victimization" but on its neglect of ecological concerns. Blair is also committed to microinvestment and small business as a source of community renewal, and this, as we will see, does have real third way potential.[18] Problems arise because the third way is also committed to globalization, and has already, as we have seen, effected cutbacks in health, education and other spending on human needs. In the US under Clinton, no legislation was enacted which assisted time – for nature or people to reproduce and regenerate – rather than space for capital expansion. The thrust of modern capital is toward deregulation in trade and investment: hence the GATT, the NAFTA, the WTO agreements (existing and proposed) and numerous other bilateral and multilateral trade and investment pacts. These are the logical outcome of the demand that standards of efficiency in the speed of acquisition should be set globally. Giddens would add an economic security council in the UN (and in fact the UN organization UNCTED is already being mentioned as an alternative to the WTO). He notes that "a global commitment to free trade depends upon effective regulation rather than dispenses with the need for it."[19] But while Giddens makes suggestions in this respect, how the third way would deal with the environment is never clear, nor can it be clear, for it would conflict with the cosmopolitan policy of globalization. The most we get from Giddens is that "It isn't really convincing to suppose that environmental protection and economic development fit together comfortably – the one is bound sometimes to come into conflict with the other."[20] Sometimes? When do they not conflict? This unclarity is symptomatic of the ideological mix I mentioned at the outset. On the one hand, third way-ites recognize that the environment is at maximum risk, and even that global inequality is increasing. On the other, they put their faith in the idea that only a strong global fox can keep these scattered environmental hens in order. The inherent contradiction in third-way ideology is the awareness of the needs combined with remedies that will exacerbate those needs; and it results in prescriptions that say nothing. Cautions about dangers to the environment lead nowhere if they are attached to policies which damage it, as the debate preceding the NAFTA's passage makes clear.[21] A real third way has to begin by reversing this trend, although the need for this reversal is obscured by the glamor of the global. It is a glamor which entices social democratic more than conservative parties. Why? Perhaps because of Labour's traditional internationalism, which has survived even if protectionist policies have not. But, as we noted, abolishing or impairing both local production and welfare merely smoothes the way for the direction capital is taking anyway, a direction which requires that there are no temporal obstacles, no out-of-time moments in which the pace or cost of social reproduction lags behind that of production, distribution and consumption.

States in which labor and nature have won ground are generally less efficient when it comes to government by the speed of acquisition. Paradoxically, these are often states with a conservative image; not because, or not only because, they "treat their workers well" (which is evidently moot) but because they have the interests of particular national capitals (such as the landed aristocracy) at heart. This was the rationale for protectionism, although protectionism may be viewed as on the side of labor-power (as it has been seen) not only because it favors local manufacturing, but because it is, more generally, on the side of the natural time of reproduction – and hence more likely to be on the side of the environment. This is the subtext of "the new protectionism."[22] But modern democratic and labor parties have targeted particular national capitals. The larger the economic union, the fewer the impediments standing in the way of the speed of acquisition.

A thoroughly modern state, in short, is one which abolishes these impediments; the state which is "out of step with modern times" maintains them. Needless to say, the advantages of joining a larger economic union, like the advantages of trade agreements and related treaties governing imports/exports, are usually presented in

terms of benefits to individual member states. Indeed they do
benefit them – in the short term – in that the speedier the speed of
acquisition, the greater the profit. And the benefits will continue as
long as these unions have ready access to energies beyond their
borders, although the trend within them will be to eliminate
progressively production based on any regard for natural reproduction time. In the long term, when even the Second World and
nonmetropolitan countries can no longer provide the energies and
substances which have been depleted, or if those markets beyond
the US and Western Europe are closed off for other reasons, crisis
is inevitable. In the short term, it is plain that the state which is
efficient either at eliminating geographical impediments to the
speed of acquisition, or subsuming its own economic sovereignty in
a union aimed at eliminating them, will also have to reckon with the
palpable inefficiency presented by any concern for natural reproduction time. The reason, as should now be abundantly evident, is
that natural reproduction time constitutes a "drag" on the speed of
acquisition.

Chief among such natural reproduction "drags" today is the
reproduction of labor. This is one form of reproduction which
cannot be speeded up, unless it is through the introduction of what
I term a "lateral" labor supply, a supply drawn across space
through migration or outsourcing, rather than through the linear
time it takes to reproduce the next generation of labor-power.
While I have emphasized migration, this lateral labor supply can be
obtained through outsourcing, which is also increasing. Easy
outsourcing can offset capital's needs for migration, just at it will
influence estimates of the cost-efficiency of human reproduction.

But in general, capital, from its industrial genesis onward, has
demanded mobility on the part of its labor supply. I will return to
the relevant historical patterns shortly. In the light of the foregoing
analysis, we can see that mobility is basic: shortly, we will see that
labor adds to surplus-value and to profit not only because its energy
adds more in production than labor takes in reproduction, but
because it covers its own transportation costs, thus offsetting
the costs of the speed of acquisition. Moreover, in the third way,
as articulated by Giddens, "Government policies can enhance
portability" by introducing common educational standards,
together with "portable pension rights."[23] But portability does not
sit easily with the maintenance and development of communities
Giddens rightly finds desirable – another instance in which
expressed concerns are undermined or countermanded by the
policies advocated.

But while capital demands ever increasing mobility on the part of its workers (and it has to demand ever more mobility to keep pace with the inevitable expansion mandated by the speed of acquisition), it must also contend with the drag represented by the natural linear reproduction of labor. This takes us to the heart of why the state which is most efficient when it comes to embracing "progressive" economic unions and trade agreements will also be a state bent on lowering the cost of producing the next generation of labor-power.

Welfare payments to single mothers (or single parents) are not the only reproductive drag. Anything that tends toward giving more to the reproduction of labor on the day-to-day level, as well as the generational level, is a drag, which means that the entire apparatus of social provision is ultimately a drag; hence the cuts in everything from healthcare and education onward. Pensions are a drag, which is why portable pensions (which exist in some countries) are unlikely to be state-subsidized pensions.[24] Anything that fosters the reproduction time of other natural energies or the natural reproduction of foodstuffs and livestock, as well as the replenishment of trees, plants, etc., is also a drag. Where the generational and day-to-day reproduction of labor-power is concerned, it is plain that states obliged to show minimal respect for this reproduction, such as the former socialist states, had to run into trouble, unless they were rich in other natural energies or unless they had access to natural labor supplies. As these conditions precisely did not hold in the former Eastern bloc, its member states' attempts to keep pace with production governed by the Western speed of acquisition had to fail. Without ready access to guest workers, these states were committed to reproducing labor-power the old-fashioned way. Significantly, at crisis points in the 1980s, some guest workers from Vietnam were brought in, but not enough, and too late.

In sum: if a state strives, despite increasing government by the speed of acquisition, to be a "good welfare state," it will be "cost inefficient." Given that exchange-value is measured by energy added compared with the costs either of reproduction or of acquisition, then a lower cost of reproduction will compensate in terms of overall social cost.[25] It will compensate . . . in the short term, but only somewhat. Freely mobile cheap labor (or, failing this, unimpeded access to cheap labor) is preferable, precisely because it keeps pace with the speed of acquisition in other ways. Capital's perfect labor market would be as fully mobile as it is free, and would somehow reproduce on the run.

Deregulation and labor mobility in historical context

The third-way policies that cut back social provision or leave it stagnant build on patterns which emerge plainly in the process of industrialization. These patterns privilege space over time (to return to our shorthand) by focusing on the global speed of acquisition at the expense of social provision for reproduction. The dergulation of policies affecting the speed of acquisition through free trade accordingly is the other side of the bioderegulation of human time, in terms of time or money for the next generation. Then, as now, at the intersection between spatial expansion and generational and daily reproduction, stand women, who suffer cumulatively from the direction in which capital has been traveling since its inception. Policies which facilitate that direction have to be considered in this context, as well as in the environmental context. Both points here will become plain if we consider the genesis of labor's mobility.

That labor-power has to be free to sell itself in the marketplace is plain enough. Marx recognized longsince that, for capital, labor-power could not be constrained by feudal obligation. If labor was constrained it could not move from country to city, or from factory to factory, nor could capital "bargain" with it to keep its cost down. Worse, capital would have to provide for labor when it was old; feudal obligations, formally at least, went both ways. Hence Marx's notion that the laborer's "freedom" and "choice" are ideological terms insofar as both these "rights" serve capital. What went under-recognized in Marx's critique is just how much "freedom" in fact means mobility. In considering capital's industrial beginnings, and discussing the nonmetropolitan countries where capital's advent is more recent, the recurring pattern is one in which women stay fixed in place, coupled to the rearing of children, while only men migrate to the towns in search of work. Laborers needed to become "free" if they were to "choose' to work, but this also had consequences for what was hitherto the main site of production: the household. In household production, or petty commodity production as it has been called, women's economically productive labor was not separated spatially from their work as mothers. One consequence of this was that married women (which meant basically all women) had a stronger economic place, a direct role in production and, it appears, in selling. In Braudel's history of capitalism, the seemingly incidental references to women as vendors, up to and including the seventeenth century, are remarkable: they reveal that women were visible as economic actors before industrialization. But these "market wives, more numerous than the men," disappear from the eighteenth century onward. [26]

Marxists and capitalists alike assume that capitalism as we know it "grew" out of small-scale, seventeenth-century petty commodity production. In other words, it is assumed that small producers accumulated capital, then increased the size of their enterprises, then gobbled up other small producers. At one level, this is self-evident. At another, the idea of natural growth from small to large obscures a central fact: production governed by natural time and production based on expansion through space and speed were and are actually in competition. Small businesses, such as the household-based production that dominated England up to the close of the eighteenth century, are in competition with larger production processes in that the latter acquire their raw materials and make their profits through spatial trade, while the former depend on time – the reproduction of those raw materials close to hand. The explanation of profit outlined in the next chapter presupposes that the conflict between the large and the small is ongoing, however latent that conflict has become. Hence in the South, as noted, the historical pattern just described continues to the present. Hitherto dependent on local production and subsistence agriculture, men leave their land (usually as a result of forced sales to agribusiness) and travel to cities in search of employment, as they did following the enclosure of common land in England. Like women of the seventeenth century, women of the South are less likely to leave their villages, holding onto subsistence agriculture where they can as a food source. If they do leave, as they know, they are less likely to be employed than the men. The industrialization or so-called development that globalization fosters invariably increases the poverty of women and decreases their social influence. Poverty spurs them to have more children. Some consolation might be offered the men, and a limited percentage of the women, by the fact that global corporations do offer *some* employment. They often relocate production to the South or Third World, or former Eastern bloc, taking advantage of labor markets where they can pay less than the average $7.50 they are obliged to pay in the US or Europe.

Migrating men are caught in that preeminent tension of modern masculinity:[27] on the one hand they have to succeed in the work-place; on the other they have to be responsible fathers. Historically, in the US, the ideological weighting has shifted to financial success: one is guilty if one leaves, but is nonetheless driven to seek the other path by the prospect of shame and humiliation.[28] In between the moralistic incantations about the decline in family values, or the sociologically inspired rhetoric on choice, it would be interesting to study why men leave their families: how else, other than through an inherent dynamic, did these families come to be headed by single women? The idea that some women wish to have children without fathers is certainly true. But for others, it is not: their single-parent status is involuntary. In other words, irresponsibility on the part of the men is not the only explanation for paternal absence. Men's economic survival in some cases, economic advantage in others, is also at stake. In addition, as we have seen, some of these missing fathers are likely to have been imprisoned. In prison, they provide a cheap source of labor, whose reproduction costs for capital are subsidized by the state. Women as mothers are less able to wander. One of the additional evils of the present legislation is that, while it stigmatizes migration as desertion, it ignores the fact that it is far harder for women with sole responsibility for children to be mobile. The ideological assumption that there are enough jobs in the United States overall for the number of unemployed if they were not too lazy to go looking for them is premised on the mobility of those unemployed. In fact, nothing is more basic to human reproduction than the mother's labor, obviously in both senses of that term, but especially in terms of day-to-day work. Given that the business of substituting speed and spatial expansion for repro- ductive time has now spanned five centuries, it would also be interesting to pursue facts suggesting that the economic position of women as mothers has deteriorated consistently with capitalism, and now globalization (which means that the women of the South are subject to overlapping circles of distantiation. They are subject to the mobility and separations contingent on the division into town and country, and the loss of land to agricultural business. They are also affected by the intercountry migration and tremendous traffic in biological resources, as well as minerals and fossil fuels, charac- teristic of globalization). The comparative and historical work on the feminization of poverty has only begun. But it is clear now that the standing of women-as-mothers is linked to the time, or lack of it, accorded replenishment or reproduction in the most general sense. The division between household and workplace, and that between town and country, marks the end of much petty commodity or household-based production. It is in household production that, according to Clarke and others, women as mothers had a better economic place. This contrasts with the notion that the position of women has progressed in recent centuries.[29] Instead women-as- mothers lose a place rooted in natural law, as well as a better economic place at the beginning of that uprooting when households struggle to be more than places of consumption, when production gets faster, and the problem of reproduction is solved by spatial expansion, except at the human level, where reproduction is slow, too slow to keep pace. As I noted earlier, petty commodity – or household – production is not simply a progenitor of big capital. Where it is based on allowances for natural reproduction time, it is a system opposed to it.

The third-way conquest of time and space

In the above light, we can see why the conquest of time and space is basic to capital's national and global interests, and why third-way policy serves those interests via its current policies on space and time. On the one hand, those policies lead to an increasing liberalization of trade and investment, with punishment provisions for those nations that brook it. On the other, we can see how the time limitations on welfare benefits, and the continuing cuts in healthcare and education, are central at an inherent dynamic level, and why the temporal temptation to which Clinton succumbed has also enticed Tony Blair, following that recent tradition in which social democrats, joining the trickle-downers of the new right, have defaulted on maintaining the balance between human needs and speedy profit. Nonetheless, I reiterate that the numbers of women on welfare, and their increasing immiseration, should be viewed as exemplary of a trend with a much broader basis. Close to home, that trend is evident in the general increase of female single-headed households (which extends well beyond those of welfare recipients). If, as I have suggested, the situation of women-as-mothers is deteriorating economically, that deterioration accelerates to the extent that the household ceases to be an economic partnership. Chapter 1 showed that this caesura takes various forms: a commuting partner, a migrating one, no partner at all. Historically, when the household remained a site of production – an alternative to the household as the place of consumption – human needs, human biological needs, had priority for more people. This priority is reduced the more that spatial acquisition substitutes for natural reproduction. But because the communities, the people, and the natural resources broken up in this process in the North still had the South to turn to for the labor and natural reserves the North had exhausted on its own terrain, there were safeguards for human needs, safeguards dependent on imperialism and the general exploitation of the South. But as the South, in turn, cannot exploit the North, and cannot really exploit itself as the North is already doing so, there are no such safeguards protecting, even in part, the human needs of its peoples.

We have seen that cutbacks in health, education, social security and pensions all suffer while the welfare of corporations flourishes. We have also seen that, while they are the least significant in terms of expenditure cuts, the new financial strictures against unwed mothers and restrictions on migration are paradigmatic, indicative of the fact that keeping down the overall social cost of generational reproduction is critical to capital's logic of speedy reproduction and unfettered spatial expansion, just as the costs of day-to-day reproduction may be borne more and more by workers in a way that substitutes time for money, so that the wage appears higher than it is in real terms.

At the same time, the fact that women and men are both subject to the rule of exchange-value pressures the patriarchal relation that kept women dependent economically on men. As far as I can see, this is the most important contradiction thrown up by the way global capital breaks apart traditional commitments. Its significance lies in that it brings the situation of women as mothers and workers into sharp relief. Women can make money in the marketplace, but that activity is at odds with rearing children without fathers (a growing demographic reality where fathers change towns and/or partners). The fact that the solution to this situation has to be one in which women are economically empowered as mothers is directly tied to localization. Globalization leads to the breakup of communities and displacement in the North and South, but its most serious effects on human beings are on women.

In the preceding chapters, I have tried to show how the exploitation of the living energy of human beings is what makes common cause between the vast majority of women everywhere, neocolonial peoples, and people in disadvantaged race and ethnic groups (insofar as this disadvantage is a matter of economic class) – and common cause between these groups and other endangered species, whose energy is exploited in comparable ways. What remains to be done is to show how this common cause is anchored in an economic analysis in which human labor and natural energies can be substituted for one another in producing profit. I explained at the outset that I would use Marx as a template for this, while differing from him in citing natural energies and substances as sources of value comparable with labor power. In Marx's initial terminology, this means changing the definition of variable and constant capital. Variable capital originally meant labor, and Marx found its variability in its living quality, which distinguished it for him from the dead objects of technology and labor. Constant capital was composed of these dead objects, and their deadness meant they could add no vital energy of their own. I have redefined variable capital to include living nature as well as labor, and the energy nature provides. Much of the explanatory appeal of extending the definition of variable capital will already be apparent. By extending this definition, making nature as well as labor a source of energy, we are able to account for the rush to produce and reproduce more rapidly which underpins pollution, genetic engineering and climate degradation through increasing transportation. We are also able to see why the reproduction costs of human labor power, the costs of raising and educating children, and keeping its workforce healthy, are cut back as the speed of production increases in relation to the time of human reproduction. It remains to see how revising the definition of variable capital provides an effective counter to the view that technology alone is the source of profit, and hence to the basic assumption of trickle-down economics.

8   The source of profit

The mainstream twentieth century view on profit is that it is produced by technology, entrepreneurship and clever investment.[1] In this chapter I will argue against this conventional wisdom by showing that technology of itself produces no value. I will show that value, on the contrary, depends on natural matter and energy. No matter how great the technology, it will of itself feed no one. The only thing that will do this is food. Now the technophile's reply here is that technology can make food from, say, plastic. But to this objection we reply that plastic comes from petroleum, and petroleum from the earth.[2] Our technological food, like any other technological product, always has two ingredients. One is the substance provided by nature. The other is the energetic power of transformation, the process whereby one thing is turned into another. Of course the process of transformation involves and usually depends on technology. But the point is that technology would be nothing without the human or natural energy that is the condition of all transformation. This is true of all technologies, from the flint I use to shape my rock to the nuclear power plant that makes my electricity. There is no source of power apart from that derived directly or indirectly from human and natural energies. Energy cannot be produced without the ingredients nature provides: electricity uses the natural movement of existing electrons, solar power the sun, and so forth.[3] We humans create nothing from nothing; only living nature can do that. When any technology "produces" wealth, it has to use both matter and energy. No matter how creative the entrepreneur, he or she must also use the material nature provides. It may be that the entrepreneur's own energy is involved; it undoubtedly is in most cases, and there are some so-called service industries where one mind and one body is all that is needed to make a profit. But these are exceptional, or severely limited in scale (and hence in profit). When they expand, they do so through using more human energy and matter – derived always from nature in the last instance.

The denial of living nature as the source of profit, and the insistence that profit's true origin lies in technology, has infiltrated scientific and legal thought so deeply that scientists have been granted patents on genes they have *altered*, but obviously not *made*.[4] There is a direct confusion between the technological intervention, as such, and the living thing that makes that intervention possible. Variety lies in the genomes of these living things far more than it does in the techniques used to uncover them. But, despite the obvious, the belief that variety is a human intervention rather than a natural given persists. Commenting on the US Supreme Court case (Chakrabarty) in which "the very logic of previous rulings preclude claiming a discovery of nature as an invention," one scientist wrote:

> let us get one thing straight: Ananda Chakrabarty did not create a new form of life; he merely intervened in the normal processes by which strains of bacteria exchange genetic information to produce a new strain with an altered metabolic pattern. "His" bacterium lives and reproduces itself under all forces that guide cellular life . . . we are incalculably far away from being able to create life *de novo*.[5]

When confronted with the material reality underlining profit, many start exclaiming about the Web. All you need to make a million, they say, is a good idea and some new software, or an idea for a net browser. What matter and energy is involved there, apart from cyberspace? In fact a great deal of matter and energy is involved: chips are not all there is to the hardware of computation. There is an electromagnetic web of connections whose nature and effects are, as yet, unclear,[6] and computers do use twenty percent of all electricity consumed. Even so, the roller-coaster price of stocks in Web and internet companies, prices that are now declining, may indicate the uncertainty over whether their price has any relation to their value. And it is this relation that is the nub of the matter. Like the belief that technology produces wealth, currently popular views on the determinants of price also neglect the role that energy and substance play in the production of goods and services.

The monetarist belief is that price is determined by equilibrium, by a balance between the price customers are prepared to pay, and the price for which vendors are prepared to sell. But, even in monetarist accounts, there is a sneaking suspicion that price has to be tied to something other than preference. This "something" used to be gold. Gold is a substance; it has matter. But, of course, tying value to gold is not the same as tying value to the natural order of matter and energy overall. Capital was never prepared to do this, never prepared to acknowledge the fundamental role nature and labor play in the production of value. But at least gold was a reality checkpoint.

Although globalizers pretend that matter and energy are irrelevant to value, market behavior often contradicts this belief in practice. When there is no apparent natural matter or substance in a product, buyers sometimes get nervous. Hence the investment moves away from Web technologies, hitherto selling sky-high, and into small businesses dealing in tangibles.[7] It was as if, somewhere, investors sensed that there is more to the determination of price than the happy meeting place of sellers' and buyers' preferences. We return to incomprehensible oscillations in price – and how price escapes from real value in a spiral of inflation – in the next chapter. The point here is that, if substance in the last instance is always derived from nature, if energy too ultimately depends on human beings or other natural sources, then these things are the real source of value. Without them, even the cleverest entrepreneur has nothing, technology can do nothing, and investment, eventually, will yield nothing. But the source of value is obscured by the belief that these things do it by themselves. Moreover, what is promised by way of technology's capacity for solving our problems often has no relation to reality. We are told that, even if we exhaust the earth's resources, the conquest of outer space will make up for the deficiencies with mines on Mars and colonies on the moon. Alternatively we will be able to shape the barest elements of matter into new forms, producing food, clean air and water. Claims like this may ultimately be founded, and I am an enthusiastic supporter of inventions and technologies that take polluted matter and turn it into something good. Hope may indeed lie in reparative technologies.[8] I want to stress this, as this book is not an argument against technology as such (unless the human species continues to show itself incapable of handling the apple of knowledge).

But the value produced by reparative technologies is currently not an incentive to their research, let alone their adoption. If it is right that value depends on matter and energy – and I will try to show here that it is – then capital's attitude to reparative technologies will depend on whether they, too, can provide matter and energy for production. As we will see, the more readily a natural source can release energy, and thus the less expensive the technology necessary for securing that release, the more desirable it is (for instance, fossil fuels are generally preferable to human energy). Similarly, in production, the more one kind of matter can stand in for others – at less cost – the more interesting it is to investors. Either the energetic potential of toxic waste, or its use as a new form of matter, will determine its value. But the energy costs involved in transforming toxic waste into that form have to be weighed against its energetic or material potential after that transformation has taken place. So far, these sums are not looking promising. However, the immediate point is that profit can continue to be made at the present rate only at the expense of the environment. This is because there are laws governing the conversion of matter and energy into value, and value into price. Uncovering those laws means tracing their forebears in classical political economy. In the first instance, this means reworking Marx's labor theory of value, then returning to his theory of profit and my revisions of it, and thence to why it is that capital must use more of nature than it can allow to regenerate or reproduce. On this basis it will be clear that there are two axes of profit, one of which enhances use-value, or at least stays in relative equilibrium with it, the other of which depletes it.

The labor theory of value

What precisely does reworking Marx's labor theory entail? I will briefly sketch the theory at issue, then summarize my reworking of it. Let us bear in mind throughout that what connects my reworking with Marx's original theory is a similar logic: Marx realized that the source of value is hidden, and that capital, like third-way economists, deludes itself as to this source. For Marx, labor was the key to this hidden source, but not in a way that was obvious or transparent. By my argument, the source is nature as well as labor. But in both Marx's account and this one, the real source of value – in labor or nature – is obscured. We will see that, while Marx was wrong in assuming that labor alone was the source of value, his reasoning about the mechanisms of concealment still holds.

Marx's fundamental premise is that the exchange-value or value of a commodity is measured by the labor-time embodied in it. He turned value into a far more interesting concept than it had been hitherto, but the idea of value based on labor had a long and reasonably illustrious career before the tedious theories of twentieth century economists took hold. Thus John Locke, who argued that it is labor that puts the difference of value on every thing . . . let any one consider, what the difference of an Acre of Land planted with Tobacco, or Sugar, sown with Wheat or Barley, and an Acre of the same Land lying in common, without any Husbandry upon it, and he will find, that the improvement of labor makes the far greater part of the value.[9]

Out of the hundred parts of value in any one thing, ninety-nine parts were due to labor, for Locke, but the hundredth part, tiny as it is, was nature's work. But Locke took both nature's and labor's contribution at face value. So in different ways did Marx's pre-decessors and contemporaries in the field of classical political economy (among them Adam Smith and David Ricardo). Where Marx differed was in seeking beneath the surface for how, exactly, labor led to profit. In this search, paradoxically, Marx reached a conclusion which led him to neglect nature's contribution to profit altogether. We will follow him to this conclusion, and then see how his logic can be extended to the very nature he discounted.

Marx believed labor was unique in the determination of profit because it was the only living factor in production. Nature and technology are assumed to be "dead." Because labor lives, it is capable of giving more than it takes. The palm trees I cut for my hut can give nothing more than their wooden substance, and they cost the same as all palm trees do in this neck of the oasis. But the labor I buy to build my hut is another story. I can get more from it than I paid for it. This is not just because living labor can push or be pushed beyond human limits (although this is certainly true); it is because labor can give more energy than it requires to keep going. Labor's value is set by subsistence needs, but the energetic capacity it carries within itself exceeds its value. I will retrace the steps Marx took to reach this conclusion more slowly.

As we saw at the end of the last chapter, the idea that labor is the only living factor in production is tied to the idea that profit consists of both a variable and a constant factor. The variable factor is labor; the constant factor encompasses nature and technology. Nature (as raw materials) and technology are grouped together on the "con-stant" side of the equation in the determination of surplus-value or profit. Profit or surplus-value is made because what the variable factor, labor, adds within the production process yields more than the cost of labor-power, a commodity that is paid for at its value just like any other commodity. But, despite this unacknowledged debt to labor, "The capitalist does not cheat," wrote Marx. "Our capitalist" pays for labor at its value, just as he pays for palm trees at their value. Those who believed that capital's profit relied on cheating missed the point. That point, for Marx, was precisely that labor, unlike the constant capital of nature and technology, has the unique property of giving more than the cost of its replenishment requires. But then, one might ask, what determines the value of labor-power? The short answer is that it depends on the cost of reproduction – meaning both the day-to-day revival of the laborer and the reproduction of the next generation: the things we earlier defined as human needs when discussing health and welfare. But it costs more to produce some labors than others. This is due to the education factor, another aspect of human needs or human reproduction. The labor-time involved in producing an engineer is, unfortunately, less than that involved in producing a journalist. But as one form of labor costs more than the other, how can labor be the common measure of value? Marx's answer was to propose that the real measure of value was something he called abstract labor-time. If you strip labor-powers of all the different training and skills that make them distinctive, you have "human labor pure and simple."[10]

> All labour is an expenditure of human labour-power, physio-
> logically speaking, and it is in its character of being identical, or
> abstract human labour that it forms the value of commodities.[11]

This physiological dimension is stressed by Marx many times over. Abstract, meaning identical, human labor is identical because it has a physiological property in common: raw physicality, the lowest common denominator of human labor power. While tailoring and weaving are qualitatively different activities, they are each a productive expenditure of human brains, nerves and muscles, and in this sense are human labor. "They are but two different modes of expending human labour-power."[12] In the last instance, Marx says directly that "Labour-power itself is energy transferred to a human organism by means of nourishing matter."[13] Abstract labor, and its correlate concept, abstract labor-time, in terms of its physicality, is anything but abstract. Yet Marx will also say that it is entirely a social affair, that not an atom of matter enters into abstract labor-time's composition.

This apparent contradiction comes about through the temptation (to which I have yielded) to differentiate abstract labor from the notion of abstract labor-time (this is done by the commentators). Marx habitually refers to abstract labor-time, rather than abstract labor, because labor does not add value in a vacuum. The measurement of the value labor adds also depends on the technology that either does, or does not, enable labor to produce within a certain time. The time in which production takes place has to be as rapid as contemporary technology could make it. So if I spin cotton by hand, my thread will be no more valuable than the same length of cotton spun on a wheel. If the wheel is the fastest form of technology, it plays a critical part in determining value. It determines what Marx called the "socially necessary labor-time" of production, the time period in which production should take place if it is to be competitive. In other words, abstract labor-time is itself measuring two things. As the measure of socially necessary labor-time, abstract labor-time measures the speed with which a technology abets the production of exchange-value. But it also measures the difference between what labor adds in production compared to what it costs to reproduce labor-power. What labor adds in production is a matter of energy. How fast labor can produce depends on technology, which is to say it depends on time.

One complicating factor is that Marx used the term "abstract" labor to distinguish the activity all labors have in common (labor in general) from "concrete" or useful, particular labor. The distinction runs in tandem with a distinction between use-value and exchange-value. In both cases, and this is where the confusion comes in, the material and substantial category (use-value, concrete labor) appears to be opposed to the abstract or immaterial one (abstract labor-time, exchange-value). Moreover, and this is also confusing, the general term (abstract labor, exchange value) is opposed to the specific term (concrete, useful). If I make a fence, I am performing useful or concrete labor. My fence has use-value. But, provided I am paid for it, my fencing can also be reckoned in terms of abstract labor-time. If my fence is made for the market, or could be co-opted to the market, it has exchange value. In this case, the value of my labor is determined by the amount of labor-time embodied in it. It is determined by something that is able to be measured because of a hypothetical common denominator.

Attention by commentators has focused on how there are use-values which lie outside the market. In other words, not all use-values have exchange-value (at least, not yet: Marx cited streams of water as examples of use-values lacking exchange-value. But as freely available water becomes polluted, pure water comes to have exchange-value). On the other hand, exchange-values must have use-values: all commodities have a "twofold nature." For Marx, this is critical. Exchange-values must always have use values, in two senses. First, a particular commodity has a particular use-value. Second, to have a use-value, a commodity must be material, or (as one can now say in the age when energy and matter are inter-changeable) have energy. "The ever-lasting nature imposed condition of human existence" is that existence is material and energetic. Marx's own materialism was based in nature. It is only later Marxists who have reduced materialism to the social matter of technology.

Just as there are two sides to value: use (material) value and exchange (temporal) value, so there are two sides to abstract labor. On the one hand, abstract labor is, as we have seen, the common energetic property all labor has in common. On the other hand, it is the measure of exchange-value. Abstract labor measures exchange value as abstract labor-time. The neglect of the time in "abstract labor-time" has led to many a misperception of Marx's political economy. It has led to a debate among Marxists, who see the idea that abstract labor is the measurement of labor-time, and the idea that abstract labor measures concrete labor by comparing the physical expenditure of energy with its particular elaboration as somehow opposed.[14] They forget that abstract labor, like value, has two sides. Abstract-labor is material; abstract labor-time is the measure of exchange.[15] To resolve the abstract labor debate, we have to note – first – that yes, the two-fold nature of commodities is reflected in the difference between concrete and abstract labor. But we should note as well that abstract labor itself has two sides, which can also be figured in terms of energy/matter on the one hand, and time on the other.[16] In more detail: I can compare the time I take to rewrite a computerized reference with the time I take to do it by pen. I can compare the time I take to drive to work with the time my trusty donkey requires for the same journey. But I cannot compare my donkey travels with my computer reference writing in terms of the "socially necessary" labor-time both tasks consume, because I cannot write references on my donkey or ride my computer. Both tasks may take half an hour, but this of itself tells me nothing about their value. The time component in the measurement of abstract labor is necessarily particular rather than general. It is always time-specific. I can compare disparate tasks only in terms of the energy expended. After writing a new reference by hand, I feel just as tired as I do after riding a donkey to work and back. Energy expenditure is readily commensurable, in other words, which is why Marx defined abstract labor as "the expenditure of human labor, pure and simple."

The element that is precisely not commensurable is the all-too-human product of technology: the socially necessary time of production. This varies, which is why value is measured not only by labor but also by time. For Marx, the exchange-value of a commodity was determined by the labor-time embodied in it. Socially necessary labor-times vary according to whatever technology has the cutting edge in a particular industry. They vary not only in terms of the difference between gardening hooks and tractors, but in terms of the difference between tractors and microchips. As with any notion of a natural reproduction time, abstract labor-time is also measuring a variety of production processes, in which various technologies and hence various times of production are involved. Accordingly, abstract labor's claim to be a common measurement can only be based on the notion that the measurement embodies human energy: labor as energy is commensurable between as well as within production processes. Socially necessary labor-time is not.[17] Having extracted from the abstract labor debate the notion that the only common or abstractable element is human physiological energy, we will now place that notion to one side. I return to it below, in the context of how far natural energy from other sources can be substituted for human energy, offsetting a decline in capitalist profit.

Profit in Marx

Having established that abstract labor-time is simply the expenditure of human energy, exercised within a certain time, we now turn to why time is also critical. Human energy has to be expended within a given technological time, otherwise the commodity produced by labor will not be profitable. Profit, in short, depends on labor power and time, and, of these, the greater is labor-power. Provided the right time of production is respected, meaning competitive technologies are used, labor-power will add value. Those competitive technologies, I suggest, include the degree of education of labor-power, as it is this that enables labor to move faster and more efficiently in relation to certain tasks. But all the competitive technologies and education in the world will not make a profit without the sheer physiological energy of human labor-power. At least, so Marx thought.

But as capital spends more on its constant outlay to keep pace with the available technologies (which determine socially necessary labor-time) and less on its variable outlay, it spends more on the constant capital that does not add value. Because the variable component (understood as labor-power) is the source of value, the rate of profit will tend to fall. Paradoxically, while technology might seem to make money (an illusion that keeps contemporary economists enthralled) it does so at the expense of profit. This tendency is offset where capital does not pay in full for the reproduction cost of labor-power, meaning that it forces wages down below subsistence level.

For Marx, "the immiseration of the working class" would result from this countervailing tendency, where capital deals with the cost of technology by reducing wages. It would happen in the heartlands of capital, the advanced West. But it did not happen there, and the question is, why not? I can answer this by saying that other natural energies as well as far-flung labors have substituted for the exploitation of local labor. But leaving that aside for now: in Marx's account, even the trend to immiseration will only postpone the crises of capital: capital cannot avoid the compulsion to spend more on its constant outlay.

That is to say: the central contradiction of capitalist production lies in the fact that capital has to outlay ever larger expenditures on technology. By such expenditure, and only by it, can capital maintain or acquire its competitive edge in any large-scale production and distribution process. In Marx's account, capital survives and prospers when it produces and distributes in the shortest possible time; it loses otherwise. When capital is unable to spend more, relatively, on labor, its profits should decline. But the belief that the rate of profit will tend to fall has not been borne out wherever production flourishes and profit grows on the basis of "natural resources" rather than labor-power. We need to see why this is so.

Revising Marx

My revision of Marx's theory begins with the definition of variable and constant capital. Variable capital for Marx is labor power, "pure and simple." Constant capital is dead labor: Marx taught that nature, like technology, was worth no more than the labor-time embodied in it. I will argue here that there is every reason to include nature together with labor on the variable side of the fence, and to leave technology as the only "constant" in production. I propose instead that constant capital be defined solely as technology, which truly adds nothing substantial in terms of energy. It is not living. It is only the congelation of dead labor and dead nature.

By what warrant do we make these changes? Apart from the empirical problems with the labor theory of value, the grounds for revision are there in Marx's notions of abstract labor-time and labor-power, which are energetic notions at their core. When Marx asked himself what labor-power was, he said explicitly that labor-power is energy. The energetic connotation is even clearer in German: the word for labor-power is *Arbeitskraft*, and *Kraft* has more the sense of energy and effort, of the thing you use when you push yourself to the utmost, than the more abstract "power." While an English physicist speaks of force, a German refers to Kraft. It is Kraft or energetic power which is now depleted in human beings by their attempts to keep pace with, or breathe, drink and eat, in a polluted economy. As we have seen, the exchange value of labor-power can be calculated only when all useful concrete labors are reduced to their common denominator of energy – sheer physiological force and capacity. It is labor-power's energy that enables it to embody more of itself in the product than it costs.

But, and this brings us to the crucial facts, there are other natural sources of energy aside from labor-power, and other things which share the living quality of labor in that they can give more than they cost. This is why variable capital has to be redefined, as labor- *and* nature-power. Just as surplus-value is realized through the disjunction between the cost of reproducing labor-power and what labor adds in production, so also is surplus-value realized through the disjunction between the reproduction of other natural sources capable of adding energy and what these sources add in production. Just as capital makes a profit because the reproduction cost of labor-power is less than the energy labor adds in production, so too do other natural sources add more than capital pays for their reproduction. The difference is that capital never pays for the reproduction costs of nature, unless it has no option under what I have termed the law of substitution.[18] Under the law of substitution, capital will always take the cheapest of the suitable energy options available. Nor, to be valuable, need these other natural energies and substances remain untouched. These energies can be transformed many times over, removed more and more from the natural state from which they are initially extracted. They are transformed by technology as human energy is transformed by education, and their energies converge in the new product that could not exist without nature or technology: the commodity. Natural sources stay valuable as long as they are capable of adding energy; and their value in this respect may be enhanced or diminished by the intervention of human labor, and by the other natural energies they are mixed with.[19] The way that various combinations of energies and technologies enhance or diminish value overall will be plainer if I explain why I use the terms "natural substances" and "natural energies" interchangeably.

The negative energy capability of substances

Energy and matter, as everyone knows after Einstein, are the same thing. Matter is energy in an apparently congealed state. Energy can be concretized in matter. Matter and energy exist on a continuum in which substances, such as wood or coal, can be transformed into energy, while energy transforms one material thing into another. It is at this level, the level of transformative power, that we can speak most readily of some other form of natural energy substituting for the pure physiological energy that is labor-power. But not only energy is at issue here. Substances are also involved in that (a) they can be transformed into an energy source and (b) some of them require less energy expended upon them. The nature of some substances renders them more malleable than others: in this respect they have what one might call a "negative energy capability." That is to say, while they do not release energy as such, they require the expenditure of less energy in getting them to the point where they can release value for capital.

The work that is done, say, in transforming coal extracts into cloth will demand more levels of transformation and more energy than the transformation of cotton into cloth. In the second instance, nature has already done the work of producing the ingredients to be used in production. Capital recognizes nature's work, and the negative energetic capability of certain substances, insofar as it welcomes means (genetic modification among them) for speeding up the production of agricultural and other naturally occurring commodities, both for direct consumption, and in consumption for production.[20] Capital takes nature's production process and speeds it up in two ways. Either it keeps the general design and accelerates it, or it alters that design to the same end. Ten big tomatoes produced by genetic modification may be equivalent to twenty small tomatoes produced more rapidly by the enhancement of short-term soil fertility, and so forth.

At this point, a Marxist might object that nature becomes a "raw material" only when it has labor mixed into it in some form. Nature as such does not enter the production process. At the minimum, labor-power removes nature from its place of origin to the place of production. In fact this is not strictly true, but the general point remains: "raw materials" demand labor-power to come into existence. My point is simply that some of the raw materials, by their nature, require less labor and/or technology for their transformation. Oil, for instance, is capable of releasing crude energy with the minimal technology of a spark of flint. It is easier to obtain a fire by this means than it is to gather driftwood. The negative energy capability of a substance depends on the ease with which it can be transformed into energy that substitutes for human labor, such as electrical energy (remembering that fossil fuels are the main source of electricity). Some technology is used for all transformation, including the technology of human education. But human labor requires least technological expenditure, for it can be harnessed and trained to tasks while remembering the actions required to make those tasks more efficient. (Technological education, as noted in Chapter 6, is not the same thing as the exercise of the imagination.) In addition, human beings are more portable, and can take themselves to work.

Nature, as I have stressed, does not take itself to market, or to the place of production: keeping pace with the speed of acquisition means that natural energies have to be acquired at a constantly accelerating pace, and this goes hand in hand with the imposition of portability upon them. From this perspective, transportation is itself a form of transformation, which begins the moment the substance is uprooted from the earth or extracted from water or air. In other words, unless the focus of labor is agrarian, the moment of labor's first intervention is simultaneously the first moment in which a given substance or potential force is removed from its conditions of reproduction. Labor-power is unique both because it adds energy, and because of its self-actualizing portability: it is the instrument of transportation. Not only this, but it covers its own transportation costs, making it doubly attractive as a source of energy. But while labor-power takes itself and the "raw materials" to the place of production, once the "raw materials" are there, some of them contribute more than others in terms of energy, and this ability to contribute is in their nature, not in what labor-power has done to them. This is the point about "raw materials" and "nature" as sources of surplus-value: they are precisely sources of energy. As they are transformed, they abet the process of their transformation, and even substances such as rocks, the most inert and inanimate of things, abet it if we think of energy and matter as an ultimately quantifiable continuum. But the point here is that their transformation not only results in a commodity with exchange-value. That transformation also impacts the reproduction of the next generation of use-values, and the reproduction of nature as the overall condition of use-value and hence of exchange-value. Capitalism, as a mode of production, must diminish the overall quantity of use-value in that it diminishes the stock of nature, replacing it only with the overproduction of human energy with a diminishing education (and, for that matter, given the effects of pollutants on intelligence, a diminishing educational capacity). Other modes of production, such as localized feudalism, maintain some equilibrium between human production and natural reproduction.

When the quantitative dimension of use-value overall is ignored, when the "everlasting natural condition of human existence" is treated as infinite, it is possible to gauge the production of profit solely in terms of exchange-value. But this means ignoring the extent to which different natural substances have various negative energetic capabilities. They are ignored in this way when they are reduced to the constant factor "raw materials." Then their contribution to surplus-value can be gauged, as it has been by Marxists, solely in terms of the labor-power that has carried them to the place of production. Or, from a different standpoint, profit can be gauged in terms of the technology that has speeded up the extraction and the transformation of natural energies and substances. In both cases, nature is treated as if it were the dead factor in profit. The extent to which nature, like labor, is variable is overlooked. But nature, too, gives more than it gets.

Against my argument, it may be objected that capital recognizes these differentials between natural things when it pays more for some raw materials than others. But this exactly proves my point. While capital recognizes energy differentials, it still assigns the profit to be made from them to technology, and so cannot explain the real relation of energy to profit, anymore than the labor theory of value has been able to account for the cost of raw materials on the basis of extraction alone: it can be just as difficult to extract dross as diamonds. While one can maintain that the labor is really in the looking, or, from a different perspective, that value is determined by technology, the fact is that radar and other research instruments which make looking less arduous have not reduced the cost of diamonds, which are valued industrially precisely for their energy configurations.

Another objection: At this point there may be mutterings that I have turned the labor theory of value into yet another account of supply and demand. As we will see below, there is a sense in which this is partially true. But what my argument does, and the vagaries of supply and demand economics do not, is to keep the twofold nature (use value and exchange value) of commodities constantly in view, which means focusing on the material level of energy and substance as well as exchange. Insofar as a commodity has use-value it cannot be immaterial; it has to consist of energy and/or matter. It is this materiality which is forgotten by those who rely on time management, or who teach that "technology" can make us rich all by itself. "Out of nothing, nothing can be created," wrote Marx, quoting Lucretius.[21] What supply and demand does not and cannot account for is the real cost of these "raw materials."[22] "Supply and demand"[23] economics goes searching for new supplies of the raw material, and when it has exhausted one repository it moves on to another. It ignores the real cost of these raw materials, which is determined by the time of their reproduction. This real cost has to catch up, if only because we run out of supplies, although we also become ill. When the real cost catches up, capital has its reckoning with nature.

The law of substitution means capital tends to use energy sources whose reproduction time it can discount, unless for some reason paying for reproduction is essential to a continued supply of a needed energy source. Supply and demand is always constrained by the law of substitution, which of itself points to why natural energy and matter is the source of value. If one cannot obtain the supply of energy at an acceptable cost, one has to find a substitute. But one also has to know how much of that substitute one needs. The question of *quantities* of energies means that value depends on supply only in a trivial sense: it ultimately depends on how much of *this* supply replaces *that* supply, and the exchange-value of those amounts cannot be determined by "supply" or quantity itself as an abstract factor. It has to be determined by energy, and how much value a given energy adds in production within a given time.

So if capital can have oil at half the price of electricity, it will take the former. For that matter, if I am doing brute labor, hauling coal or timber, with no exercise of my mind or will permitted to me, I might as well be the oil that fuels a tractor doing the same work.[24] Capital will also use human labor-power rather than technology when labor-power saves production costs in other ways. Thus sugar cane growers in South Florida have found it, generally, more profitable to use human labor than machines to harvest their crops, since, despite the costs for the wages, housing and food for the immigrant workers, the damage the machines do to the fields makes it more profitable to hand-cut their crops.[25] But in general, capital seeks to avoid paying for the costs of reproduction. This is basic to why capital tends to substitute space for time. If the social rate of production means that more commodities make it to market if they depend on electricity rather than oil, then, even if oil has the edge in terms of real value, electricity will be preferred. However, if the real value of electricity forces itself on the particular corporation using it, then it will shift to oil. At the same time as it outlays more on energy based in fossil fuels, capital seeks to cut its labor costs. For instance, one recent study in the US found that employers threatened plant closings in approximately half of all union organizing campaigns. And 12 percent of all employers actually closed their plants in response to organizing drives.[26] In instances where workers are demanding better compensation for their reproductive needs – healthcare, retirement, better wages, etc. – employers either consider moving, or actually move, to a location where workers will demand less for their reproductive needs. Indeed we can speak of a law such as the law of substitution precisely because it encapsulates the deeper law of profit. By profit's decree, space substitutes for time because the exploitation of various natural sources, including labor-power, has to accelerate in order to sustain the production of surplus-value.

The putative Multilateral Agreement on Investment (MAI), and treaties like it, extend the range of options available under the law of substitution, in that they facilitate the replacement of reproduction time by spatial reach, providing new sources of variable capital. But this facilitation in turn means that capital acts like a herd of grazing locusts, leaving behind barren earth in one place, and moving on to another. A recent study reports, for example, that the oil industry spends $156 billion each year in search of new reserves of oil and gas. Over 6,000 companies are involved in exploratory projects for new sources of petroleum.[27] As current reserves are depleted, the oil industry must go elsewhere. Indeed, the pursuit of new, not-yet-extracted oil and gas is a high-stakes, high-budget component of the international oil industry and a hostage of war.

As already implied, none of this is to challenge the idea that, if the expenditure on constant capital over variable capital increases past a certain point, the rate of profit will decline. The point is that the rate of profit will fall only where constant capital is really "fixed" in relation to labor-power, fixed in that no other natural force – disguised as constant capital – figures in production. But once those alternative energy sources add less than the cost of the technology used to convey them, or once they decline, the law of the falling rate of profit will once more apply. Consider the computer industry. Computers employ 2 percent of the population in Europe and the United States, but use 20 percent of the electricity. The Internet alone uses 7 percent of the electricity consumed in the United States, which is phenomenal when domestic usage is still limited to 20 percent of the population. As we have seen, the Internet demand for electricity is growing at a rate which means that coal, that most noxious of fossil fuels, is the one thing that can satisfy it. The computer industry, in short, is one where the contribution of nature to the production of surplus-value is greater than the contribution of labor-power. But it is also an industry where it might be easy to write off electricity to "constant capital," then puzzle over the evident profits. Where human energy does not stand in for other sources of energy (and all sources of energy, as we have seen, are ultimately derived from nature), profit indeed will be made. But, if there is no natural check on it, it may be made at a rate of consumption which outstrips the rate of reproduction of that energy source. Where reproduction does not force itself into account, capital fails to look ahead. It is too busy making money precisely because it does not pay for that energy source at its value (cost of reproduction). Hence, in part, the electricity crisis in California in 2001, where the profit from electricity is insufficient to satisfy private producers running out of hydroelectric sources.

As we have seen, escaping the real cost of the reproduction time of natural substances leads capital to extend its spatial reach, in search of new options under the law of substitution. Under the law of substitution (which underlies the push for more free trade and fossil-fuel electricity – Chapter 2), there is no regulation of energy sources based on their rate of reproduction rather than the rate at which they can be consumed in production. Capital, unless it has to, does not pay for the reproduction cost of natural sources of energy, which means that the reproduction time of these energy sources is not taken into account. As a rule, they are consumed more rapidly than they can reproduce.

In terms of explaining the world, Marx's theory does not work. But it almost works. By keeping Marx's logic, but varying the key players, everything shifts. In other words, if constant capital is redefined as technology, and variable capital as labor plus nature (with certain qualifications), then the equations concerning surplus-value take on more explanatory force in relation to the present-day realities of capital. This new value theory accounts for the tendency toward environmental degradation of capitalist cultures and explains why it is inevitable (and it accounts for how it is that, without appearing to have completely immiserated their working classes, the advanced capitalist cultures nonetheless, for a time, supported an enormous middle class). However, this should not blind us to the extent to which the apparent comfort of those middle classes is based on accumulating debt, and on the extent to which the middle classes are joining the working class in forms of immiseration that Marx had not foreseen. For instance there is the immiseration involved in making a body ill, not only with its own violation of its bodily rhythm, but with that same body's constant and often involuntary ingestion of a bombardment of toxins. This bombardment, like the denial of human fallow time in the learning process (Chapter 6), progressively depletes our intelligence as a species.

This theory accounts for these new forms of immiseration at the same time as it sheds light on that favorite theme of modern critics,[28] the elimination of time in favor of space. This is revealed as the inevitable consequence of the speed of acquisition, manifest in an ever-expanding reach through conquest or trade agreements – anything that facilitates the more rapid acquisition of energies and the substitution of one energy source for another. Capital is not only seeking labor-power and markets through imperialism (although it is certainly doing that); it is also seeking to exploit other natural sources of value. In that capital's continued profit must be based more and more on the speed of acquisition, it must expand more and command more unregulated distance, and in this respect space *must* take the place of generational time. This is the core contradiction, or inherent dynamic, in capitalism today: you must go further in space to obtain your raw materials, and, in doing so, you cannot stay home to reproduce. The process of reproduction is thus "out of time," which means that, in the event that the natural process of reproduction cannot be speeded up, the cost of natural reproduction has to be reduced to make up for its drag on exchange-value.

But the exhaustion of real resources, and the cost of that speed, return in a declining profit margin. That decline can be figured in terms of the cost of the technology needed to extract and convey energies from greater distances – that is to say, the cost of transport and communication. It can and should also be figured in terms of the real reproduction costs of certain energy sources. Some of these real costs are felt even in the fantasmatic world of capital, which still has to reckon with those energy sources it cannot replace. Capital would have to pay still more of those costs if the new protectionism (integral, as we will see, to the real third way) is implemented. It would have to pay more insofar as it would have to wait for more things to reproduce at their natural rate.

But, as production stands, the source of profit from nature is concealed in that its real cost is always deferred, never taken into account unless it has to be. This endless deferral means that it is all too easy to take technology (which, by its speed, makes deferral possible) for the source of profit in itself, when it is merely means. As the means, it enters into how profit is calculated, just as it enters into estimates of labor-time. Technology sets the pace, but it is the product rather than the determinant of the economy that demands that pace. The growing global economy makes or at least selects the technologies which increase that pace. As we have seen, cars driven by fossil fuels stay in use, despite technologically sophisticated alternatives, while vehicles transporting goods and services for profit are exempt from any restrictions on their speed. Transport and communication, increasingly privatized, have become a popular target for global investment. As the regulators of speed, hence of profit, they are judged likely to remain profitable in themselves.

The two axes of profit and production

So far we have focused on the real cost of natural things and human labor: the cost of their reproduction. But this is not the way capital reckons its costs. In general, for capital, the value which natural energy sources and substances add in production is derived from a contrast not with their reproduction time (unless that must be paid for) but with the speed at which these sources can be acquired.[29] This is because deriving energy sources at greater speed is a key component in racing to market (in the shortest possible – or socially necessary – time), but, even more importantly, it is linked to avoiding the real costs of those energy sources. While labor-power may have to be paid for at its value, trees are rarely paid for at theirs. The capitalist definitely does cheat on trees, and on other dumb living things. By avoiding full or even part payment of the cost of their reproduction time, our capitalist enhances his or her profit, in the same way he would if he succeeded in immiserating the working class by paying them below subsistence wages.[30] Hence there are two axes of profit and production: first, the axis of the speed of acquisition, which generally works by spatial acquisition; second, the axis of real time, or the reproduction axis, where surplus-value is measured as it has always been, in terms of the cost of reproduction. These two axes match the dimensions we are drawing out in relation to real time and speed, respectively: as we have seen, goods and labor can be acquired either by being temporally reproduced (their reproduction time is allowed for) or by being acquired at greater speed, either across space or by other means which discount the real time of reproduction. Invariably, when it can, capital goes for speed, because it cannot afford to wait. Reproduction time will be constantly pressed to give way to speed. On the spatial/speed axis, the axis which NAFTA, GATT and a MAI (if it is acceded to) operate, natural time is disregarded entirely.

Energy, or the value added in production, is measured only against the speed of acquisition, although it should be measured against the time of its reproduction.

Speed is basic to the conventional understanding of profit and a focus of critiques of modernity, from Baumant to Virilio especially; the latter's analysis of speed focuses on militarism and the media, but his distinction between vehicular and metabolic time parallels mine between the time of production and that of reproduction. Speed in getting to market, speed in the technologies of production, speed in acquiring the raw materials of the production process, speed of labor: these things are fundamental in the mainstream understanding of profit. They are the rationale for economies of scale and the mechanized mass-production process, whose contribution to bioderegulation was discussed earlier in relation to electricity, and in terms of how humans became adjuncts to the machine, attempting to keep pace with machine time. The economics of mechanization and automation now deserve more explicit attention.

Starting with Henry Ford, mass production became "virtually the only production system practiced by large U.S. manufacturers."[31] The reason? Output to time ratio increased with mechanized production: it became the new arbiter, for most commodities, of socially necessary labor-time. In this method of production, the cost of producing an item is lowered by producing large quantities of standardized items; "high product volumes drastically reduce manufacturing costs through economies of scale."[32] Any complexities or custom work would upset the production process and result in higher costs. The more standardized a product, the more automation can be used to produce it: "to realize the lowest possible costs, hence the largest market, the production process should be as automated as possible. This means high fixed costs but low unit costs, further reinforcing the need for high volumes."[33] Mass production evidently increases the speed at which items are produced: "when Ford's engineers introduced the assembly line . . . the amount of labor-time spent in making a single car dropped from 12 hours and 8 minutes to 2 hours and 35 minutes." Six months later, the average labor-time dropped to one hour and thirty minutes.[34]

Mechanized production, by accelerating the speed of production, accelerated the profit. But it did so only insofar as the cost of the new mechanized technologies did not outweigh the natural energies and human energies consumed in the production process. Profit depends on natural energy sources, including human labor-power, but profit margins depend on the cost of these energy sources compared with the value they add in production. The reason that mechanized production processes entail globalization from the outset is that mechanization is profitable only if the energies and materials it consumes can be processed at a profit greater than the cost of the technologies required to process them at the fastest possible rate. Processing at the fastest possible rate is the condition of successful competition, whose other condition is that the energies and materials with energetic capability called on in production give more than the cost of their acquisition requires. While labor-power's cost is determined by the cost of its daily and (up until this historical point) generational reproduction, this is not true necessarily for the cost of other natural energies and energy sources. These are commonly acquired below their real reproduction cost; consequently the speed of their acquisition, by this argument, will often take over as one measure of profit. That is to say, the speed of acquisition can be regarded as the measure of short-term profit. Long-term profit, on the other hand, is set by the disjunction between the energy added in production and the cost of reproduction. This gives us the real measure of the cost of these natural resources, as it does the cost of labor-power.

There is ongoing debate as to how we should cost the natural energies and substances depleted by production. By my argument, the real cost of natural energies and substances is determined by their reproduction time, in the same way that the real cost of labor-power is determined by labor's reproduction time. I am also saying that profit is made because of the gap between what these natural things add in production and the cost of reproduction. This is the law Marx uncovered in the labor theory of value. In this argument about nature we are merely extending it. However, that extension gives us a means for establishing the real cost of the environmental resources used in production. By my account here, the cost of clean air would be the cost of reproducing clean air from air that has been damaged. The real cost of oil would make it suitable only in the rarest circumstances, while the cost of solar energy would be zero. This has evident consequences for social policy, but this is not the social policy which is being pursued as the third way, as shown in the last chapter. Instead, support for globalization from right and center means that reproduction time will be disregarded, as this occurs wherever the speed of acquisition can substitute for reproduction time. Exchange-value is produced regardless of whether its origin is temporal or spatial; this is why I have insisted on the speed of acquisition as a measure of exchange-value. Capital's interest is always geared to the speed of acquisition: this mode yields more profit, precisely because the reproduction time of natural resources and, where possible, human labor, need not be paid for at its value. Yet, as indicated earlier, the fact that capital is geared to speed in this way means it has to diminish the basis of use-value and hence the basis of profit overall. The speed needed to maintain and extend the global reach of corporations is critically dependent on technology, so dependent that technology itself is often taken for the source of speed, rather than the energy consumed in the process of getting this or that from A to B, just as it is in the production process itself.[35]

9   Price, inflation and energy

To go online and buy products, or book airline tickets, is to perform delivery work. Such work is squeezed into the time once given to rest and revival. The turn of the century has witnessed a shift in the burden of service labor, from producer to consumer, that is impacting almost everybody. If you live in the so-called advanced West, you must have been spending more time doing telephone work, pressing "1" for this option or "6" for that option. When you do this, you are also making money (for someone else) insofar as you are saving labor and/or delivery costs. The automated telephone services are becoming more threatening: they used politely to offer you the option of staying on the line if you had a rotary phone, and some of us who did not have rotary phones nonetheless stayed on the line. The shrillness (in the US) of the upgraded automated systems – where you are firmly and reproachfully instructed that resistance is futile, and to start pressing options *now* – reflects capital's need to cut delivery and distribution costs, as well as labor costs. Automation does not only cost jobs; it also yields means for sliding more of the residual labor of production and distribution under the door of exchange. The consequences of automated speed, in fact, are that in addition to having to look harder for a job, and having less chance of finding it, a person spends longer in the unpaid labor of consumption.

When the consumer carries part of the cost of distribution, as at the supermarket, online, or on the telephone, then the consumer also contributes to short-term profit.[1] But when consumers do this, they offset the escalating costs of distribution (the prerequisite for exchange), which has to keep pace (from capital's point of view) with the speed of production. Keeping pace is difficult precisely because production can outstrip human capabilities. Not only does the speed of technology as such move too fast for human time, but the cost of the other ingredients entering production is out of line with the cost of human labor-power. This is because the raw materials entering production have to be consumed at a speed which will justify their escalating acquisition costs, and one cannot consume human labor rapidly enough to keep pace. Where that labor is unavoidable in order that the transaction be successfully completed, it is shifted over to the consumer's side of the exchange, using his or her energy-time, petrol and electricity. Later in this chapter I will suggest that the unpaid work of consumption escalates as profit based on the speed of acquisition takes over from profit grounded in the reality of value. But this is only one of the ways in which the reality of value is catching up with the fantasy world of technology. Other consequences of ignoring reproduction time can now be situated theoretically. These consequences range from inflation to new forms of human immiseration. The first section of this chapter frames the explanatory issues here in terms of how we measure price in relation to speed, and how finance games can only be played where price is divorced from value. The second section situates the discussion in the context of inflation. The notion of a war between the speed of acquisition and the need for reproduction time explains inflation, and also why immiseration is increasing. As I show in the concluding sections, it does so because it draws lines between speed, as something that dimishes real value while increasing price, and time, as something that enhances real value while remaining invisible.

Speculations on price

What this theory and the accounts of contemporary mainstream economics have in common is an emphasis on speed. Speed in getting to market, speed in production, speed in acquisition: all these are recognized. Together, they constitute "the speed of trade," which in turn is recognized as one of the two critical economic issues confronting today's governments. The other is the speed of finance capital. Finance capital was an issue at the Florence conference I mentioned before. Both Jospin of France and Cardoso of Brazil said that the speed of finance capital was too fast for the speed of trade. "After each crisis, it is clear that capital flows have to be connected with direct production, that is, trade flows," said Cardoso. Jospin's conclusions were similar. He argued that the speed of capital flows had accelerated too fast in relation to trade flows. Cardoso's and Jospin's concern with finance capital flows is entirely, so to speak, on the money. Brazil's economy had been devastated by financial speculation in 1994, while Indonesia and other parts of Asia are still suffering from more recent "casino capitalism." But what needs to be stressed is that, while both Cardoso and Jospin were concerned about the speed of finance capital, they overlooked what "speed" does at a third level – the reproduction of people and natural resources. That is to say, these heads of state could see that finance capital causes havoc (the most recent instances being in Asia – due to flooding by American currency – and Russia) but overlooked the level of bioderegulation of human beings and other natural life forms.

Finance games in all their manifestations, from futures markets to casino capitalism, can only be played in the gap between value and price. The havoc they cause would certainly be decreased by reconnecting flows of finance capital with trade flows, but this cannot happen with globalization, because it widens the gap between value and price. Both by Marx's and this account, real value formed out of labor-power and other sources of natural energy rarely translates directly into price. In Marx's account, supply and demand can temporarily send profits, or surplus-value, scampering into certain sectors of the market, until competition reasserts a more normal approximation of price to value. In my account, something similar occurs, except that it takes longer, and price has more autonomy (relative autonomy) from value. As the next section draws out, the separation of price and value is perceived by all varieties of economists as critical to understanding inflation ("the most intractable problem of economics"). Hence attempts to tie the amount of money in circulation to some value standard. As Soros has it, "The value of money depends on the value of the goods and services for which it can be exchanged." This is in the context of the idea that one of the functions of money is "as a store of value."[2] Marx too proceeded on the assumption that money is a store of value. It is a store of value because it is "the phenomenal form" of the abstract labor-time that is the measure of exchange-value. The standard Marxist view is that price corresponds to value if the price of a commodity, multiplied by the value of money, equal the labor time embodied in the commodity. Price deviates from value if the commodity's price, multiplied by the value of money, is greater or less than the commodity's socially necessary labor-time. The mechanism of the deviation overall is also the mechanism for the equalization of the rate of profit on stocks of invested capital across different sectors in capitalist production. Surplus-value in Marx's account can flow to various sectors, and artificially inflate prices within them, but competition evens things out. Surplus-value as the measure of price asserts itself in the long-run. The process Marx describes fits with the empirical world of capitalism in relation to supply and demand. When profit rates in one sector go beyond the norm, capital flows into that sector, competition escalates, and then prices drop back or closer to the preexisting norm. Where problems arise in Marx's account of value and price is in the idea that absolute surplus-value asserts itself in the relatively short term. By this argument, it must assert itself in the long-run, insofar as capital runs out of natural resources which supply energy more rapidly than labor-power, such as oil. But the short-term effects of natural energies substituting for those of labor-power have been to offset the falling rate of profit, as we have seen.

The sums that need to be done to predict when the falling rate of profit will assert itself in the globalizing world have yet to be attempted. When they are, we will see that it is one thing to insist on the reproduction time of all natural sources and energies as the measure of their value, and another to find a way of comparing them, because their times of natural reproduction vary greatly. The natural reproduction time of oil is infinitely longer than that of wood; coal has the millennial edge on labor-power. When value was measured solely in terms of labor-power it was possible to have a measure whereby each commodity could be evaluated in terms of the labor-time it embodied. As we have seen, this is the measurement Marx called "abstract labor-time."

Yet, as I have argued, the measure of real value (based on natural substances and energies) can be given in terms paralleling that of abstract labor-time, because the energy component in labor-time is precisely not unique to labor. Labor is not the only source of natural energy. If labor as energy can be compared across a range of tasks, so too can labor as energy be compared with the energy derived from other natural sources. In short, the various natural energies (and their comparative value) could, in principle, be measured quantitatively (provided one has an agreed-upon unit of energy–time measurement). Where natural energy overall is concerned, the possibility for a quantitative measurement exists in that, in all production processes, a given amount of energy is needed to transform such and such a raw material into this or that particular product. And as I have already suggested, the human energy required for transformation, if indeed any human energy as such is required, would depend on how far the "raw materials" themselves also adapted – or released energy – in ways needed for the process of transformation.

Thus the question becomes whether substitutable natural energies can be measured correctly, in the same way that labor-time can be measured, at least in principle. And the first part of the answer, as we saw in the last chapter, is that they can be measured on the basis of their interchangeability. But this answer is insufficient. When we are talking of their interchangeability we are also talking of exchange-value. And this exchange-value, as we have also seen, is determined in two ways. One is the real time of reproduction. The other is the cost of acquisition compared to the value added in production; exchange-value measured in this way is measured by speed as well.[3] But the cost of that speed in turn is measured by the cost of acquisition of the energies it consumes (mainly fossil fuels, or electricity based on them). The full implications of this for use value and exchange value come into play precisely because inanimate natural energy sources are the preferred source of artificial speed. While they – rather than, or as well as, labor-power – are a source of energy, they become that source only when their physical structure is manipulated. That manipulation leads to the release of energy by fossil fuels, and then to the production of waste. In turn, this diminishes the organization of living matter, which is integral to its capacity for adding exchange-value. So, while enhancing exchange-value, speedy acquisition based on fossil fuels diminishes use-value.

Because this revised value theory factors in distance traversed in relation to speed of acquisition and value, it points to two potentially competing economies, only one of which is on the side of life. The other, deathly (and as we are about to see, inflationary) economy makes the inanimate *appear* animate. It makes things move from its own standpoint. But it does not add to the common stock of use-value; it diminishes it. Here the power of human design and imagination is the fulcrum on which the production or negation of use-value turns. The power of animation is certainly within us, as well as in the energy source we release. But when human animation turns to the diminution of use-value, through using natural sources more rapidly than they can reproduce themselves while increasing the quantity of disorganization – through, in other words, producing exchange-value by the speed of acquisition – it *simultaneously* produces an inflated price together with air and climate damage. Which is why the human species showed itself prescient in naming the gap between value and price "inflation," meaning hot air.

Inflation and a new periodization of the stages of capitalism

Traditionally, one of the explanations for inflation is that it is produced by putting more money into circulation, which leads to an increase in price. Hence attempts to tie the amount of money in circulation to some value standard. As we have seen, Marx too proceeded on the assumption that money is a store of value, but one of the weaknesses in his political economy is that he cannot explain it. However, once inflation is tied to price and value to reproduction, the apparent inevitability of inflation is tied to the apparent inevitability of expansion. Price measures distance, and value time. In support of this notion, one can consider the following.

Inflation and increases in prices existed before the eighteenth century, but it was in that period that they became noticeable. They accelerated with industrialization, have ebbed and flowed since, but have steadily increased throughout. Inflation always gets worse. I am proposing now that this steady asymmetry is due to how the speed of acquisition takes over as a variable factoring price. In this connection, it is interesting that Braudel's research, and that of others, indicates that increases in price seem to depend on increases in the distance traveled by a particular commodity. This is so, however, only insofar as trade is a measure of distance traveled, for it is trade, rather than distance as such of course, that is measured. "In the eighteenth century, one can undoubtedly say that *almost* everywhere in Europe, *large-scale* profits from trade were superior to *large-scale* profits from industry or agriculture."[4] While data is limited, I would interpret Braudel's rare generalization in terms of the speed of acquisition (trade) yielding greater profits than production taking account of natural reproduction time (agriculture and some forms of industry).

By this argument, price increases have afflicted us more steadily since industrialization because accelerations in the speed of transportation (and with it communication), and the consumption of more energy in the process, have also been relatively steady (except for periodic crises). We can explain these price increases because we have supposed that the speed of acquisition must function as a measure of value additional to the rate of reproduction. These two measures fight it out, with the speed of acquisition winning when prices rise and inflation accelerates. At such times, the speed of acquisition takes over from the measure of real value – the abstract labor-time or "energy-time" embodied in a particular commodity – as the determinant of price. Of course the problem with the "socially necessary" speed of acquisition, as the determinant of price, is that, as long as it has apparently endless resources available to it, it can ignore reproduction – in reality, and as a measure of value. In these periods, especially the period that is now coming to its close, the economy "booms." There appears to be no impediment, other than trade, labor and environmental regulations, standing between having the whole globe to play with and booming profit. This illusion is fostered by the fact that money is measured not only in relation to value (energy), but in relation to speed, or *the socially fastest means for getting commodity X to point Y, which increases together with its cost*. This, incidentally, is another reason why finance flows might get ahead of trade flows. Changing cost is accurately reflected in real terms insofar as perennial increases in the cost of speed reflect more consumption of oil and fossil fuels (and nuclear fission). In turn, these costs are passed on to enterprises and other consumers via a spiral of price increases commensurate with the greater quantities of energy consumed in the manufacture of the speed not only of production, but of exchange, distribution and consumption. But when the reality of reproduction time asserts itself as the ultimate measure of real value – in any way – there is recession or crisis, of which the 2000–01 Californian blackouts were illustrative. Real exchange-value can assert itself within a sector of production, or overall. But under globalization, or other systems of extension to lesser extents, value is viewed through a refracting lens, in which price is first referred to speed, while speed in turn is determined by the social rate of its production (technology), insofar as this sets the rate of exploitation of a natural resource.[5]

Periodization

We can view the different stages or phases of capitalization in terms of this struggle between natural time and speed, or the spatial acquisition of resources and goods. In fact an advantage of this rewritten value theory is that it makes variations in spatial organization direct actors in the process of capital accumulation, together with the accumulation of interest through time. It makes access to resources – through territorially organized space – as crucial as limiting labor costs. Both are conditions of profit, and one can reformulate the periods of capital in terms of the tension between production based more on real production time or value based on the speed of acquisition. This reformulation leads to a reperiodization of capitalism based on spatiotemporal variables. This reperiodization links questions of boundaries (nationhood and so forth), colonization, and other imperializing spatial moves directly to capitalization. It is based on establishing markers of that tension pertaining to real production time, on the one hand, and speedy acquisition, on the other. Among the markers of acquisition, for instance, would be enclosure acts and specialization, centralized and mechanized production processes, level of transport and communications, free-trade agreements and literal acquisition (as in the conquest of territories). The markers of real production time include wages, environmental restrictions, and the level of social and healthcare provision. In the time remaining to this book, I can only sketch out that reperiodization in broad outlines, but it may go something like the following.

Throughout the last thousand years, the rate of speed and the time of nature have slogged it out, from the period when usury – or interest on money loans over time – became widespread, a period beginning in the eleventh and especially the twelfth centuries. The practice of lending money for interest was condemned widely as a perverse imitation of nature by which money too had offspring (interest). Practically, if not theoretically, this was the crucial factor in the accumulation of capital.[6] It was a factor in which something other than natural wealth determined the degree of profit. That is to say, for the first time since the fall of Rome, wealth depended on something which based its calculations on the calendar, rather than on the good fortune bestowed by nature.[7] But my point here is that, broadly speaking, capital, from the eleventh to the fourteenth centuries, was accumulated through turning calendar time into money. The same period gives us the birth of trade with specialization – that is to say, price based on acquisition rather than reproduction.

It is only with distance or some degree of separation that the middleman, first incarnated in peddlers and traders, comes into existence. As he grows, so does the distance he commands, and the size of the middling company he keeps. The burghers are born, and then the bourgeoisie. Specialized crops were produced from the twelfth century: they made it easier for the new class of merchants or middlemen to gather their merchandise in one place before shipping it elsewhere. Evidently, if one has to go from farm to farm, and from town to town, gathering produce, the process takes longer than it does if production is concentrated in a particular place. While specialization was severely restricted until the Enclosure Acts, and other forms of land concentration in the seventeenth and eighteenth centuries, its prior existence testifies to the awareness of how specialization cut costs and speeded up production and distribution. Specialization, and extended networks of transportation, went together with urbanization. Cities expanded along with trade, as they continue to do. They were the residence of choice of the new middlemen.

Time – calendar time – and traversing space – the manmade map – are now significant. Both circumvent nature, and both contain within themselves the structure of a different economy where time is at war with space. There is a first approximation of a periodization of that war in Box 1.

Box 1 An initial approximation.

STAGE 1: *Usury*: Capital accumulated through interest (or turning time into money).

STAGE 2: *Distance trading* (basically, according to Braudel's research, contemporaneous with Stage 1): Capital is directed more toward investment in trade and specialization within reach of available transport (from the feet of peddlers onward). The new middlemen come into being.

STAGE 3: *National boundaries* come into being for the first time since the Roman empire: in other words, the spatial territories in which reproduction time has to be respected by tariffs or similar devices begin to be redrawn, a process extending from the twelfth century to the nineteenth and settling into briefly familiar constellations only after the First World War (which territorial and imperialist disputes of course provoked). Middlemen acquire more influence.

STAGE 4: *Colonialism*, after researching and improving the speed of shipping.

STAGE 5: *Specialization* is accelerated through spatial enclosures or concentrations in land use.

STAGE 6: *Free labor* (contemporaneous with Stage 5) Labor power begins to move.

STAGE 7: *Industrialization* accelerates consumption of natural resources; territorial expansion also gathers steam. Territorial wars begin. Carbon deposits in the atmosphere commence rapid growth.

STAGE 8: *Imperialism and the war between space and time, 1834–1929*: Struggles between free trade – spatial expansion and the speed of acquisition – and welfare and labor protection – the right to reproduction time – commences. The higher cost of labor is offset by the law of substitution as well as imperialism. Free trade accelerates – and is accelerated by – concentrations of capital in the first monopolies and conglomerates, but national capitals are dominant. The victory of free trade leads to war. The split between finance flows and trade flows results in crises (depression).

STAGE 9: *The truce between space and time, 1933–1965*: The welfare state is introduced as a temporary outcome of the struggle between space (speed of acquisition) and living time. Protectionism and isolationism put breaks on free trade. The policy of full employment (Keynesianism) places checks on spatial expansion. War breaks the UK's economy and accelerates the growth of the EU. The Welfare state culminates in the struggle between production based on speedy acquisition and demands for human reproduction and regeneration time. International economic agencies after the Second World War attempt to overcome national incentives to war by economic cooperation transcending national issues. They succeed.

STAGE 10: *The Pyrrhic victory of space, 1965–present*: natural time is losing out to speed of acquisition altogether. Free trade advances with globalization, and time for human and natural reproduction and regeneration decreases as it does so.

In this initial approximation of a periodization, I have used language referring to wars and truces between space and time. Of course this language is inexact, in that "time" is shorthand for natural, cyclical time, while "space" stands in for speeding up production and acquisition. But the idea of a war between space and time will do as shorthand for tracing out the struggles that ensue not only between labor and capital, but between environmental survival and the depletion of the conditions for life.

Today, of course, the problem is that the traditional remedy for inflation, the IMF's favorite medicine, discounts the real factors producing inflation, insofar as its remedy is to "raise interest rates and reduce government spending."[8] In some instances, this means curtailing the cost of human reproduction and abolishing social provision, as the IMF did recently in Indonesia with disastrous results. As I have shown, one reason that the traditional medicine works is that it reduces the existing levels of social provision, and hence the cost of human reproduction, although capital continues to draw on human energy. The same effect is achieved by "reducing spending on wages." The medicine cuts the spending on human time, and, through this immiseration, things look up – for capital. But because the remedy works, we see high labor costs as the cause of inflation, when, in reality, inflation is caused by the escalating distance between price and value, where rising prices lead to an increased money supply, and more financial games. In this respect, as in others, government policies directly reflect the Pyrrhic victory of human speed over natural time. They perpetuate the steady increase in prices which they are meant to control, at the same time as people, especially women, work longer while living in unhealthy conditions, keeping up with a system whose profit demands that it function at an inhuman pace.

Regardless of which course we take in the future, labor-power, like nature, is in trouble today, either because it attempts to keep pace with the boom rate of the global exploitation of nature, or because it is already being called upon to substitute for other sources of energy whose cost of acquisition is removing them from the game. In a world where automation and artificially directed energies require ever more expenditure, it must try to eliminate the labor that slows it down. In other words, when labor – whether mental or manual – cannot keep up with the pace of production, capital seeks to minimize labor altogether. This is the logical outcome of spending investment capital on fuel-dependent technology for improving the speed of communications and transport on the one hand, and the fuel itself on the other. The speed of production and distribution has to be phenomenal to justify the expenditure in terms of product output. Hence (among other things) passing that labor onto the consumers, who end up doing more unpaid work: on the phone, online, on something.

The classic quarternity of production, consumption, distribution and exchange is, as Marx was the first to note, indissoluble. At a certain point, distribution and consumption have to meet. That point is the point of exchange, where consuming and delivering merge in the middle ground. Now the genesis of capitalism, as discussed above, involves the exploitation of the middle ground, especially in relation to trade, specialization and distance. If the modern-day middleman can get the consumer to do his own work of delivery, he makes more profit. But this profit is precisely not a matter of exploitation at the point of production. It is rather that the technologies and distribution costs of producing profit at a rate based on speed are such as to reduce profit margins. Or they preclude human labor as too slow, or too costly. Where consumers pick up the labor of distribution, these costs are reduced accordingly. From having done nothing except the work of distribution and exchange, the middleman now passes even that work on to those who live on the other side of his profit.[9]

Before Marx, it was assumed that the point of exchange was the point of profit. As noted already, while Marx relocated that profitable point in production, he also agreed that maneuverings at the point of exchange meant that a particular capitalist could take advantage of market vicissitudes. The point of the distinction between absolute and relative surplus-value was to underscore these dynamics. That is to say, absolute surplus-value accrues from the point of production, relative surplus-value from that of exchange. My reworking of value theory gives more autonomy to the sphere of relative surplus value, in line with emphasizing speed as a factor determining short-term profit. To illustrate this, one need only note how the Internet, the World Wide Web, was not a drain on energy when it was a only a method of communication rather than a medium of exchange. But the minute it becomes a medium of exchange, the consumption of electricity, and the coal that feeds the production of electricity for internet consumption, accelerates dramatically. "One pound of coal [is burnt] for every two megabytes of information moved over the internet." Ordering a book on Amazon.com, for instance, typically involves shifting 1 megabyte of information, or burning half a pound of coal.[10] In consequence, while it appears that the Internet is responsible for one-half of all growth in electricity demand, in reality most of this is due to financial transactions downloading web page information and filling out forms online, whereas ordinary email is modest in its requirements.[11] However, the immediate issue is how far exploitation at the point of exchange has increased and, with it, the autonomy of relative surplus-value. And the point to referring to Internet transactions in this context was to illustrate how far exchange is now the cover for a certain variety of transaction in which the consumer labors and the corporation benefits, a transaction which takes place according to the laws of time and space governing relative rather than absolute surplus-value. In terms of these relative laws, any profit made at the point of exchange enhances the profiteer's margin, insofar as it secures for him or her a greater share of absolute surplus-value (and this remains the case even if the price is only temporary, even if that price holds only as long as absolute surplus-value has not asserted itself).

In the end, the relative autonomy of the sphere of relative surplus-value is why mainstream economics works. By mainstream economics, I mean all those economic theories that exclude environmental and reproductive factors as externalities. These exclusions, rather neatly, make them theories of the relative, theories of the contingent fluctuations in human time wars with nature, and the human regulation of space. They work, as theories, provided that they exclude the sphere of reality or reproduction, and they do not work whenever that sphere irrupts into their world of human space and human time. But just as mainstream economics cannot deal with the irruptions of the sphere of real value, so too did Marx underestimate the force of relativity. He did not anticipate the extent to which relative surplus-value would take on a life of its own, putting literal distance between itself and the source of real value, which was the addition of energy at the point of production. Nor could he foresee how far the rapid transit and transportation over these new distances was accomplished by releasing the energy locked in inorganic fuel at tremendous environmental cost. Marx did, however, point to the "metabolic imbalance" capital occasioned through overuse of the land, and located the cause of the imbalance in the speed of the production process. [12]

To sum up so far: I have suggested that capitalism is an economy of spatial extension in which one mode of making profit feeds directly into price, and a certain notion of relative surplus-value. I have suggested that this capitalist economy competes with, rather than being an aspect of, an economy based on absolute surplus-value, or natural reproduction time. While this understanding of relative surplus-value radically revises Marx's, it is also compatible with it. For Marx, relative surplus-value was the result of competition's presence or lack, of supply and demand and other variables. For us, it is the result of spatiotemporal variables increasing the distance between the point of acquisition and that of production. In this account, far from being a vicissitude of absolute surplus-value, relative surplus-value undermines it. It does so because relative surplus-value depends on a mode of production that extinguishes real value. Relative surplus-value, in other words, is at war with the source of absolute surplus-value, in that the means for traversing space and communicating through time simultaneously (insofar as they depend on fossil fuels) diminish and degrade nature and human health or energy. This is general or absolute damage. It is damage additional to the specific injuries inflicted on natural resources by overusing them or using them up in the pursuit of profit based on the speed of acquisition.

In the terms of this reworked value theory, absolute surplus-value asserts itself when resources run out or territorial and local restrictions are instituted. We are beginning to face the cost of replacing current energy expenditure based on fossil-fuel consumption, including the costs of war. Moreover, were real or absolute surplus-value to assert itself fully, we would face unparalleled (if temporary) crisis. This is because the value of fossil fuels has been calculated on the cheap and on the side, rather than on their impossibly long reproduction time, which would make them utterly precious – as they are becoming, as a stake in a war for fuels to burn more fuel. It is precisely toward such a scenario that the dynamics hitherto consigned to "relative surplus-value" take us. Because they threaten to take out the source of use-value overall (nature and human health – or energetic liveliness), these dynamics involve more than fluctuations. They precisely involve a competing economy based on its own spatiotemporal variables, the history of which can be traced out in terms of a struggle between natural time and the speedy acquisition of space. As time loses to space, the immiseration of living species intensifies.

Immiseration

Marx's quintessential insight was that capital paid for labor-power fairly when it paid for its cost of reproduction, but that labor gave more energy than it cost, even when fairly paid. Labor, paid an adequate wage, could keep at it, producing far more than its own cost (including the next generation of labor-power), for about forty years. The wage, or subsistence cost of labor, would pay for that forty years; and, under the social democratic contract, taxes on those wages and corporate taxes paid for the new generation's education and upbringing (in part), and for old age healthcare and basic living costs.[13] The welfare state brought into being by the trade unions and liberal pressure ensured that the cost of reproduction included provision for new workers and old age. But what constitutes an adequate replenishment if labor is worn out before its time? If it is exhausted by drains on its adaptive energy, those apparently fixed quotas of energy with which humans are born, which are used up at varying rates as we age? "Enough that they live healthily and they age securely," was the answer, at least after the second war in the welfare states of Western Europe, the United States, Australia and some of the former Commonwealth. It is no longer a sufficient answer, as the growth in various forms of immiseration reveals.

Immiseration may take the form not only of economic poverty but of exhaustion. In this respect – as well as the poverty so massively underestimated by social theory last century – Marx's predictions concerning capital's tendency to push down real wages in "the heartlands of capital" are coming very true. But the reason Marx gave for this immiseration is only partly right. For Marx, as we discussed, immiseration came about through the fact that capital had to spend more on constant capital or new technology. But, in our account, that expenditure is offset by the value added by nature, which also gives energy. It would follow that it is only when natural energy sources run out in the West that constant capital expenditure necessitates a more thoroughgoing immiseration of workers there as well. Already, the immiseration faced today is manifold in its reach and its effects. The idea that labor is entitled to replenishment is no longer taken for granted.

The energy labor expends in surviving is going somewhere, but it is not translating into take-home profit in terms of pay or time for enjoyment. "The little boats are [not] floating as the trickle down picks up": the wealth accumulated through globalization is concentrated. But the demand for energy, as surplus-value, is such that it appears that a need for the immiseration of more people may be asserting itself. Whether this is due to a demand for enhanced profit, or to declining profits, would in turn depend, by this account, on whether energy sources other than labor-power are drying up or becoming prohibitively expensive. If the latter is the case, then technologies featuring human labor-power may once more come into fashion, but they will feature human labor-power pushed to its limits.

For Marx, immiseration meant pushing human needs below subsistence. But human beings who are immiserated in this or other ways do not die immediately. In Yemen, for instance, the life expectancy is thirty-eight, so that people take approximately thirty years to die when they are not provided with adequate nourishment, and adequate water, air and shelter. The point is that the effects of immiseration in this analysis extend far beyond the short term – as one would expect, given that human energy and human matter, like those of all living things, exist on and in a continuum, in which poverty contributes directly to aging and mortality.

While the labor theory of value might lead one to think otherwise, there is nothing inherently protective of human life in capitalism. When capital could acquire more slaves if it worked its existing slaves to death, it did so. It changed policy when it was no longer as easy to acquire new slaves. In other words, where slave labor could be imported cheaply and was readily available, plantation owners worked their labor to death; the average life expectancy of a young African was seven years from the date of his or her enslavement.[14] When the labor ceased to be readily available, breeding by slaves was mandated.[15] This is indicative of the general principle: when capital cannot substitute space for time, and only when it cannot, it allows for the real time of reproduction.

So it is that, in the world where conquest by speed substitutes for reproduction, reproduction itself becomes a drag. For instance, human reproduction – the production of a new or refreshed laborer – drags insofar as the other elements involved in the production of exchange-value can be brought to the workplace more speedily. Hence the attempts to lower the social costs of reproduction, through making lone mothers work in and outside the home; through neglecting healthcare and education and even pensions. Hence deregulating trade, enabling you to cross borders daily; hence, when you do not pay for labor's or nature's reproduction, traversing the globe in search of labor and nature paid for by somebody else. Hence the increasingly nomadic world of modern capital, and the increasing portability of all things, especially labor-power. Hence the fact that laborers and workers sacrifice refreshment and regeneration time in order to keep pace.

As a rule, governments do not admit to the peoples they are meant to protect that health is endangered by the present economy. It is telling that the clearest admission by any government official on health damage came from the director of the Russian Academy of Medical Sciences, Vladimir Pokrofsky, in 1992, when the academy released figures showing birth defects in 11 percent of Russian infants, 55 percent of schoolchildren suffering health problems, an increase in early death and illness for those under forty, and Russian life expectancy falling overall. Pokrofsky's admission was made easier by the fact that he could blame a system which was then (publicly) universally condemned: "The new generation is entering adult life unhealthy. The Soviet economy was developed at the expense of the population's health."[16] But what was developed was the same system of industrial centralization, speeding up the exploitation of natural resources together with production (and the waste generated by rapid production), that we have in the West. Since global capitalism embraced Russia, life expectancy for Russians has declined further, and more rapidly, than it did under communism, which provided social services.

The economic libertarian, the believer in the completely free market, is (let us not forget) making the market the arbiter of life and death. Some will live under the regime of unregulated capital – for a while. More will die, as capital attempts to speed up their natural time of reproduction in other ways. The consequences of this for human life are plain enough. But in the same speeding up lies the incentive for fertilizers increasing soil yield without regard to their long-term environmental consequences, and, among other things, genetic engineering and genetic modification (GM) for agriculture. Then again, if social policy and social organization allowed for reproduction time, they would have to oppose short-term profit based on the speed of acquisition. This does not mean opposing all market mechanisms, let alone all technologies. It means supporting production processes which take account of reproduction time. These also go to market, and compete. But they do so in a way which allows life, the basis of all profit, to continue to exist.

10　The prime directive

A global economy, in which control is centralized but transport and communication networks expand, is the most recent manifestation of capitalism's dual tendency to concentrate control and ownership while reaching ever further in the quest for materials and markets. With the one hand it restricts; with the other it reaches out, by war as well as trade. This economic system of concentration and out-reach contrasts with a more venerable form of market economy based on household and small-scale business production. We can call this economy the small business market economy, and reserve the name capitalism for any economy which disregards the rate of reproduction of human subjects and natural things. Accordingly, real resistance to multinational capital now must take the form of protecting, improving and increasing small-scale production in the South, and, in the North, exploiting the contradiction – never sufficiently understood by Marx – between big business and small business. Small business interests, insofar as they depend on natural reproduction time, and whether they realize it or not, are opposed to those governed by acquisition through space. Given this fact, and I have shown that it is indeed a given fact, we should note at the outset that the line to be drawn among businesses, between those which abet the sacrifice of natural time and those which oppose it, obviously favors small businesses. But a small business is just as capable as the big brothers it often emulates of substituting space for time. The crucial questions are: what natural resources (if any) does a business use, how does it use them, and from where does it obtain them? Is it directly affected if these resources are exhausted, or can it simply go and get them somewhere else? If it is directly affected by the loss of natural resources, it is more likely to be on the right side of the line.

Not that this perspective on the matter is clear to small businesses, who usually hope to become big ones. Just as the myth of the upward mobility of the working class is stressed, and stories told of the "man who makes it from nowhere against the odds," so are the success stories of the occasional small business. Marxists describe the small-business class, the petty bourgeoisie, as "notoriously vacillating": first on the side of labor, now on the side of capital. But these vacillations can be explained by the fact that neither capitalism nor socialism addresses the real interests of most small businesses. Where they have been directly addressed, it has generally been by fascist or populist (and usually racist) parties, who co-opt them to the interests of big business, obscuring the real spatiotemporal conflicts between small and large enterprises.[1] Occasionally small producers have found their own voice. They were the driving force behind the Levelers movement in the seventeenth century, when the conflict between large and small-scale enterprises was early enough to be visible.[2]

For our purposes, the significant thing about the older, more competitive economy – which survives in those small businesses still grounded in real reproduction time – was that it was *slower*. The dual tendency toward centralized control and far-reaching extension is increasingly rapid because it works by accelerating the speed of production at the expense of reproduction. An economy based on household, sustenance and small-scale production was also based on the reproduction rate of nature. Just as nature took time to regenerate, so did her stewards, even if the idleness was enforced. At the outset, we supposed that, like nature, human beings have biological rhythms which require a certain down time. When the rate of production is constrained by natural rhythms, human beings are enabled to rest and recreate. They are forced into enjoyment, which releases one from the paranoid mindset engendered by bio-deregulation. The restricted pace of life regulated by natural rule, or the "prime directive" (see below), also allows for meditation, prayer and reflection. Slow time or downtime was, and in some parts of the world still is, seen as the condition of creativity. In India recently I was told that computer programs would soon produce new sari designs. They do not do so as yet. To this day, sari designs are produced when the sari maker goes to the temple and meditates, and asks God to send her a new sari design. The advantage of the computer programs, says their advocate, is that they will allow for the more rapid production of sari designs.

At what point the tension between an economy based on the rhythms of nature and its victorious, expansive rival became explicit is unclear. Perhaps it was never especially explicit (although aspects of the Levelers movement lead one to think otherwise). What is clear is that the connection between profit and distance trading was in place long before the rise of capitalism proper – that is to say, capitalism marked by the subsumption of the labor process through specialization. We have established that the embryonic form of capitalism began with the birth, or rebirth, of trade in the Middle Ages. This went hand in hand with the expansion of roadways and wharves, and the beginnings of specialization. While there are anti-technological accounts which assume that extension, or traversing greater distances in search of raw materials and markets, began with industrialization, this is not so. As this book has established, the quest for more preceded as well as followed the introduction of industrial technology. That quest was embodied in the building of roads and wharves from the twelfth century.[3] This was the other side of specialization, and the move away from a local economy toward accelerated production. Hence reversing the accelerated pace of production with its overconsumption of energies means moving back toward a local and nonspecialized economy. This was precisely what Gandhi advocated.

Gandhi and the advocacy of localism

Before small was found to be beautiful, and well before current debates on the wisdom of large-scale economies, the Mahatma Mohandas Gandhi argued that it was essential to maintain the integrity of local village production or there would be no real progress. By real progress Gandhi meant moral progress, which "is the same thing as progress of the permanent element in us."[4] As much because of his emphasis on the moral as because of his views on how this progress could be achieved by *Satyagraha*, or nonviolent resistance, Gandhi's economic program has been labeled utopian and cast aside by Marxists. Gandhi's conclusions are less utopian insofar as we have reached the same conclusions through an analysis of the underlying dynamics of capital, based on reworking Marx's labor theory of value. Underlying the political economy of time and space, grasping its direction, means identifying the points of resistance of it in the present, and how they might lead to a better world.

Marx and others have dismissed utopian thought on the grounds that it only posits what an ideal future would be like. It does not explain how we get from here to there. Famously, Marx insisted that scientific socialism, unlike utopian socialism, had to proceed on the basis that capitalism's own contradictions were the condition of a new world order.[5] By exploiting these contradictions, present in the here and now, it would be possible to move in a different direction, toward a socialist future. Specifically, Marx argued that a *contradiction* between the forces and relations of production was at issue. The forces of production, meaning the technology and raw materials used in the production process, *had to be increasingly centralized* in order for capital to continue to make a profit. But this increasing centralization brought the workers exploited in that production process into larger conglomerates, which meant they had more contact with one another. This increased the chances of a revolution taking place, although Marx, despite the attribution to him of a linear, evolutionary thinking, was never fully confident that socialism would triumph over the alternative of barbarism.[6] Nonetheless, from the traditional Marxist standpoint, the centralization of production was the necessary if not sufficient condition of revolution: accordingly, any revolutionary program and any revolutionary party had to advocate both industrial development and centralization. This advocacy is directly at odds with Gandhi's view that "industrial centralization" is precisely what is destructive to true human progress. It is also, in the Third World and feudal countries in which all communist revolutions have taken place, an attempt to graft an industrial production structure onto an economy which has not experienced capitalism.

Gandhi, by contrast, wanted to resist the centralizing dynamics of extension and retain the rural India of small holdings. Land ownership in India is still predominantly local. This puts India, as well as other Third World nations, at a distinct advantage when it comes to reversing course. It is easier for those who still practice local production to return to it. It is also easier for them to perceive that the "turn" needs to be made. Gandhi anticipated the need for reversal – or rather, in the case of India, the need to halt. He saw production, consumption and centralization as inextricably linked factors in a process that threatened to destroy genuine progress and actualization of human potential. According to Gandhi's theory, capital has to speed up production, and, whenever production is speeded up, so is consumption. Gandhi assumed, too, that this speeding up is a necessary concomitant of centralization and that localization resists it. "When production and consumption both become localized, the temptation to speed up production, indefinitely and at any price, disappears." One might say the temptation literally disappears. It disappears in the form of the usurer and merchant trader, who introduces the first dislocation between the time of reproduction and the time of production by buying here and now, and selling there and later.

Consolidation of control and extension necessarily accompanies exploitation for profit. Extension, specialization and concentration necessarily extract more from nature than they return in terms of real value or the time of reproduction. These things must speed up production and hence the extraction of raw materials to keep pace with that production, insofar as the distribution costs (embodied in the state infrastructure of transport, communication and the like) have to be paid for by taking more from nature than can be returned. Moreover, as Gandhi also reiterates, pressure to speed up production will always speed up consumption. The waste produced in the West illustrates how speeding up production and consumption reinforce one another. The dreams of wealth and "choice," which enticed so many in Eastern Europe, ignore the underlying economic dynamics which mean that wealth and choice on the US model are impossible on a global scale: the US "standard of living" rests on the speedy extraction and consumption of labor and nature internationally. It cannot be emulated, as critics of imperialism have argued, without emulating the exploitation it rests upon. But, as we saw in the Introduction, what these critics of imperialism have missed is the way in which the exploitation of nature offsets the exploitation of labor. In some respects it sustains that exploitation, insofar as state infrastructures exploit natural resources more directly and are usually somewhat constrained in relation to the exploitation of labor.

How, then, is globalization to be opposed? The implication of this analysis is that the only way out is to limit the scale and scope of production, making or, in cases like India, keeping production local in scale while improving its technology. The law governing such production would be this: the real reproduction time of the natural resources consumed in production must be allowed for, which means that time, the time needed for replenishment, would take over from space, reversing the logic of multinational capitalism. The corollary of this law would be that the resources used for production have to be produced within a given locality or, at the least, a designated region. This would mean that those engaged in production have to be concerned with the reproduction of resources close to hand. Of course, this means that the protection of environmental needs is built into the production process itself: if you cannot go and get it over there, you have to wait. Production is slowed down, but so is the consumption of natural resources, which in turn relieves the pressure to consume personally. As Gandhi pointed out, the other side of speedy production is the increase in personal consumption. The significance of local production, small in scale and scope, is precisely that it slows down both production and consumption. Even Gandhi's resistance to the spread of the railroad has its points: its facilitation of long-distance transportation makes it as much a servant of speedy exploitation as of community and communication. But, as the railroad is the least obnoxious means of land transportation, I stress here that I am only making a general point, which is that Gandhi's conclusions are less utopian than their detractors have claimed.

As shown above, those willing to specialize were those organized by middlemen long before industrialization. The technology of industrialization brings this class of merchants, the middleclass, to power, but it does not bring the bourgeois class as such into being. The fact that the bourgeoisie is born of the merchant traders, or middlemen, tends to make one overlook how this class constituted an innovation long before the innovation effected by the birth of free labor. In fact, free wage labor can be seen as one variation of that innovation. The innovation? The introduction of distance between the place of production and the place of consumption, via specialization designed to speed up the rate of distribution in such a way as to compensate for the distance covered. Each specialized division of labor is governed by the logic of assembly-line production – whether it is for mental or manual labor. At the same time, each specialization effects a separation, and more distance, between producers and the final product. Members of the new middle class multiply on the basis of specialization on the one hand, and of extension on the other. Each separation they effect between production and reproduction strengthens their own position.

To reduce these degrees of separation is to begin to retrace the steps taken toward concentration and extension, by going back to more varied ownership and more local production. It is in this way that this analysis bears on understanding the dynamics of big and small business because it helps show that not all small businesses have a common cause, nor do all large ones. Let me stress here that there is nothing inherent in small business that counters the spatio-temporal dynamics leading to unstoppable pollution and gross exploitation of the majority of human beings. Smallness is a necessary but not a sufficient condition of an effective alternative to global capital.[7] This has special relevance to social orders which are not yet fully centralized and still predominantly local.[8] In this respect immediate hope lies in the South and Third World, in those lands which do not have to reconstruct the basis for a sustainable future. But the task for the First and Second Worlds (the former Eastern bloc), while more slow and more intricate, is not impossible. Building up "small business," the logical source of opposition to big capital, can be a creative task for the larger enterprises themselves. In both North and South this goal requires keeping one's eye on the dynamics of extension in relation to profit, an eye on where one stands, and having a principle with which to counter them. I return to this principle, here called the prime directive, shortly. What needs to be stressed first is that resistance to capital and exploitation can be implemented only in the context of a policy of reversal, of turning around. There is no other way to counter the overconsumption of natural substances and energies, to close the degrees of separation, and the increasing exhaustion of human labor-power in production.

The real third way and prime directive

The argument in this book so far has shown that globalization is born of speeding up time while extending further through space, increasing the degrees of separation in relation to control (few have more) and in relation to geography (more people and things have further to go). This dynamic informs the shift from competitive capitalism to monopoly capitalism, and from monopoly capitalism to global capitalism.[9] This same dynamic is responsible for consuming more of nature than we allow to be replenished, for stress and related illness, and for the destruction of air, water, food and climate. It is this situation which can be countered, without loss of the lives of human and other species, only by reversing course.

To go back into the past deliberately, not out of nostalgia but out of the desire to keep living, is to follow a path which is exceedingly well signposted, simply because the different stages of concentration and expansion are so clear.[10] If the short-term aim is the restoration of competitive capitalism, in which national capitals predominate, then direction follows as the night the day. Overall, the way out of the present mess is to reverse the concentration of wealth on the one hand, and the distance over which natural resources can be obtained on the other. But the way that this can be done is to begin today as if it were yesterday, in the process of being put right. Where once we would have endorsed some deregulation, now we turn to the new protectionism

I want to be clear about what I mean by "going back deliberately." By going back, I do not mean returning to the most primitive mode of production we have on record. I do not mean re-creating the most ancient economies or the early market society of the fourteenth to seventeenth century in England and much of Europe. The difference between then and now, naturally, is technology, which is the key to why nostalgia is not at issue here. To re-create the form and scale of an earlier market is not to advocate that its technology be reinstituted. Whatever genuine technological advances we have made (from solar and wind power to anesthetized and sterile surgery) we retain and build on. But we cannot capitalize upon them, for to do this is to use up more of nature than we return, in one form or another. The creative endeavor of combining technological brilliance with a commitment to sustaining the conditions of human creativity in all its unpredictable variety, which is what a local economy is and does, will be an ongoing process of discovery. It will also be a process of careful selection and participant approval. For while technology can be brilliant, it can also be unnecessary. Unnecessary technologies invade one's life more and more in late modernism, where (for instance, in the business of computer software) there is the constant demand that one adapt to new technologies and innovations, to the point where those supposedly helpful innovations impede one's progress or task.

By going back, I do not mean foregoing the real advances in civilization in the last two centuries. Rather, these social advances are the motivation to go back, deliberately, to an older form of economic ownership. While we may be aiming for the dismantling of large corporations and the flowering of small businesses, this does not preclude capitalizing on the advances in fair labor practices. Organizations hitherto devoted to labor standards, such as trade unions, can facilitate their members forming small businesses of their own.

In going back, we do so self-consciously, so as to correct the mistake that led to the current mess. That mistake is evident in the formal downgrading of the social and economic power of women as mothers. This is not to say situations where women worked either in the home or near to it, in an economically productive way, were or are unflawed. But these flaws, for the main part, originate in the stresses caused by the surrounding economies competing with local markets based in household production. If the significance of the potential of the household and of mothers, in this respect, is acknowledged before the journey back begins, and if household-based industries (whether they are single-family undertakings or neighborhood cooperatives of single mothers) are promoted in socioeconomic policy and supported by the elimination of all but minimal taxes, for instance, then we will not repeat that mistake.

Going back, in this conscious way, is both revolutionary and pragmatic. The paradox – and hope – of the present analysis is that it makes the union of two traditional opponents desirable: on the one hand there are the advocates of distributive justice, who couch their advocacy in the universalist language of rights, and sometimes still brandish the dream of world socialism; on the other, there are the locally or regionally minded, who are traditionally conservative. If there is a real third way, these are its adjoining territories: an emphasis on regionalism (first, then localism) without the conservatism. But this reverses the traditional associations. Regionalism has been advocated by the Republicans, insofar as they stress federalism, in the US. It is generally opposed by social democrats, although this is changing. In Britain, a limited regionalism has been the province of those few in the Conservative Party opposed to European economic union, who are today fewer yet in number. Now, a more widespread political union might actually be useful if it is counterbalanced by strong local economies. But the EU tends the opposite way, retaining the nominal political sovereignty of its member states while moving to economic homogeneity. That said: the EU does limit the advantages of trade to a region – a substantial region, but at least one in which distance is limited. Whether it can protect the natural reproduction time of the resources of its member states is another question, but one which could, as I suggested, be pursued in its policies. On the other hand, as we have seen, sectors of the EU are fostering the next Multilateral Agreement on Investment (MAI). The EU is an organization that can go either way, for or against the speed imperatives analyzed here. The attempts by Oscar Lafontaine and other serious social democrats to maintain historic levels of social provision are indicative: they explicitly flag the choice involved. Thus Lafontaine's insistence that "tax co-ordination" in the EU has gone "in the completely wrong direction" . . . taxes paid by immobile workers on consumption and wages as well as social security contributions were "always co-ordinated in an upward direction." But taxes on "mobile factors" in the economy, such as assets, capital and company profits "always go down."[11] What goes up, like what goes down, aids the speed of acquisition while lessening the overall cost of reproduction. That the EU might take the alternative direction is possible, but it is more likely if the dynamics embroiling its decisions are clear. Then the nature of the ongoing struggle waged by Lafontaine (among others) could be clarified: it is the Herculean task of making the EU an organization committed to the real reproduction time of the peoples and natural substances of its member states.

Were the EU to take the path to becoming a political and ethical union of local economies, this could bring social democratic aspirations for the EU into line with some of those opposed to the union.

For let us recall here that an emphasis on limited as well as national regionalism is a concern not only of conservatives. An emphasis on the small-scale (regional and local) characterizes ecological and appropriate technology movements. Some opponents of MAI pacts believe that production should be "local" and small in scale.[12] Yet this belief exists alongside the assumption that, with a little good-will, capital could somehow clean up its act. If only for this reason, there is a marked difference between intuitive beliefs about the "local" and an analysis of inherent dynamics in capital (which I have attempted here). That difference makes it possible both to draw lines and to predict trends.

As to the short-term issues: in the light of the foregoing theory, it is clear that means of regulation should be reinstituted as one retraces one's economic steps. This applies not only to the relation to nature, but to the broad apparatus of the welfare state. Obviously, I do not think the welfare state should be abolished; any institutional tendency that countermands the gallop of acquisition across the globe is a tendency toward long-term survival. But there may be alternatives which also work against that tendency in more creative ways. One can envisage "small business" grants for the ownership of certain enterprises by local households, groups and cooperatives, enterprises whose nature fits with approved guide-lines geared to establishing regionally based production. The third way's one deviation from a checklist for globalizing capital is its stress on "microinvestment," which has been shown to be used to great advantage by women in particular.[13] "Regionally based production" means that the natural raw materials needed for the enterprise are also reproduced within the same region. Regional production does not mean "the end of all trade": it means the end of trade which does not allow for reproduction time. A region might produce and allow for the reproduction of silk, and trade it where it will. But Silk Enterprises of London could not exhaust the worms of China and then move on to those of India and Japan.

The possibilities of the present need to be pragmatically evalu-ated, but they can be seen through the long view, the view that has a regionally based, self-sustaining economy as its ideal. It is perfectly possible to encourage a policy of reinforcing national and regional production and reproduction of resources that is local in scale, and environmentally realistic in terms of time. There are still real choices to be made even within the context of dependency, real dependency, on global trade. To take up the existing historical options for the local in scale, even if doing so goes against the trend, is to strengthen the options for taking a better route at a later point, when it becomes economically essential, as it must (it is already essential environmentally). In short, the distance of the ideal from the present reality should not blind us to the fact that buried in the present are possibilities for reversing a global trend toward distanciation. They are evident in the resistance by regional manufacture and the trade unions to the NAFTA and the successful resistance to the OECD's MAI. Structurally, there is potential in the growth of small businesses.[14] At the same time, changing the position of women means not returning to regional and local production as it was. Under the seventeenth century's patriarchal contract, the woman was formally subordinate to her husband, even if she was economically better off, *qua* mother, than she is now. But without her formal subordination, the suppression of household and small-scale production by large-scale capital would have appeared as the defeat for women it was.

In sum, the closer to home one's energy sources and raw materials are, the more one's reproduction costs stay in line; paid and domestic labor will be less exploited, and the environment less depleted. Apart from the moral issues about providing for the next generation at this level, the replenishment of natural resources becomes an evident necessity when these resources are close to hand. Also, pursuing policies today which attend to local production and reproduction of resources deals with the effects of increasing environmental exploitation effects, which will sooner or later ramify on the cost of commodities. Multinationals will exploit the circumstances where local production has ceased. They already exploit it when they can. They are claiming, through free trade, their right to exploit it further.

I have tried to show here why capital *must* be governed by the speed of acquisition and expanding scale, why it *has* to negate reproduction time, and why, accordingly, it will not act against its own economic interests by respecting environmental measures,[15] or trade agreements that protect small-scale or even national enterprises, let alone countenance care for the reproduction time of working women and many men day-to-day, or the next generation. But in the small-scale and regional, in the residues of the welfare state and protection policies, in the efflorescence of small enterprises owned increasingly by women, enterprises which, when they exploit neither labor nor nature, are in opposition to large-scale capital's laws of motion, in these things lies more than a democratic alternative. In them lies the hope of life over death. Death's war on life, as I have argued in the companion volume to this book, should be taken literally.

Religious and reasoned judgment

With the anxiety and growing terrors about survival, there is a resurgence of religiosity. As we saw at the outset, both sides in the current conflict term the enemy the evil one. Insofar as they take each other's lives as well as their own, either by economic policy or by suicide bombing, they are technically insane, a danger to themselves and others. They see this in one another, and correctly call the madness evil, but they do not discern it in themselves. If they reason deductively from the facts now known, they will see on the one side that short-term greed is making their own peoples ill, as well as impoverishing the rest of the world and destroying the air and climate that sustain most life. They will understand the desperation that informs terrorism, when the terrorist says he is bringing the economic and other violence visited on the South back home where it originates, and remaining just as unaccountable. They may even understand that the West appears Satanic to more and more in the South because they take the struggle of life against death basic to all religious thought literally.

The fact that faith is invested in prophecies such as those in Revelation should not blind us to recognizing the conditions described in the Book when they are coming into being around us. They come through the perverted work of human hands, rather than by the fiat of angels. But while an angelic fiat can only be reversed at the discretion of angels, the work of human hands can be redirected by human agency. In recognizing the patterns before us, in exercising the human ability to reason deductively in relation to the known facts, we come to the conclusion that, unless we reverse course, most species on the planet, together with our own, are condemned to near extinction.

At all times of famine and refugee floods, humans concentrating on surviving have little time for the preservation of knowledge. Where civilizations have regressed to barbarism, the first casualty is the means to understand the patterns of causality that have led one to the place of loss or suffering. But that place is not yet a universal one. This is the moment where assessments can still be made, before the time to study and think is truncated even further by violence and the fear of loss of life, as well as its actual loss through war, illness, famine and exploitation. If correct and reasoned assessments are made, if the sums once done are respected (as in the minimal case of implemeting the Kyoto Protocol by the appointed time), then the exercise of judgment helps us avert judgment.

But where the religiosity of both sides is divorced from the exercise of reason, where it is twisted by hysteria, paranoia and suspicion (either at personal or political levels) then the line of accountability leading to the moment of real judgment is obscured. The false cause of all our ills is meant to be homosexuality, understood as the epitome of "sexual perversion." (In this respect, one wishes that the fundamentalists would pay more attention to the letter. The Jewish Bible condemns "sodomy," not "homosexual perversion," which is how sodomy is translated in new user-friendly Bibles. There is a difference between sodomy and homosexuality (where sodomy is often eschewed). Only an understanding of sexuality as goal directed as human male heterosexuality would translate (and thereby interpret) "sodomites" as "homosexuals." The translation issues here are confusing however: surely the Latin would have to be *fundamenti*?)[16]

The real line of accountability leads straight back to the West, and a global economy that ostensibly benefits the West while promising all good things but delivering waste to the rest of the world. Following that line back to its sources, which is what this book does, enables us to see this, and to see too that the prophesied disasters of Revelation follow from the unrestrained growth of this economy, which emerges as the very devil. But where the Christians of the United States are led to believe that the devil is in Iran, Iraq, Syria and North Korea (having fled Afghanistan) the faith that might give them strength to reason and reverse course is under-mined by fear.

When Christ said that revelation will come from the Jews, for it will come through Truth or Reason as well as Faith, He did so in the context of the one religion which privileges the exercise of reason. Judaism traditionally seeks to know God through deduction in relation to truth as well as spirit. In some cases, that deductive, reasoning tradition is allied with the belief that one will also come to know God through science and empirical knowledge. Spinoza's philosophy testifies to that tradition. Christianity is meant to be an extension of that tradition, not to resist reason and succumb to paranoid projections, as at certain points Christians have done, although the exercise of reason should help them recognize that the disasters prophesied in various religions are our own work.

Despite the deflection of attention away from the earthly causes of the present destructiveness, there is a tradition within Christianity which accepts that hell is something we make on earth, that Revelation is a book about the present, judgment is now, and that it is up to us to build the new earth. One of its proponents, Christopher Rowland, suggests that judgment has been present as two principles in history, that which destroys and that which redeems, and that these principles can be actualized to various extents.[17] Rowland's argument is based in religious exegesis. I have tried in this book to make the same case from the standpoint of social and political theory, showing how that which destroys is identical with the action of global capitalism. From this most unmetaphorical perspective, the good news is that, if the disasters are our own work, so accordingly is the new earth that is built after them. Revelations does not refer only to the loss of land and the death of the sea, in a way suggestive of the preamble to the Kyoto Protocol. It refers also to the world that will be built after that judgment, the new earth, where water has no cost.[18]

Building this new earth is a human endeavor. In this endeavor, the prime directive serves as a principle which can be argued for on the basis of reasoned analysis, and which is also consistent with reversing course, as we shall see in a moment. The term "the prime directive" is borrowed from the television series *Star Trek*, set in the twenty-fourth century. From the perspective of the twenty-fourth century, it will be plain that we either reversed course peaceably or had the reversal imposed upon us by the consequences of our own actions. In the *Star Trek* universe, we reversed of our own accord after a terrible war. As we did so, we built a world where poverty is unknown, where exploitation of humans and animals has been abolished, and where money does not exist. The prime directive outlined here has similar ambitions. For my own part, its conception was the result of inspiration in the strong sense, but the claims of this principle can also be defended reasonably, as a touchstone for reversing the trends evident in the facts surveyed in this book.

The prime directive

As a principle, the prime directive can be applied in the temporary business of re-regulation, as well as civilly and religiously. As we have tried to show here, going back deliberately means going forward. It is the only reasonable way to proceed, if one regards civilization as the accumulation of advances which affirm the health of life, broadly defined, rather than the wealth of nations, narrowly defined. It is also a way of proceeding that is not utopian, as it requires nothing of anyone other than turning around, and undoing yesterday's decision today, where that decision conflicts with the prime directive. It offers scope for those currently employed in most professions. Indeed, the employment of OECD and other agency officials and scientists initially would have to stay at current levels, because so many of the breed would be required to determine how the prime directive would hold in particular contexts.

The prime directive: we shall not use up nature and humankind at a rate faster than they can replenish themselves and be replenished. By this commandment, the prime directive recognizes that we are using ourselves up as well as our environment, and that by using up our environment we are exterminating ourselves, as if we have unconsciously condemned ourselves to extinction after a period in hell. For, if we live by reason rather than faith, this is the inevitable conclusion. If we live by faith, we might reasonably recognize that the only judgment inflicted upon us is our own.

In an amplified form, the prime directive means that 1) the human species, as the condition of its stewardship of nature, will take no more from nature than can be justly replenished; 2) all living things shall reproduce at their natural rate and their just measure. The natural time of any living thing shall not be altered, nor the form given it by its genetic code. The idea of a just measure is simply that the reproduction of a living thing should not disturb the just existence of other living things, meaning the extent to which all things exist in an ecological balance with others. So that if rabbits, for example, are disturbing the ecology and life chances of other species in the Australian bush, their reproduction within it at the rabbit rate is not justified. And if human beings are proliferating at a rate that disturbs the ecology and life chances of their habitats, their reproduction at whatever rate suits their convenience is also unjustified. At the same time, the reproduction of things which have been unjustifiably reduced, such as rainforests, should be encouraged so that they may return to their just measure, meaning the measure at which they best serve all other things in concert, not merely the human being.

To cease altering the rates of reproduction of living things is to guarantee that just measures will obtain. Not altering those rates means not altering the intertwined and harmonious speeds with which life in its varieties reproduces genetically, as well as not transplanting different species to an environment in which they multiply more rapidly than is their given lot, or changing their given conditions of reproduction in a way that enhances that reproduction while depleting that of others. For the same reason, any new genetic combination should be the work of nature in concert, rather than the product of the human imagination alone. New genetic combinations which are unrehearsed distort an environmental balance. When these new combinations, conceived from the human standpoint, meet human desires at the expense of other living things, the living conditions of the many are sacrificed to the profits of the few.

The nostalgia issue and the political standing of the directive

The desire to return to a previous stage of things is immensely powerful in the human psyche, and it may be the case that the pull exercised by nostalgia is another instance of the death drive Freud identified. This is the major difficulty I foresee with reversing direction. The temptation to interpret that reversal as an appeal to patriarchal values is huge. But it is not the point. The point is to return only to that which is lifegiving, not to that – anything – which led us to the present impasse. This means relying on reason rather than on repetition. It is vital at this point in history that the left identifies with logic, and that those in the left who think of themselves as committed to reason revise their association of reason and progress. To say we need to "go back, slow down," will be portrayed as antiprogress. But progress lies in straining the human imagination to its limits in cleaning up the mess – while retaining the information that mess has yielded.

One of the ever-present problems of revolution is that revolutionaries, in their need to keep control, constantly think ahead of the game. (Insights of the libertarians and situationists bear on this control issue, and we return to them.) In projecting ahead as to likely contingencies, in believing that it is protecting either revolution or revelation in this way, the controlling agency is in fact deadening the future creativity of generations to come. This entails prescribing the appropriate course of activity in situations which might never arise, and, worse, using that possible future contingency as a means for not taking good action now. This is what may be gleaned most positively from the contemporary awareness of contingency.[19] We do not need to say what will happen – then and if. We need to say only we are stopping.

It is not possible for us to see past the first steps in reversing course. It is not possible, first, because things will look different from there. But the second, and more pressing, reason why only first steps may be predicted is that effects and attitudes will change as surely as the views to be contemplated in the future. In arguing this, we begin by acknowledging the postmodern insight that one cannot make history go according to plan, and that theories which are interpreted this way yield something equivalent to the dictatorship of the proletariat. They tend to authoritarianism because they are trying to control events in a pattern that prohibits the creative response to new circumstances (creative responses such as Mandela's and South Africa's Truth and Reconciliation Commission). Such responses alter how things are done, sometimes for the long *durée*. We suppress popular as well as personal genius in its many forms when we try to provide for all eventualities.

But a goal or a direction is a different thing. If there is a direction that favors life, and one that favors illness, we take the former. How we implement that direction is another thing. This in fact was the practice in 1999 at the demonstrations in Seattle, attempting to disrupt the meeting of the WTO. The aim was to shut down the talks. The means were as varied as the groups represented, who would undertake tasks listed on a central plan but carry them out in their own way. Agreement in the aim; autonomy in the action.

A directive can only be articulated in relation to circumstances. That is to say, the context for each decision guided by the prime directive will change. This should go without saying. To understand how to replenish a diminished natural resource, we have to know the context. But we are safe if we undo today what we did yesterday. If yesterday we felled trees, today we plant them. The earth is astonishingly recuperative, and will bound back like the life force it is. It will do so in creative ways we cannot anticipate.

For this theoretical generation, the difficulty with the concept of the prime directive is that it is a universal. But it is the universal to end universals. The prime directive is a universal that guarantees the continuity and specificity and endurance of biological and cultural diversity. Moreover, its implementation would mean returning economic power to progressively decentralized localities. Each country, each locality has to have its own limits. This is what stops the prime directive from being authoritarian. This is the one general program which has the demise of an overarching economic authority built into it. In opposing this authority we do not need a new division, we do not need an emphasis on division at the expense of unity. We need a unity of all those who have been stigmatized because of their differences, who affirm these differences as a manifestation of the spirit of life. However, it is my belief that this affirmation, together with the real economic democracy it presupposes, can be accomplished only when a spiritual authority – and corresponding collective conviction – develops which is equivalent in force to the centralized, global economic authority under deconstruction. I also believe that a spiritual resistance is the only resistance that can effect a reversal of course in the United

States, although reason of itself may accomplish the same task in Europe.

This spiritual authority does not require a new religion as such. It requires actualization, so to speak, of the prime directive, which can be found latent in the cardinal teachings of all religions. The prime directive – thou shalt not use up nature and people at a rate faster than they can be replenished – underpins the Judaic tradition that forgave debts every seven years and returned land to its former owners every fifty years. Aside from the spiritual and cultural significance of these traditions, they also made centralized economic ownership impossible.[20] Christianity banned usury or the lending of money for interest, and the effect of this ban was to block the accumulation of capital. The new school of "Islam economics" also recommends slowing down the exploitation of nature, and offers the most explicit condemnation of globalization to date. All the great religions of the West and the Book insist on restraining human free will in terms of how it *paces* itself.[21] Human free will is distinctive from natural will in this: it can alter the rate at which it produces itself, and the ratio between its requirements and the requirements of other living things. If God allows us liberty in this respect, surely we have it in relation to setting our own deadlines (the first rule of good pedagogy) – a matter again of good judgment. The Kyoto Protocols are significant as a contract with ourselves by which we guarantee a future for those unborn. If we continue not to honour that contract, we deny them that future. For this, we will certainly be judged, and judged because we knew, but did not stop.[22]

This prime directive can be actuated as an exhortation for some ventures and a prohibition on others. If the followers of all religions were to feel themselves bound by the prime directive in the transactions of everyday life, this would generate the kind of spiritual force that underpins all justified revolutions, and do so fast enough to enable us to reverse course in time, which at least means honoring our own deadlines. Being fast to the right end is not the same as being speedy. Being fast is the result of a clear head and clear direction, without the need for escape time generated by physical and mental depression. Moreover, uncovering and implementing the directive within the religions of the North and South would strengthen their dialogue with one another at a time when the stronger their combined social force against globalization, the better the chances of a victory for life over death.

The attack on life (hence an attack on the Holy Spirit in Christian theology) effected by capitalism has come second to sexuality and the regulation of others' bodies as a matter of encyclical concern. It

is as if an unconscious knowledge of bioderegulation as a phenomenon affecting future life *tout court* is displaced onto perceived
sexual irregularities.[23] Rather than policing the deregulation of
natural life and reproduction overall, one concentrates on regulating reproduction in its most narrow human form. The flowering
of anticapitalist liberation theology and Protestant critiques of the
"market as God" testify, however, to the fundamental opposition in
Christianity to greed at the expense of others. Yet the most public
form of concern with the right to life is directed (with a boggling
lack of compassion) toward those who suffer the most in everyday
life under globalization. It is directed for the main part toward poor
women with children, for poverty or lack of means and the consequent harm to existing children is the main reason given for abortion.

The prime directive in practice

Not that the religions alone are the only means for implementing
the prime directive. Among the most significant forces of opposition are the various women's movements, the environmental
movements, the unions, the small-business federations, farmers;
and perhaps there will be alliances with true conservatives. There is
also the realm of personal action. Interpretations of the prime
directive in secular and political contexts will vary vastly. At the
minimum, it means no more than pointing to the fact that one's
professional and personal actions today are geared to more
replenishment of nature than they were yesterday. For instance,
where once we would have signed a free-trade treaty, now we do
not. Where once we would have let local manufacture decline by
shifting production elsewhere, now one takes the most profitable
point closer to home (which means less profit for some, more for
the majority). There are decisions that will discommode only those
capitals who depend on multinational spending for class labor
especially. Cheap resources will immediately be subject to higher
tariffs, which means that the national capitals, which survive the
retrenchment on free trade, or retrench themselves to survive, will
look for better environmental alternatives.

What these policy reversals would mean, in every instance, is
returning gradually to production regulated by the rule of natural
time. This is utopian, in the positive sense of the term, insofar as it
means envisaging a better world. But provided it is possible to see
how one gets from A to B, it is not utopian in the negative sense of
that term. In the Third World, how one gets from A to B is plain.
Provided the ideology of development, large-scale industrialization

and trickle-downdom is resisted, then one keeps a small-scale, self-sustaining economy and improves its technology, and reinstitutes that economy where it has been lost. It is in the heartlands of capital that reversing large-scale industrial centralization will be most difficult. But there is a beginning to be made in reversing direction on the question of free trade, for only by this means can the Kyoto Protocol, and the series of deadlines the human species gave itself, be honoured.

Any treaties or agreements which will lessen the time for nature's replenishment (in relation to the rate of her use) violate the prime directive. Now, if I am a major political party or president holding office, it may be that the most I judge myself able to do is to refuse to sign any more deregulation agreements or legislation. But in this, I am observing the prime directive. The point about it is that, even if the choice for life it makes is no more than refusing to advance its destruction, that choice is to be respected. It may be all a body can do while maintaining immediate responsibilities and vows.

Take another example: an immediate decision on subsidy cuts. If one was adhering to the prime directive, it is probable that this decision would not be in favor of those cuts. But as something that happened recently, or is only happening now, this reversal creates far fewer problems than one entrenched in the bureaucratic accretions of years. Reversing subsidy cuts, maintaining cuts in personal taxation while changing tax laws in relation to corporate or business size (scaling them up according to size, rather than down), is the kind of administrative short-term reversal which is within the scope of even the least social of social democratic governments and, for that matter, Burkean conservatives. It is not real conservatives who will have problems with the directive; it is the new right. But the fact that the directive can apply in any context means that it is possible to push for its implementations in diverse contexts without changing their diversity. For instance, rather than found another political party, political activists would build on those aspects of party policy which already inclined toward the directive. Take American isolationism. No one has a friendly word now for American isolationism, understood in the political rather than the economic sense. But genuine economic isolationism for the US would be far the best strand of Republicanism to win through. It appeals to people both because it means that American resources are contained within the US, and because it means that the US cannot extract wealth from other countries. Isolationism means no imports as well as no exports, and should mean no financial imports as well: under economic isolationism, profits made abroad cannot be returned to the US. This would mean an end to confusion, at home and abroad, about whether the US was protecting its own investments or protecting the right to self-determination of other countries. There is nothing here to prevent one country requesting aid of another. But the request has to be real and it has to be premised on the economic self-containment of the country requesting the aid. Where the premise of economic self-containment is given, the nature of religious and political unions among nations can become imaginative, at least possible.

If observation of and commitment to the implementation of the directive leads any politician or policy maker beyond their present affiliations, it should not be without a conversation with those who still adhere to those affiliations. In short, one can always act where one is today. One could add caustically that it might take a lot of creativity to devise ways to shrink holdings while maintaining full employment and satisfying shareholders. But the challenge is less if the shareholders themselves are seeking to invest in funds which adhere to the prime directive (as the huge pensioner funds might, if organized),[24] and if groups within the existing firm are encouraged to diversify, forming or reforming smaller enterprises. The voluntary reduction in scale – and transfer of shares where appropriate – toward smaller enterprises born from within the original enterprise does mean less for some, but it does not entail the devastation following complete expropriation. Toward that expropriation we are most surely heading if we do not go back of our own free will, if only because there will be no other way for life to continue.

My point here is that one way of reversing course can come from the choices of politicians constrained by pragmatism. But if these politicians continually take the pragmatic path away from the prime directive, then the prime directive may be implemented by more direct means. If I am fed up with the bad faith of leaders who license the escalation of fossil-fuel consumption every year, together with increasing poverty, I may leave the path of reform for that of the revolution in Mexico. If so, I will be demanding that the conditions necessary for the daily and generational reproduction of people be changed now, and that this can be done without further violation of nature's need for replenishment only by rapid redistribution of income. In either of these extreme cases, that of the pragmatic politician reversing by slow means or the revolutionary, there is nonetheless an attempt to observe the prime directive. The point is that the commitment to observing the prime directive, like the true character of both governments and revolutionary movements, will emerge from how they act this very day as well as the day after that or the day before. Observing the prime directive means never justifying a means by an end, for the choice of means today determines the quantity of life surviving (as good energy or specific species) in any form. The idea of the prime directive and the term itself may be used in bad faith, but a truth or a lie is "know(n by its) fruits." Where the prime directive is observed, there is more healthy or good fruit, more diversity of fruit, and that fruit is closer to home. Even the most literal literalist will have no problem with this one.

Let us say that our revolutionary bid in Mexico is successful. How, then, do we handle the redistribution of income? Would it be by the violent expropriation, which devastated not only the plantation owners in Cuba, but the owners of small family businesses? Because, if the answer to this question is yes, we are violating the prime directive on two other fronts. First we are destroying the fabrics of life without giving those affected negatively an opportunity to negotiate for their own contribution to the realization of the prime directive we claim to be implementing. Second, we are assimilating small businesses with larger ones, when the former are often the lifelines for the success of locally based production. Reappropriation in the first instance can be done more gradually – say on a time scale which redistributed profits at the rate of their accumulation, provided that all those affected had a significant say in their redistribution.[25]

And what, then, is the alternative? For the very rich literally to take off into the stratosphere, living in protected bubbles that seal off the effects of pollution, consuming highly prized organic foods and filtered water, while desperately investing in the conquest of galactic space? It is a possible future; sometimes it seems a probable one. But would it be a good life up there, cast out from the green forests and fresh oceans that no longer exist, aware however dimly that in the muck beneath people still struggle for air and food and water? An orthodox Marxist would say that the rich can take this path and only this path, because they will not be parted from their money: "social being," they tell us, "determines social consciousness." Yet there are significant exceptions, in that many of those who take up the cause of the working class or the poor are themselves of aristocratic and upper-middle-class origin.[26] If they can betray their class, why not others whose wealth is meant to restrict their ability to reason? Inquiries into why those who have stepped beyond the spheres of self-interest have done so return the answer that their circumstances afforded them the luxury of time to reflect. Nothing interferes with thinking like anxiety, and freedom from the anxiety over day-to-day survival is perhaps the greatest freedom.

The good in all social movements and political organizations, like one of the great goods in all religions, is a commitment to the prime directive. It is just that the language for expressing it varies. This might be borne in mind by those who ask what the prime directive will mean for our intellectual, cultural and spiritual life. Will it mean that we are slowed down, with the worst of the stagnation that term implies? The slowing down that the prime directive foretells is not a slowing down of advances in civilization, but of the things that impede civilization. As Gandhi so perfectly articulated the point, it is centralization that works against spiritual growth and local economies that foster it. The prime directive takes our energies and directs them where they should go; instead of flinging them any which way, it concentrates them in those spheres which lead to reversing course, mitigating the destruction of life. Human betterment, whatever it means, cannot be separated from the just exercise of our stewardship in relation to nature, and the re-regulation of the body.

The modernist insistence that, *pace Star Trek*, we *are* alone in the universe is the insistence that faith is the consequence of a childish projection onto an anthropomorphized good parent in the sky. Paradoxically, the existentialist notion that one should give up such projections and rely on one's reason is consistent with the proposition that one avoids judgment by exercising it. To grow up in reality means assuming the consequences of one's actions. Religion, as a matter of reason, asks for no less.

Notes

Preface

1 Bush recently named Iraq, Syria and North Korea as terrorist-affiliated states in his January 29, 2002 State of the Union address.
2 Even if one stands back from the Arab-Israeli conflict on the grounds that a Jewish homeland was a necessity following Nazism, the illegal occupation by Israel of the West Bank (as former British foreign minister Douglas Hurd terms it) – at the time of writing – is not.
3 On the broader argument on how Islam has been reduced to an homogeny only equaled by similar reductions in Christianity, and its critical voice silenced by parody, see Susan Buck-Morss, *Islamism and Critical Theory* (forthcoming). This wise and brave book engages with Islamic feminism as well as drawing out the critical diversity in Islamism and its potential relation to a global left.
4 For the most recent figures, see: United Nations Department of Public Information, *The Feminization of Poverty*, Press Kit: Geneva, 2002. For more analysis of earlier data, see Gertrude S. Goldberg and Eleanor Kremen (eds), *Feminization of Poverty: Only in America? (Contributions in Women's Studies, No. 117)* (Westport, CT: Praeger, 1990) which draws out the structural similarities between the situation of women as mothers in the United States and that of the poor – women as mothers – in other countries. The essays in this collection also gives the lie to the notion that the majority of single mothers are cavorting teenagers.
5 *Il Corriere della Sera*, Nov. 14, 2000.
6 English Conference of the Parties third session Kyoto, 1–10 December 1997. Kyoyo Protocol to the United Nations Framework Convention on Climate Change.
7 Stephen Castle, "Pressure mounts on Bush as EU agrees to Kyoto cuts", *The Independent*, 5 March, 2002.
8 The U.S. attitude is entirely self-centered. Consider the following "Differences in the cost of energy will affect the outlook for US jobs, consumer prices, investment, technical change, and economic growth. Whenever use of a factor of production such as energy is restricted, economic performance falls for some period of time, the price of

energy and other goods and services rises, and consumption and employment decline. Hence the various cases affect the national economy to varying degrees." A Briefing Paper on the Energy Information Administration's Analysis and Report. Prepared for the Committee on Science, U.S. House of Representatives, Washington, October 1998, p. 1. http://www.eia.doe. gov/oiaf/kyoto/kyotobtxt.html (Preface).

9 These are specific references from the Revelation to John which seem to have to do with the present. "The moon turned completely red like blood" (6:12) (pollution, smog); "The sky disappeared like a scroll being rolled up" (6:14) (ozone depletion); "Hail and fire, mixed with blood, came pouring down on the earth" (8:7) (acid rain); "Something that looked like a huge mountain of fire was thrown into the sea. A third of the sea was turned to blood, a third of the living creatures in the sea died" (8:8–9); "A third of the water turned bittter, and many people died from drinking the water, because it had turned bitter" (8:11) (dumping in the ocean, pollution); "every living creature in the sea died" (16:3) (poisoning the waters with pollution, rising heat destroying coral and then upwards); "A third of the sun was struck, and a third of the moon, and a third of the stars, so that their light lost a third of its brightness; there was no light during a third of the day and a third of the night" (8:12); "The sunlight and the air were darkened by the smoke from the abyss" (9:2) (smog, pollution); "They were burnt by the fierce heat and they cursed the name of God" (16:8–9) (ozone depletion, global warming). The references to the great whore as "the great city that rules over the kings of the earth" (17:18) augur ill for capitalism; when this city is destroyed, "The merchants of the earth also cry and mourn for her, because no one buys their goods any longer" (18:11) John makes it clear that this earth is at stake explicitly when he adds: "The time has come to destroy those who destroy the earth!" (11:18).

10 *Genesis*, 21:9–21.

1 Introduction

1 Definitions of terrorism are fungible and change according to political necessity. The strategic use of violence against civilians dates as far back as the Romans, but the modern concept of "terrorism" was first used in the context of the French Revolution: the term terrorism first appeared in a dictionary in 1798. Caleb Carr, *The Lessons of Terror: A History of Warfare against Civilians* (New York: Random House, 2002), pp. 6–7. While the French Revolution introduced the concept of terrorism into political discourse, the *People's Will*, a populist movement inspired by the writings of anarchist Mikhail Bakunin and Sergei Nechayev, as well as a certain interpretation of Rousseau's "general will," introduced a notion of revolutionary terrorism and a basic cell structure (which continues to be influential). What constitutes the People's Will as a terrorist organization is that they perceived the deaths of the uninvolved and innocent as "an inevitable part of the

merciless revolutionary process". Thomas P. Raynor (ed.) *Terrorism: Past, Present, Future* (New York: Franklin Watts, 1987), p.33. There is either revolutionary terrorism, or terrorism sponsored by the state. This distinction between the two lies at the heart of difficulties in establishing a clear-cut definition of terrorism, and is further complicated by terrorists who target particular groups within the same civil population or country (as with the IRA, who define themselves are revolutionary terrorists, and the Ku Klux Klan, established in 1867). The distinction between state and revolutionary terrorism governs many of the definitions of terrorism found in contemporary writings, although it is confused when the appellation, "terrorists" is so often used in the service of state terror:

> The words "terror" and "terrorism" have become semantic tools of the powerful in the Western world. In their dictionary meaning these words refer to "intimidation" by the "systematic use of violence" as a means of both governing and opposing existing governments. But current Western usage has restructured the sense, on purely ideological grounds, to the retail violence of those who oppose the established order.
>
> Noam Chomsky and Edward Herman, "The Washington
> Connection and Third World Fascism" in *The Political Economy
> of Human Rights*, Nottingham: Spokesman, 1979 (2 vols),
> vol. 1, pp. 85–6

Jack Goody notes that the word was used in this way by the Nazis against the French resistance, by the French against the Algerians, and so forth (unpublished paper, "What is a Terrorist", 2002). Netanyahu offers another definition: "Terrorism is the deliberate and systematic murder, maiming, and menacing of the innocent to inspire fear for political ends" (Benjamin Netanyahu (ed.) *Terrorism: How the West Can Win* (New York: Farrar, Strauss, and Giroux, 1986), p. 9.

2 Species are dying out at up to 1,000 times faster than their rate of extinction prior to the twentieth century, due principally to the decimation of rainforests. UNEP, *Global Biodiversity Assesment* (Cambridge: Cambridge University Press, 1985). Web estimates of the rate of extinction for all species, including plants and inveterbrates, range from 137 per day (the UNEP figure) to higher.

3 Control of land by corporations and the introduction of genetically engineered seeds are held responsible. The genetic engineering giant, US corporation Monsanto, has brought into the major national seed companies of both India and Brazil. Initially, five hundred farmers died in Warangal, India, in 1998, but the suicides (mainly by means of ingesting pesticides) continue and have now passed one thousand. Glenn Davis Stone, *Anthropology News*, vol. 43, no. 5, May 2002.

4 These cuts are detailed in the next chapter, and developed additionally in Chapters 5 and 6.

5 The growth of Islamic-identified terrorism is tied to increasing unemployment in the South. Not that the terrorists who come to

prominence are unemployed necessarily. "The suicide bombers who had trained as pilots in the US and Germany came from a new generation of Islamic militants. They were educated, middleclass, with jobs and families and girlfriends." Ahmed Rashid, *Taliban: the Story of the Afghan Warlords* (London: Pan Books, 2nd edn, 2001), p. vii.

6 Matt Born, "What the Middle East Papers Say," *Daily Telegraph*, Sept 29, 2001 (the online version of this article deletes the references to globalization).

7 Western Europe follows not far behind. In 1989, the ratio of the usage of the world's resources by the world's richest 20 percent to that of the world's poorest 20 percent was 59:1. This may be contrasted with the 1960 ratio of 30:1, the 1970 ratio of 32:1, and the 1980 ratio of 45:1. See United Nations Human Development Programme, *Human Development Report 1992* (New York: Oxford University Press, 1992).

8 John Gray, *False Dawn* (New York: The New Press, 1998), pp. 114–15.

9 James Petras and Henry Veltmeyer, *Globalization Unmasked: Imperialism in the 21st Century* (New York: Zed Books, 2001), pp. 30–1. *Globalization Unmasked* offers one of the most thorough nuts and bolts accounts of the many issues that accompany globalization and its alternatives – with special focus on Latin America – including transitional strategies back to local and regional economic control. Other examples of current globalization theory include *Empire*, which addresses how global capital is transforming labor and civil society through flexible, decentered power networks that the authors call "Empire." See Antonio Negri and Michael Hardt, *Empire* (Cambridge, MA: Harvard, 2000). Of more interest for managing to combine empirical tracking with theoretical concern is Paul Hirst, *From Statism to Pluralism: Democracy, Civil Society and Global Politics* (Bristol, PA: UCL Press, 1997).

10 André Gunder Frank and other Latin-American thinkers delineated the dependence of the centre on the periphery as a trade phenomenon, and their influence in this and other respects is evident throughout this book. H. Fernando, F. Cardoso and E. Faletto, *Dependency and Development in Latin America* 1969; André Gunder Frank, *The Development of Underdevelopment*, 1966; and *Capitalism and Underdevelopment in Latin America: Historical Studies of Chile and Brazil*, 1967; also Ernesto Laclau, *Feudalism and Capitalism in Latin America*, 1971.

11 Rashid, *Taliban*, pp. 145–6.

12 Ibid.

13 Unocal suspended its participation in the CentGas consortium in August 1998 and formally withdrew from that consortium in December 1998. Statement on Afghanistan and the Taliban, <www.unocal.com>.

14 "Green-washing" of course means "white-washing": presenting a green image at odds with the reality. Green-washing means covering over environmental damage with expressions of environmental concern. The term is analyzed in Joshua Karliner, *The Corporate Planet; Ecology and Politics in the Age of Globalization* (San Francisco, CA: Sierra Club Books, 1997).

15 See Alex Callinicos, *Against the Third Way: An Anti-capitalist Critique* (Oxford, Basil Blackwell, 2001).

16 Review of John Gray's *False Dawn*, *New York Times Book Review*, June 1999.

17 "Dig more coal – the PCs are coming: Being digital was supposed to mean less demand for hard energy. It isn't turning out that way." *Forbes Magazine*, May 31, 1999, pp. 70–2.

18 Hilary F. French, "Reconciling Trade and the Environment," *State of the World: Worldwatch Report* (New York: W.W. Norton, 1993), p. 160.

19 General Agreement of Tariffs and Trade (GATT), *International Trade 1990–1*, vol. 2 (Geneva, 1992).

20 Manufacture has increased in the South, but primary products tend to dominate. "More than 98 percent of the total exports of Bolivia, Ethiopia, Ghana and Nigeria fall into this category, for instance, compared with 24 percent of US exports and only 2 percent of Japan's" (French, "Reconciling Trade and the Environment," p. 161). Between 1990 and 1998 world merchandise exports have increased by a total of 6.5 percent annually. In particular agricultural products have increased 4 percent annually, mining products 5.5 percent and manufacturers 7.0 percent. The total value of world merchandise exports (agricultural, mining and manufacturers) is 5,270 billion dollars in 1998 (WTO Annual Report, 1999, chart II.1).

21 Lester R. Brown, "A New Era Unfolds," *State of the World*, p. 13.

22 Like other African countries, including the Ivory Coast and Ghana, Nigeria has now become a net importer of timber (French, "Reconciling Trade and the Environment," p. 161). "Of the 33 remaining Third World exporters of forest products, only 10 are projected to still be in the position by the end of this decade [the year 2000]" (Brown, "A New Era Unfolds," p. 15).

23 The world export of commercial services (transportation, travel and other) amounts to 1,320 billion dollars total in 1998. Their annual growth between 1990 and 1998 is 7 percent. In particular transportation's annual growth is 4 percent (WTO Annual Report, 1999, table II.5). For 2000, it is still too early to make a detailed review of world merchandise trade by product group. The WTO nevertheless anticipates an enormous growth in oil transportation: "Partial informations indicates that rebounding oil prices have led to an increase of world fuels exports in excess of 20 percent" (WTO Annual Report, 2000, p. 9).

24 Richard Rosecrance, *The Rise of the Virtual State: Wealth and Power in the Coming Century* (New York: Basic Books, 1999); for something more nuanced, see Antonio Negri's and Michael Hardt's descriptions of immaterial and material labor (*Empire*, pp. 290–4).

25 Martin Khor's Third World Network and its website (*www.twnside. or.sg*) addresses many of the issues addressed in this book from the perspective of the South. Vandana Shiva's work is also invaluable, and referred to below. For other concrete accounts of the impact of globalization on the South, see Sarah Anderson (ed.), *Views from the South: The Effects of Globalization and the World Trade Organization on Third World Countries* (Oakland, CA: Food First Books, 2000).

26 Anthony Giddens, *The Third Way* (Cambridge: Polity Press, 1998), p. 24. See also pp. 43–4. "No one any longer has any alternatives to capitalism. The arguments that remain concern how far, and in what ways, capitalism should be governed and regulated."

27 John Gray, *False Dawn* (New York: The New Press, 1998), p. 21.

28 John Vinocur, "War Transforms the Anti-Globalization Crowd," *International Herald Tribune*, Nov 2, 2001, p. 1.

29 Gray, *False Dawn*, p. 9.

30 As we will see in the next chapter, even if all are affected by air pollution, they are not affected equally. Class position is a key variable: cf. Val Plumwood, *Environmental Culture: The Ecological Crisis of Reason*, London: Routledge 2002.

31 In a kind of absolute and relative value of health, we might say that while some might escape for sometime from the bioravages of pollution, none can be protected entirely or forever.

32 George Soros, *The Crisis of Global Capitalism: Open Society Endangered* (New York: Public Affairs, 1998), p. 111.

33 Ibid., p. 112.

34 Paul Hawken, Amory Lovins and L. Hunter Lovins, *Natural Capitalism* (London and New York: Little, Brown, 1999), p. 7.

35 Teresa Brennan, *Exhausting Modernity: Grounds for a New Economy* (New York and London: Routledge, 2000). Marx was constrained by a worldview in which man, the towering subject, stood alone against a world of objects. Nature was an object for Marx. Labor was a subject. In his account, only a subjective factor such as labor was capable of adding value. Yet Marx stressed again and again that the reason labor could add value – where technology and money could not – was because labor was living, a living energy. But labor is not the only thing that lives. Nature also lives, although Marx overlooked this when he consigned nature, like technology, to the realm of objects and reified things.

36 Gray, *False Dawn*, p. 89.

37 French Prime Minister Jospin's and Brazilian Prime Minister Cardoso's addresses to the "Third Way" conference, Florence, Italy, November 1999.

38 Jeremy Rifkin with Ted Howard, *Entropy* (New York, Viking Press, 1980); Jeremy Rifkin, *Time Wars: the Primary Conflict in Human History* (New York: Henry Holt and Co., 1987).

39 They include William Blake, Peter Kropotkin, William Morris, Leo Tolstoy, Gustav Landau, and more recently, Gandhi. More recently still, they include Lewis Mumford and famously E. F. Schumacher.

40 M. K. Gandhi, *Economic and Industrial Life and Relations*, ed. V. B. Kher (Ahmedabad: Navajivan Publishing House, 1959), 3 vols.

41 Giddens can be also described this way: he wants the United Nations to take new incentives to regulate the global economy, and of course he too wants tax reforms. I mention Giddens in this context because the fact that he takes the same path to solutions as critics of the third way points to how much they have in common. The difference between them lies in the targets and degrees of taxation, and the role ascribed to international fiduciary bodies. It does not lie in any structural challenge.

42 Fernand Braudel, *The Wheels of Commerce: Civilization and Capitalism: 15th–18th Century*, vol. 2, trans. Sian Reynolds (Berkeley, CA: University of California Press, 1992).

43 Umberto Unger and Cornel West, while acutely sensitive to the disparities of class structure, manage to avoid mentioning the environment in *The Future of American Progressivism* (Boston: Beacon, 1998).

44 Lawrence H. Summers, Memorandum on GEP, Dec 12, 1991.

45 Jose Lutzenburger, letter to Lawrence Summers in "Mr. Summers Supreme Neo-Liberal," <sawsj-members-request@lrrc.umass.edu>.

46 Amartya Sen and Martha Craven Nussbaum (eds), *The Quality of Life (Studies in Development Economics)* (Oxford: Oxford University Press, 1993).

47 As if to illustrate the central thesis of this book, the new US president has passed or repealed legislation affecting each of the conditions of life in turn with astonishing rapidity, and then gone directly to war. Within the first three months of the president's term, (1) we witnessed the refusal to ratify the Kyoto Protocol on carbon dioxide emissions, on the grounds that the economy could not afford the luxury of leaving the climate relatively intact or stopping the proliferation of air diseases; (2) following the attack on air and climate, President Bush repealed the standard for acceptable levels of arsenic in water; and then (3) he turned to food, arguing that the salmonella test on school lunchmeat was no longer necessary because of the delay it imposed on distribution, which in turn led to unacceptably low profit margins.

2 Daily life in the West

1 John Gray, *False Dawn* (New York: New Press, 1998), p. 132.

2 Juliet B. Schor, *The Overworked American – The Unexpected Decline of Leisure* (New York: Basic Books, 1993).

3 Jeremy Rifkin, *Time Wars* (New York: Henry Holt, 1987), pp. 14–15. There are many overlaps between Rifkin's thought and my own. On reflection, I wonder if all I have added to his perception is the economic analysis.

4 British workers are twenty-five times less likely to relocate than their American counterparts. D. Puga, *The Rise and Fall of Regional Inequalities* (London: Centre for Economic Performance, 1996), cited Gray, *False Dawn*, p. 112.

5 None of this is to argue against the idea or pleasures of hard work. It is to argue against the appropriation of these and other virtues in the service of capitalism, so that those who do not work day and half the night for "the economy" guiltily believe themselves to be shirking. Intensity of effort, surely, belongs with creative work, or labor righting wrongs.

6 The core contradiction in capitalism is that speed, as one of two key components in production, sets a pace which exhausts the other component, so that the overall source of profit – energy in diverse natural, material forms – is consumed more rapidly than it can sustain itself in order to make an unrealistic profit. (By unrealistic, I mean a

profit based on the irrational destruction of the natural reality on which it is based.)

7 My thanks to Ian Patterson for this example.

8 "Air Pollution Worsens in Italy's Big Cities," Xinhua News Agency, May 11, 1998: Item No: 0511063. Only a third of the 900,000 people who commute to Milan take public vehicles.

9 Deborah Williams, "House Hunters Flocking to the West: Cheaper prices, Better Road Links Prove a Magnet," *South Wales Evening Post*, Dec 23, 1998 (Housing Section), p. 7.

10 Ibid.

11 *Journey-to-Work Trends in the United States and its Major Metropolitan Areas* 1960–1990, in the United States and its Major Metropolitan Areas 1960–91. Bureau of Transportation Statistics. National Transportation Statistics, published in 1998, by the United States Bureau of Transportation Statistics. <http://www.bts.gov/NTL/DOCS/473.html>, p. 28.

12 *Journey-to-Work Trends*, p. 11.

13 "Those workers whose jobs were located outside their counties of residence rose from 9 million in 1960 to 27.5 million in 1990, again by 206 percent." Ibid.

14 Ibid.

15 One could as well date the deregulation experiment from Bretton Woods in 1947, and of course deregulation continues to accelerate beyond the present.

16 *Journey-to-Work Trends*, p. 11.

17 William Julius Wilson, *When Work Disappears: The World of the New Urban Poor* (New York: Vintage Books, 1997), pp. 41–2.

18 Ibid., p. 39.

19

> Studies of automobile drivers have shown significant relationships between exposure to traffic congestion and a variety of adverse physiological reactions. For example, researchers have reported a significant and positive correlation between high traffic volumes and increased heart rates, blood pressure, and electrocardiogram irregularities. Studies also show that chronic exposure to traffic congestion, especially over long distances, long waits, and frequent trips, increases negative mood states, lowers tolerance for frustration, and can even lead to more impatient driving habits.
> (*Transportation Implications of Telecommuting*, April 1993, <www.itsdocs.fhwa.dot.gov/jpodocs/repts_te/68j01!.pdf>, p. 84)

See also US General Accounting Office (GAO), *Traffic Congestion: Trends, Measures and Effects*, Report to the Chairman, Subcommittee on Transportation and Related Agencies, Committee on Appropriations, US Senate GAO/PEMD-90, November, 1989.

20 Dick Murray, "Who Takes You to Work? Just the Job," *Evening Standard*, May 18, 1998, p. 2. The RAC says "It's all tied up with population changes – car use went down in London when businesses and people moved out. Now the reverse is true."

21 "In the European Union, as regards fatalities only, we still accept about 123 a day, just under 45,000 a year . . . the total cost of the adverse environmental and health effects of transport, including congestion, is estimated as up to 260 billion ECU." Press Release, WHO/57, "Averting the Three Outriders of the Transport Apocalypse: Road Accidents, Air and Noise Pollution." Robert Coleman, director-general of the Transport Division of the European Commission for the European Forum on Transport, Environment and Health jointly organized by the European Regional Office of the World Health Organization (WHO) and the Austrian Ministry for the Environment, July 31, 1998.

22 Saskia Sassen, *Globalization and its Discontents* (New York: New Press, 1998).

23 Although he admires the "incredible rapidity with which thought circulates in the midst of these [frontier] deserts" as well as the "great rapidity" with which they pass along the roads. Alexis de Toqueville, *Democracy in America*, trans. Henry Reeve; rev. Francis Bowen and Phillips Bradley (New York: Vintage Books, 1945), pp. 328–9, *n.* 6.

24 Juliet B. Schor, *The Overworked American*. For related, and illuminating perspectives on the same question, see Arlie Hochschild, *The Second Shift* (New York: Avon Books, 1990); Gary Cross, *Time and Money – The Making of Consumer Culture* (New York: Routledge, 1993); and Leland Burns, *Busy Bodies: Why Our Time Obsessed Society Keeps Us Running in Place* (New York: W.W. Norton, 1993).

25 Schor, *The Overworked American*, p. 29.

26 Louis Uchitelle, "Increase in Productivity," *New York Times*, Nov 13, 1999, p. C1.

27 Cheryl Russell "Overworked? Overwhelmed?", March 1995, <http://americandemographics.com/publications/ad/95_ad/9503_ad/9503 AD03.htm> US Census Bureau Current Population Survey (CPS).

28 *Journey-to-Work Trends*, p. 11.

29 Not that these figures go uncontested. It has been argued that, according to people's diary notes rather than the Census Population Survey, women especially are working less, so that "working more" may be a matter of perception. This is less likely if one takes account of how consumption, the time spent in provisioning, requires more work, while living costs are rising. Diary notes do not take account of, say, having no time to write in one's diary, or increased telephone time: the hours spent wending one's way through the "options" merely to correct a computer error, or pay a bill. Paying bills, like provisioning or "shopping," cleaning, cooking and above all childcare, are all part of the labor of consumption. Russell, "Overworked? Overwhelmed?".

30 "Lower Wages, Longer Hours, Hinder Women's Progress," Press Release, International Labor Organization, July 30, 1996. <http://www.ilo.org/public/english/bureau/inf/pr/96–25.htm>.

31 Ibid.

32

In developed countries, women work at least two hours more weekly than men, though 5 to 10 hours more per week is not unusual. In Australia, Canada and Germany, the hourly work loads of men and women are roughly equal, but in Italy women work 28 percent more than men, in Austria 12 percent more and in France 11 percent. In Japan, the time women spend on unpaid work is nine times greater than that of men.

(Ibid)

33 "Global Employment Trends: The Outlook is Grim," Press Release on the *World Employment Report 1998–99*, International Labor Organization.
34 John Gray, *False Dawn*, pp. 116–17.
35 "Global employment trends."
36 Ibid.
37 John Gray, *False Dawn,* p. 113.
38 See the discussion in Chapter 5.
39 The quotation is from Blair's guarantees in relation to welfare reform. UK Department of Social Security, *New Ambitions for Our Country: A New Contract for Welfare*, Green Paper, Foreword by Prime Minister Tony Blair. UK Department of Social Security, March 26, 1998.
40 Jane Humphries argues that the "family wage" was a gain in working class struggle at the beginning of the nineteenth century, precisely because it meant that work at home could offset living costs, while capital was deprived of an additional worker producing profit (or surplus value). Jane Humphries, "Class Struggle and the Persistence of the Working Class Family," *Cambridge Journal of Economics*, Vol. 1, No. 3 (1977), pp. 10–37.
41 My point here is not that women should be servicing men, children and other women at home. Quite the reverse. The point is that, as the vast bulk of household work and childcare is of course still performed by women, the accelerated entry of women into the workforce worldwide over the last forty years means that women have no time to spend on housework without spending more money on it (or becoming exhausted).
42 The trends toward fast foods, which require homogenous ingredients, reinforces the concentration, or consolidation of farms. Two-thirds of the forests in Costa Rica have been cleared for grazing cows to feed the nearly insatiable Western demand for hamburgers (with English-speaking countries – especially but not only the US – eating the most). The money spent by Australians eating at McDonald's increased from $670 million in 1992 to $935 million one year later. Kristin Lyons, "Agro-industrialization and Social Change within the Australian Context: A Case Study of the Fast Food Industry," in David Burch *et al.* (eds), *Globalization and Agri-Food Restructuring: Perspectives from the Australasia Region* (Aldershot: Avebury, 1996), p. 241.
43 "Browning the Land," *The Times*, Nov 23, 1998.
44 The tendency to drive alone increases when the women are in middle-class "professional/manager" employment. Elizabeth K. Burns, "Women's Travel to Inner City Employment," <www.fhwa.dot.gov//////ohim/womens/chap10.pdf>, p. 167.
45 *Journey-to-Work Trends*, p. 33.

46 See Teresa Brennan, *The Transmission of Affect* (Ithaca, NY: Cornell University Press, 2003).

47 Cf. Luhmann's work on systems.

48 Robert Sapolsky, *Why Zebras Don't Get Ulcers* (New York: W. H. Freeman & Co., 2000), p. 65ff.

49 *The Independent* [London] March 22, 1998, and Press Release, WHO, Washington, DC and Geneva, Switzerland, June 4, 2000.

50 In 1997, 44 percent of adults reported having a longstanding illness. In the same year 15 percent of men and 19 percent of women reported having had acute sickness in the two weeks preceding the interview. Interestingly, between 1994 and 1997, even though the majority of interviewed people maintained their health was good, the number of people who thought about bad health increased. Health Survey for England 1997, <www.doh.gov.uk/HPSSS/TBL_A5.HTM>.

51 See Chapter 4.

52 Sapolsky, *Why Zebras*, p. 273.

53 Like most aspects of modern life, caring for the body has its contradictions, otherwise known as choices. It is possible to learn more about the real laws of the human body and mind through this process. But saying this does not make up for the sheer time expenditure involved in maintaining health by alternative or regular means.

54 *Journey-to-Work Trends*, p. 26.

55 John Gray, *False Dawn*, p. 118 (citing "Center for Disease Control and Prevention," in turn cited in *International Herald Tribune*, Feb 8–9, 1997).

56 The leading feminist theories of the day neglect how more and more women annually, of more and more cultures and classes and races, are being universalized by the real category of poverty. Significant exceptions however – among the theorists – are Val Plumwood, Susan Buck-Morss, Drucilla Cornell, Juliet Schor, Martha Nussbaum, Rosi Braidotti and Ehrenreich herself.

57 Barbara Ehrenreich, *Hearts of Men: American Dreams and the Flight from Commitment* (Garden City, NY: Doubleday, 1984), p. 46.

58 None of this is to put the need to go to the limit – at times – in question. The case concerns why one goes to the limit.

3 The war on the atmosphere

1 World Resources Institute, "Rising Energy Use: Health Effects of Air Pollution," <http://www.igc.org/wri/wr-98–99/airpoll.htm>, May 9, 2002.

2 The situation is most serious in metropolitan areas of California, Arizona, the Northeast Coast (from Washington DC to Massachusetts), Texas, Illinois, Wisconsin and Georgia. United States Environmental Protection Agency, *National Air Quality and Emissions Trends Report, 1998*, EPA-454/R-00–003 (Research Triangle Park, NC: Office of Air Quality Planning and Standards, EPA, 2000), pp. 2, 66.

3 Roger Highfield, Christine McGourty and Adrian Berry, "Air Pollution is 'Health Threat to City Dwellers'" *Daily Telegraph*, Sept 3, 1993.

4   Canada is a case in point. Canada's national health agency, "Health Canada" found that as many as 1,800 Ontarians per year were dying prematurely from poor air quality. According to the Ontario Medical Association,

> at current levels of exposure, pollutants such as ground-level ozone, inhalable particulates and total sulfur compounds are responsible for adverse health effects in Ontarians. There are concerns about whether the existing standards for environmental exposures provide adequate protection and about the potential risks of new and unevaluated agents.
>
> (B. Ted Boadway, Judith MacPhail, Carol Jacobson, "Ontario Medical Association Position Paper on Health Effects of Ground-level Ozone, Acid Aerosols and Particulate Matter," *Canadian Respiratory Journal*, Vol. 5, No. 5 (1998), pp. 367–83)

The Health Canada study cited above resulted in Canadian Environment Minister Sergio Marchi unveiling car emission rules that aimed to "reduce illnesses caused by air pollution." Andrew Duffy, "Marchi Targets Highway Smog: New Car Emission Rules Aim to Reduce Illnesses Caused by Air Pollution," *Ottawa Citizen*, March 3, 1997, p. A1. One very recent study on asthma and air pollution in Italy (part of the European Community Respiratory Health Survey) notices the relevance of asthma in the region of Emilia Romagna in northern Italy, but – strangely – does not connect it with air pollution. It is affirmed:

> Bronchial Asthma is a socially relevant disease in our territory (more than 7% of interviewed people had a diagnosis of asthma in the course of their life and 3.8% had asthma attacks in the last year). The relevance of allergic rhynitis, often associated with asthma, has a major prevalence: more than 15%. . . . While there is a negative role of air pollutant elements in the aggravation of the disease in people already affected by it, the eventual role of pollution in the determination of the disease remains to be established.
>
> (R. Dallari *et al.*, "L'asma bronchiale nella popolazione adulta del distretto ceramico modenese. Risultati preliminari," *Sviluppo sostenibile: Noi e l'ambiente*, No. 62 (2000))

5   In 1993 there were more than 100,000 hospital admissions attributed to asthma – up 7 percent from 1992. Asthma is also a deadly disease; in 1995, 1,621 people in the United Kingdom died from it. Jeremy Laurance, "Drug Offers Relief for Asthma Sufferers," *The Independent* [London] Feb 9, 1998. One or more persons had been diagnosed by a physician as having asthma in nearly one out of ten households across seven European countries. In addition, a small proportion (4 percent) of households reported asthma that had not been diagnosed by a physician. At one extreme, the household prevalence of current asthma was 15.2 percent in the United Kingdom.

At the other, the household prevalence of diagnosed asthma was 2.5 percent in Germany. In four out of the seven European countries, household prevalence of current asthma fell in the range of 4 percent– 6 percent of households.

> Since the middle of the 20th century, worldwide prevalence and severity have started to increase considerably, especially among children – approximately 5% of Europe's population now suffers from asthma. Asthma is one of the most common chronic diseases worldwide, and represents a significant medical, public health and social problem. By reducing exposure to allergens and other sensitizing substances, the prevalence of these diseases can be controlled.
>
> (World Health Organization (WHO) Regional Office for Europe, Asthma Pamphlet (1999))

6 <http://www.environment-agency.gov.uk/ourservices/consultations/vision.htm>. The European definition of "air pollution" does not refer to any concrete diseases: rather, air pollution is

> the introduction by man, directly or indirectly, of substances or energy into the air resulting in deleterious effects of such a nature as to endanger human health, harm living resources and eco-systems and material property and impair or interfere with amenities and other legitimate uses of the environment.
>
> ("Community Legislation in Force," Document 279A1113 (01) "Convention on Long-Range Transboundary Air Pollution – Resolution on long-range transboundary air pollution"; article 1-a (<europa.eu.int/eur-lex/en/lif/dat/1979/en_279A1113_01. html>))

Moreover, the document claims to regulate, limit, reduce and prevent "long-range transboundary air pollution" at the same time as it confesses to the difficulties in locating the origin of air pollution. Air does not have boundaries. "Transboundary air pollution" means

> air pollution whose physical origin is situated wholly or in part within the area under the national jurisdiction of one State and which has adverse effects in the area under the jurisdiction of another State at such a distance that it is not generally possible to distinguish the contribution of individual emission sources or groups of sources.
>
> (See Article 1-b)

7 The Harvard Working Group on New and Resurgent Diseases, "Globalization, Development and the Spread of Disease," *The Case Against the Global Economy*, ed. Jerry Mander and Edward Goldsmith (San Francisco, CA: Sierra Club Books, 1996), pp. 160–70, at p. 169.
8 Ground-level ozone, even at low levels, is damaging to the cardio-

respiratory system and is considered in general to "pose a serious health risk." Studies have concluded that current levels of ground-level ozone can have the following effects:

> lung inflammation, decreased lung function, airway hyper-reactivity (problematic especially for asthmatics), severe asthma attacks requiring hospitalization, respiratory symptoms, possible increased medication use and emergency room visits among individuals with heart or lung disease, reduced exercise capacity, increased hospital admissions and possible increased mortality.
> (Boadway *et al.*, "Ontario Medical Association Position Paper",
> pp. 370–71)

In addition, human exposure studies have "clearly demonstrated that the lung responds to ozone exposure by irritative cough and substernal chest pain on inspiration." Hillel S. Koren, "Associations between Criteria Air Pollutants and Asthma," *Environmental Health Perspectives*, Vol. 103, Supp. 6 (1995), pp. 236–42, p. 238. There is also evidence of decreased forced vital capacity and an increase in airway resistance. A wide range of susceptibility was observed in this study. The people affected were not only those with existing cardio or pulmonary diseases. The Ontario Medical Association's findings were supported by David V. Bates at the University of British Columbia in his "The Effects of Air Pollution on Children," *Environmental Health Perspectives*, Vol. 103, Supp. 6 (1995), pp. 49–53. He found that asthma admissions for children under fourteen were "invariably higher" on days where there were high levels of ozone in the air. Other studies in Philadelphia and southern Ontario also support this result. Joel Schwartz, "Nonparametric Smoothing in the Analysis of Air Pollution and Respiratory Illness," *The Canadian Journal of Statistics*, Vol. 22, No. 4 (1994), pp. 471–87; and Koren, "Associations Between Criteria Air Pollutants and Asthma," p. 238.

9 460,000 avoidable deaths occur annually due to exposure to particulate matter; "particulate matter" is used to measure the size of pollutants without specifying their chemical content. PM10, for example, is a classification used for particles that are 10 micrometers or less in diameter, and thus able to be deposited in the lower airways of the lungs, as well as the areas where gas exchange occurs. Breathing particulate matter has been linked to chronic respiratory illness, increased respiratory symptoms, decreased pulmonary function levels, increased bronchitis, decreased forced vital capacity and increased use of asthma medication in children. Lucas M. Neas, Douglas W. Dockery, Petros Koutrakis, David J. Tollerud and Frank E. Speizer. "The Association of Ambient Air Pollution with Twice Daily Peak Expiratory Flow Measurements in Children," *American Journal of Epidemiology*, Vol. 141, No. 2 (1995), pp. 111–21. One study found that morbidity increased with PM10 respiration, across the population, not only those already exhibiting cardiopulmonary problems. These particles have been linked to respiratory irritation and disease very

similar to those induced by ozone. They are also the precursors of acid rain. Boadway *et al.*, "Ontario Medical Association Position Paper", p. 370. In addition, particulate matter makes asthma substantially worse and increases respiratory hospital admissions. Respiratory and cardiovascular mortality also increase with elevated PM10 pollution levels. The World Health Organization recently attributed 7 to 10 percent of respiratory infections in European children to particulate pollution. In addition, the World Bank has estimated that exposure to particulate levels exceeding the World Health Organization health standard accounts for roughly 2 to 5 percent of all deaths in urban areas in the developing world. From the World Resources Institute web page, <www.igc.org/wri/wr-98-99/airpoll.htm>. In 1997 the French Committee for the Prevention and Precaution of the Ministry for the Environment released a report in which it signaled the emission of fine particles as the most dangerous for the health of lungs. The fine particles are emitted by diesel engines. According to the report, the regulations existing in this field are still insufficient. (Comité de la Prévention et la Précaution, Ministère de l'Environnement, *Recommandation sur les particules fines*. Paris: Ministère de l'environnement, 1997.) In the same year another study of Paris reported that a decrease of the levels of acid pollution (SO₂ and black smoke) would decrease the number of premature deaths due to cardiovascular problems. (S. Medina *et al.*, *Impact sur la santé selon différents scénarii d'évolution de la pollution atmosphérique en agglomération parisienne. Estimations à partir des résultats de l'étude Erpurs*. Paris: ORSIF, 1997.)

10 Carbon monoxide exposure, for example, may relate to the genesis of atherosclerotic arterial disease in smokers and to increased mortality in workers chronically exposed to vehicular exhaust. Patients with ischemic heart disease exhibit angina pectoris and excess mortality from exposure. The effects of carbon monoxide on the body are seen to increase with anemia or chronic lung disease. Committee of the Environmental and Occupational Health Assembly of the American Thoracic Society, "Health Effects of Outdoor Pollution," *American Journal of Respiratory Critical Care Medicine*, Vol. 153 (1996), pp. 3–50, at p. 6.

11 Ninety-nine percent of ingested benzene is taken into the body via the air, and it has been determined that automobile exhaust is the second major source contributing to benzene exposure after cigarette smoking. In addition to the estimated 233,000 people in the United States that are exposed to benzene by working in the petrochemical and petroleum refining industries, potentially dangerous levels of benzene have been detected in urban and densely trafficked areas. Benzene can cause leukemia in humans, and is yet another harmful byproduct of fossil-fuel combustion. As with most chemicals ingested by air pollution, there is a reluctance to say that an increase in a disease is definitely caused by a given chemical factor. But there are repeated correlations, and an otherwise unexplained increase in respiratory illness. Because it is emitted through automobile exhaust and effluent from petrochemical plants, benzene is a danger not only to people

exposed in their occupations, but to those in the vicinity of high petrochemical pollution. Lance Wallace, "Environmental Exposure to Benzene: An Update," *Environmental Health Perspectives*, Vol. 104, Supp. 6 (1996), pp. 1129–35; and Song-Nain Yin *et al.*, "An Expanded Cohort Study of Cancer Among Benzene-Exposed Workers in China," *Environmental Health Perspectives*, Vol. 104, Supp. 6 (1996), pp. 1339–41. More generally, petrochemical air pollution from the petrochemical manufacturing industry is statistically linked to female lung cancer in nearby areas in Taiwan. C. Y. Yang, M. F. Cheng, J. F. Chiu and S. S. Tsai, "Female Lung Cancer and Petrochemical Air Pollution in Taiwan," *Archives of Environmental Health*, Vol. 54, No. 3 (1999), pp. 180–85.

12 Nitrogen dioxide is actually most dangerous when found at high levels in indoor air from gas stoves (which are found in about 50 percent of US households), and kerosene heaters. J. Samet and M. J. Utell, "The Risk of Nitrogen Dioxide: What Have We Learned from Epidemiological and Clinical Studies?" *Toxicology and Industrial Health*, Vol. 6, No. 2 (1990), pp. 247–62. However, significant levels of indoor pollution are from transportation byproducts. Nitrogen dioxide increases the risk of lower respiratory illnesses or symptoms for children. Asthmatics may be particularly sensitive to this gas, and exhibit decreased lung function.

13 Sulfur dioxide is directly regulated by the United States' Environmental Protection Agency's (EPA) Clean Air Act because of the dangers it entails. Healthy adults can experience increased respiratory symptoms, respiratory mortality and increased hospital visits for respiratory disease. Committee of the Environmental and Occupational Health Assembly of the American Thoracic Society, "Health Effects of Outdoor Pollution," p. 5. Asthmatics develop significant effects such as restricted air passages. Bates, "The Effects of Air Pollution on Children."

14 Boadway *et al.*, "Ontario Medical Association Position Paper."

15 One case control study and two correlational studies cited by Shelia Hoar Zahm and Susan S. Devesa have suggested that exhaust from combustion engines can increase the risk of childhood leukemia. In "Childhood Cancer: Overview of Incidence Trends and Environmental Carcinogens," *Environmental Health Perspectives*, Vol. 103, Supp. 6 (1995), pp. 177–84, at p. 181.

16 Wallace, "Environmental Exposure to Benzene." Yin *et al.*, "An Expanded Cohort Study of Cancer Among Benzene-exposed Workers in China."

17 Committee of the Environmental and Occupational Health Assembly of the American Thoracic Society, "Health Effects of Outdoor Air Pollution," p. 6.

18 There is also evidence from animal exposure studies suggesting that nitrogen dioxide impairs host defense response to bacterial infections. Ibid.

19 Eric Mann, *L.A.'s Lethal Air* (Los Angeles, CA: Izbor/Community Strategy, 1991), pp. 5, 36, 38. Russell P. Sherwin, "Findings,"

International Specialty Conference on Tropospheric Ozone and the Environment Los Angeles, California, March 21, 1990, and R. P. Sherwin *et al.*, "Chronic Glandular Bronchitis in Young Individuals Residing in a Metropolitan Area," *Virchows Archiv: An International Journal of Pathology*, Vol. 433, No. 4 (1998), pp. 341–8. Los Angeles, in 1991, had 8 million autos, trucks and buses on its roads everyday. Fifty-nine percent of the land in central LA is reserved for freeways, streets and parking lots. The various transport vehicles traveling in LA were responsible for 72 percent of the nitrogen oxides, 96 percent of the carbon monoxide, and 54 percent of the sulfur oxides in the city's atmosphere.

20 The increase of daily mortality of 3 percent has been observed in correspondence with an increase of 50 $\mu g/m3a$ over the medium level of acid pollution (FN and SO_2). Particularly, cardiovascular mortality increases of 1 to 4 percent corresponding to an increase of 50 $\mu g/m3$ over the medium level; and respiratory mortality increases of 4 to 5 percent corresponding to each increase of the NO_2 indicator. The cases of asthma hospitalization in children increase by 8 percent with every increase of the SO_2 indicator. "Impact sur la santé de la pollution atmosphérique en milieu urbain: synthèse des résultats de l'étude APHEA (Air Pollution and Health: European Approach)," *Institut de Veille Sanitaire*, Feb 3, 1998. During one week (Dec 12–15, 1991) in London the level of NO_2 was counted as 406 $\mu g/m3$ and the maximum hour level was of 868 $\mu g/m3$. The number of deaths and the number of hospitalizations were compared to the preceding week, and to the similar episodes registered in the preceding four years. The results showed that, correlated to this situation, daily mortality increased by 10 percent (Relative Risk: 1,1), and cardio-vascular mortality 20 percent (RR: 1,2). As far as hospitalization, the increase in risk was observed in people more than sixty-five years old, with an increase of 19 percent in admission for respiratory causes and 43 percent for chronic obstruction of lungs. Ironically enough, the authors concluded that air pollution and NO_2 were a "possible explanation" for these data. In Lyons, France, a similar case was observed during the week 13–17 Jan, 1997. The peak of air pollution had determined the alert procedure. The Cellule Inter-Régionale d'Epidémiologie et d'Intervention (CIREI) compared the number of school absences with the degree of air pollution, but preferred not to draw any conclusion because "the evaluation of health consequences of these peaks of air pollution in urban area is difficult due to the multiplicity of environmental and socio-demographic factors that can interfere with the study." "Pics de pollution atmosphérique et santé publique," *Institut de Veille Sanitaire*, Aug 2, 1999. The article advises us not to be blinded by these pollution peaks, because they "are not the most important risk factor for public health." In Italy 3,500 more deaths a year in eight big cities are due to smog. Research by the Organizazione Mondiale per la Sanità in collaboration with ANPA (Agenzia Nazionale per l'Ambiente) – June, 2000 – asserts that this number increases to 5,000 if more elastic parameters are used. If the maximum

level of permissible pollution established by existing laws were respected, there would be a decrease of 5 percent in the number of deaths, 1/3 less of acute bronchitis, 10 percent fewer asthma attacks. Oliva Daria, "Quell'oscuro killer chiamato PM10," *Hyperion e-zine*, year II, n. 9. The deadly effects of transportation on Italian lungs has its visual counterpart in the fast degradation of the nation's artistic monuments.

21 The health costs of traffic-related air pollution are very high. In Switzerland, they amounted to 1,600 million Swiss francs in 1993. The estimates were limited to several health indicators, including premature deaths, hospitalization for respiratory and cardiovascular diseases, and effects on patients with chronic bronchitis and asthma. Loss of production, medical treatment and administrative costs were also included. Press Release, WHO/57, "Averting the Three Outriders of the Transport Apocalypse: Road Accidents, Air and Noise Pollution," for the European Forum on Transport, Environment and Health, jointly organized by the European Regional Office of the World Health Organization (WHO) and the Austrian Ministry for the Environment (July 31, 1998).

22 M. I. Edfors-Lubs, "Allergy in 7000 Twin Pairs," *Acta Allergologica*, Vol. 26 (1971), pp. 249–85, cited in World Resources Institute, *World Resources: A Guide to the Global Environment, 1998–1999* (New York and Oxford: Oxford University Press, 1998), p. 31.

23 World Bank, *World Development Report 1999/2000*.

24 World Resources Institute, *World Resources: A Guide to the Global Environment*, p. 175.

25 The urgency of restricting pollution is felt most at times of natural disasters. After the floods that hit Europe in the fall 2000, the Italian daily *Il Corriere della Sera* wrote:

> The storms that destroyed a large part of Europe are pushing the U.E. Ministers of the Environment to cry out their alarm over the responsibility of pollution. . . . It is necessary to decrease the global gas emissions that cause overheating, in the measure of 5.2 percent within 2012 (the starting points are the values of 1990). To reach this point Europe has to decrease its polluting emissions by 8 percent, the US by 7 percent, Canada by 6 percent.
>
> (*Corriere della Sera*, Nov 8, 2000)

26 Pollutants emitted into the air by electricity generation using fossil fuels include nitrogen oxides (NO_x), sulfur dioxide (SO_2), carbon dioxide (CO_2), VOCs, carbon monoxide (CO), lead (Pb), and particulate matter less than 10 micrometers (PM_{10}).

27 US Department of Energy, *International Energy Annual 1998*, DOE/EIA-0219 (98) (Washington, DC, Energy Information Administration, 2000), p. 93.

28 Ibid, p. 294.

29 E. Eakin, "Professor Scarry has a theory," *New York Times Magazine*, Nov 19, 2000, p. 78.

30 In France, 1998–9 were the years of highest growth in the family's acquisitions in relation to the past ten years.

31 The use of personal computers, dishwashers, clothes washers and dryers has grown by nearly 5 percent a year from 1990 to 1997 in the US. However, the largest increase in appliance acquisition as such was seen in (fast-food providing) microwave oven prevalence, which increased 69 percent. In Europe we find the same trend. In 1994 microwaves were present in 66 percent of families in the United Kingdom, 71 percent in Finland, 58 percent in Sweden, 52 percent in Germany, and 50 percent in France.

32 Tim Lang and Colin Hines, *The New Protectionism* (New York: New Press, 1993), p. 34.

33 World electricity production increased from 8,042 billion kilowatt-hours in 1980 to 13,340 billion kilowatt-hours in 1997. In 1998, industrial electric consumption was 3.57 quadrillion Btu. If we consider past and predicted electricity use and its polluting effects in Britain and the US, this is what emerges. In 1993, it was estimated that fossil-fueled steam electric generation units released 5.8 million tons of nitrogen oxides, 1.9 billion tons of carbon dioxide (37 percent of all emissions), and 14.4 million tons of sulfur dioxide. Although sulfur emission caps have been placed on utility companies producing electricity, the projection of emissions by the year 2010 is estimated at 9 million tons per year of SO_2. US Department of Energy, *Electricity Generation and Environmental Externalities*, (Washington, DC, 1997), pp. 1–2.

34 In 1950, there were 70 million cars, trucks and buses on the world's roads. In 1994, there were 630 million. If growth continues at this rate, by 2025 there will be over 1 billion vehicles in use worldwide. World Resources Institute, United Nations Environment Programme, United Nations Development Programme and World Bank, *World Resources 1998–99: Environmental Changes and Human Health* (Oxford: Oxford University Press, 1998). See also "Proceed With Caution: Growth in the Global Motor Vehicle Fleet," <http://www.wri.org/wri/wr-98–99/wr98–toc.htm>, specific web page for statistics above: <http://www.wri.org/wri/trends/autos2.html>. The total number of passenger cars polluting the world in 1984 was 3,640,422,000, and it increased to 4,645,144,000 in 1993. The total number of commercial vehicles circulating in 1984 was 1,098,914,000, and it increased to 1,446,809,000 in 1993. In Europe the increase in the number of commercial vehicles does not diminish in the years of globalization; on the contrary, it increases. In the United Kingdom the number of commercial vehicles was 19,795,000 in 1984 and 24,520,000 in 1992; in France there were 30,720,000 commercial vehicles in 1984 and 40,360,000 in 1993; in Italy, from 21,821,000 commercial vehicles in 1984, the number increased to 27,630,000 in 1992. *Statistical Yearbook, Fortieth Issue* (New York: United Nations, 1995), p. 517.

35 The total number of oil tankers and ore and bulk carrier fleets, counted in thousand gross registered tons (100 cubic feet / 2.83 cubic meters) decreased between 1984 and 1993: from 15,874 to 4,117 in the

United Kingdom; from 8,945 to 4,252 in France; from 9,158 to 7,030 in Italy; from 7,005 to 1,752 in Spain. Ibid.

36 Derek M. Elsom, quoted in Highfield *et al.*, "Air pollution is 'health threat to city dwellers.'"

37 World Resources Institute *et al.*, *World Resources 1998–99*; "Acid Rain: Downpour in Asia?," <http://www.wri.org/wri/trends/acidrain.html>. Action designed to reduce the polluting impact of increased use of transportation has either been undermined by multilateral trade rules (to be discussed) or has introduced its own new pollutants into our environment. For instance, petrochemical companies are currently endeavoring to make gasoline burn more cleanly. Cleaner burning will not emit as many pollutants, goes the theory. However, cleaner fuel often means that efficiency may be lowered, because smooth engine performance requires that gasoline burn properly in the combustion chamber. In order to avoid damaging engines, other chemicals are added to the mix to make the fuel burn "efficiently"; yet these additives sometimes produce more pollutants. The story of TEL and lead is a case in point. Jack Doyle, *Crude Awakening* (Washington, DC: Friends of the Earth, 1994). The trouble with chemical solutions to chemical problems is that we learn of their negative effects only after the fact. As with lead, so it may be with the next generation of additives.

38 World Resources Institute *et al.*, *World Resources 1998–99*; "Proceed With Caution," <http://www.wri.org/wri/trends/autos2.html>.

39 As I will discuss in detail below, in the past few decades there have been massive and unprecedented migrations from rural to urban areas. Inevitably, the move to cities is accompanied by a serious degradation in air quality, if for no other reason than the increase in traffic alone. This first stage of speeding up, the urban move, is only exacerbated by the globalizing move, with its increase in heavy transportation. Devra L. Davis and Paulo H. N. Saldiva, *Urban Air Pollution Risks to Children: A Global Environmental Indicator* (Washington, DC: World Resources Institute, 1999), p. 1.

40 Energy Information Administration (EIA), *International Energy Outlook, 1999: Transportation Energy Use* (Congressional Information Service, Inc., 1999), p. 1.

41 World Resources Institute *et al.*, *World Resources 1998–99*; "Proceed With Caution," <http://www.wri.org/wri/trends/autos2.html>.

42 EIA, *International Energy Outlook, 1999*, p. 1.

43 It is acknowledged even in the WTO. International Institute for Sustainable Development Report on the WTO's High-Level Symposium on Trade and Environment, March 15–16, 1999, <www.wto.org/english/tratop _envir_e/sumhlenv.htm>.

44 World Bank (Environment Department) September 1992, cited in Lang and Hines, *The New Protectionism*, p. 46.

45 WTO Annual Report, 1998, p. 33.

46 Edward Goldsmith, "Global Trade and the Environment," *The Case Against the Global Economy*, ed. Mander and Goldsmith, p. 87. See also Lang and Hines, *The New Protectionism*, p. 62.

47 "While 50% of tonnage/km effected in the European Union involves journeys of more than 150 km, rail's market share continues to decline, falling from 32 to 15% between 1970 and 1995." "Opinion of the Committee of the Regions of 11 March 1999 on the Communication from the Commission to the Council, the European Parliament, the Economic and Social Committee and the Committee of the Regions: Intermodality and intermodal freight transport in the European Union," <www.cor.eu.int/CorAtWork/comm3/english/398–1999. html>, pp. 5–6.

48 A percentage extrapolation based on Hilary F. French, "Reconciling Trade and the Environment," *State of the World: Worldwatch Report* (New York: W.W. Norton, 1993), pp. 169–70.

49 Information on air pollution and lung disease in Third World countries is very uneven. Davis and Saldiva, *Urban Air Pollution Risks to Children*, p. 11. Even the World Resources Institute had trouble finding quality, standardized data from international collections (because there are no internationally accepted standards governing air-pollution measurements, let alone international environmental health indicators) for the brief one-year period they surveyed. In places such as Pakistan, Dhaka, Bangladesh, and Bangkok there was no reliable data available at all, while important information concerning air quality in Cairo, Istanbul, Teheran, Jakarta, Moscow and Manila was unattainable. If this is the case for a relatively short study, the difficulties for putting together the full picture on international air-pollution trends should be plainer.

50 EIA, *International Energy Outlook, 1999*, p. 6. Building new or better ports for the transportation of goods by sea destroys coastal habitats, by polluting or filling in wetlands and mangrove forests, while the bottoms of bays and lagoons are dredged to make them deeper for larger ships. Of course oil and chemical spills also increase. Karen Lehman and Al Krebs, "Control of the World's Food Supply," *The Case Against the Global Economy*, eds Mander and Goldsmith, p. 123.

51 After personal vehicles, air travel is the second most popular method of long-distance transportation. US Department of Energy (USDOE), *Transportation Statistics Annual Report 1998*, p. 10. The number of domestic trips by air increased from 275 million in 1980 to 538 million in 1996, while international enplanements in the US increased from 27 million to 55 million. Passenger miles more than doubled from 1980 to 1996. Ibid., p. 23. The increase in long-distance transportation is attributed to "income growth . . . increasing regional economic interdependency and lower airfares." Ibid., p. 10.

52 "In countries such as Venezuela, air freight transportation is expected to increase strongly, encouraged by the growing presence of foreign firms." US Department of Energy, *International Energy Outlook 1997* (Washington, DC: Congressional Information Service, 1998), p. 12. "Continued economic growth in the countries of developing Asia will require improved access to air travel." Ibid., p. 11.

53 Lang and Hines, *The New Protectionism*, p. 11.

54 European Environmental Agency, *Air Pollution in Europe* (Luxembourg:

Office for Official Publications of the European Communities, 1997), p. 25. According to the WTO Annual Report 1998, "trade growth has consistently outpaced overall economic growth for at least 250 years, except for a comparatively brief period from 1913 to 1950." This was the period between the world wars and it was due to the fall in trade, not an increase in production. Since then,

> the last 50 have seen trade expand faster than output by a signifi-cant margin, increasing the degree in which national economies rely on international trade in overall economic activity. On an annual average basis, merchandise exports grew by 6 percent in real terms from 1948 to 1997, compared to an annual average output growth of 3.7 percent.
> (WTO Annual Report, 1998, p. 33. See also chart IV.1.)

55 The US Department of Transportation measures increases in land transport by tons per mile, and increases in ocean transport by tons alone.
56 This analysis is based on figures provided by US Department of Transportation but the percentage extrapolation is mine. See United States Department of Transportation, Bureau of Transportation Statistics, *National Transportation Statistics 1998* (Washington, DC: 1998), <http://www.bts.gov/NTL/DOCS/473.html>.
57 Similarly, exports and imports conveyed by water went from 581,000,000 to 1,183,390,000 tons from 1980 to 1996, while total internal water transport went from 950,700,000 to 1,100,679,000 tons in the same period.
58 US Department of Energy, *Transportation Statistics Annual Report 1998*, p. 21.
59 The available international projections indicate that things will become worse, and indeed that they are. Ocean shipping, like rail transportation, is projected to decline compared to road and air trans-portation, and road and air transportation pollute more than transpor-tation by sea and rail. EIA, *International Energy Outlook, 1999*, p. 12.
60 See Chapter 10, below.
61 Economic Policy Institute, Institute for Policy Studies, International Labor Rights Fund, Public Citizen's Global Trade Watch, Sierra Club, and United States Business and Industrial Council Educational Foundation, *The Failed Experiment: NAFTA at Five Years* (1999), < http://www.citizen/pctrade/epijoint.html>.
62 "A Case of MAI Culpa," *Financial Times*, Oct 20, 1998, p. 21.
63 "If there is need for an agreement on FDI [foreign direct investment], the World Trade Organisation, with its broad membership and enforceable rules, looks a more suitable forum." Ibid.
64 "With luck, parts of MAI could become a blueprint for a global WTO accord on investment." "Finance and Economics: The Sinking of the MAI," *The Economist*, March 14, 1998, pp. 81–2.
65 "World Trade Group Picking up the Pieces from Seattle," *New York Times*, Dec 13, 1999, p. C2.

66 Ad Hoc Working Group on the MAI, *The MAI: Democracy for Sale?* (New York: Apex Press, n.d. [1998?]).
67 Clinton consistently sought "fast-track" negotiating authority for trade agreements. The trade agreements he wished to negotiate when he launched the "fast-track" campaign in September 1997 involved: "the inclusion of Chile in NAFTA; the Free Trade Agreement of the Americas (FTAA); a NAFTA-like pact encompassing the entire Western hemisphere except Cuba; and the Multi-lateral Agreement on Investment." Robert Collier, "NAFTA Labor Problems Haunt New Trade Debate," *San Francisco Chronicle*, Sept 10, 1997, p. 3A.
68 "The Sinking of the MAI,", *The Economist*.
69 The basic premise of the MAI negotiating text was that every investor in a contracting country should be treated in the same way. This concern with equal rights is reflected in provisions concerning National Treatment (NT), Most Favored Nation status (MFN) and Performance Requirements. The first two provisions were summed up thus: "Each Contracting Party shall accord to investors of another Contracting Party and to their investments, treatment no less favorable than the treatment it accords . . . to its own investors and their investments." *MAI Negotiating Text* (Paris: OECD, April 1998), Section III, 1 and 2, p. 13. Performance requirements were something else. Basically, these pertained to national legislation affecting the environment (investors were not required to maintain a given level of recycled or domestic content in manufacture) and labor (investors could not be made to hire "a given level of nationals"). Ibid., III (Performance Requirements), 1(b) and 1(j), pp. 19, 21.
70 The OECD's MAI was in fact far more than a pure investment agreement. Under the guise of regulating the global mess of finance capital (to which we return) the MAI as it stands would do far more. The MAI defined investment very broadly, and a note records that further work is required to determine the "appropriate treatment in the MAI [of] indirect investment, intellectual property, concessions, public debt and real estate". Ibid., Section II/2/viii p. 11 and *n*. Unless a country was protected by a prior exception clause in the GATT, the MAI would have permitted direct, unimpeded access by external "investors" to a contracting party's energy and natural resources, with no requirement that the "investor" contribute to the regeneration of those resources, including the reproduction of labor-power. The following note to the text spelled it out:

> There is general agreement that the MAI obligations . . . should apply fully to the granting of authorizations for the prospection, exploitation and production of minerals, including hydrocarbons [oil, coal, natural gas]. This is also valid for any rights granted in connection with the prospection, exploitation and production of any other natural resources. Views differ, however, as to whether additional language along the lines that proposed [sic] by one delegation or another formulation, need to be incorporated into the MAI to confirm this understanding.
>
> (Ibid., [Provisional?] Article VII, n91, p. 43)

71 "The Sinking of the MAI", *The Economist.*
72 The move was called for by the EU commission's vice-president Leon Brittan. (The document is available on the website of Corporate Europe Observatory: <http://www.xs4all.nl/~ceo/mai/eu/113invest. html>.) The EU paper echoes the MAI in calling for "a broad definition of investment"; "Most Favored Nation status" for signatories; "investment protection (expropriation compensation)"; "disciplines of performance requirements"; "Effective enforcement mechanisms"; and "free entry of key personnel," among other things. Given that this list specifically reiterates the MAI's liberal definition of investment, it is worth adding that the EU paper also clarifies the need for legal enforcement provisions by corporations against national governments. The paper writes that although State-to-State dispute settlement is part of the WTO "acquis,"

> In the investment field . . . there is the additional and distinct issue of the means available for foreign investors to enforce their rights in specific cases where they want to make a claim against the host country, typically for damages arising from a specific government action or decision.

But the EU paper wants the arbitration mechanism to be delicately considered. It would "have to reassure those WTO members (mainly developing countries) who are afraid of being 'taken to court' by big multinational companies."
73 French, "Reconciling Trade and the Environment," p. 174.
74 Demonstrating this was the overall aim of John Gray's *False Dawn* (New York: New Press, 1998).
75 French, "Reconciling Trade and the Environment," p. 177.
76 Ibid., p. 171.
77 S. Verhovek, "Pollution Puts People in Peril On the Border with Mexico," *New York Times*, July 4, 1998, p. A7.
78 The ban was on the neurotoxin MMT. It was lifted in summer 1998 after MMT's producer, US-based Ethyl Corporation, sued the government under NAFTA's provisions, claiming that the ban expropriated its future profits, and won $13 million in damages, coverage of legal costs, and a public declaration that MMT is "safe" – despite the views of the national environmental protection agency.
79 A week after this first settlement of a NAFTA case, the US-based PCB-treatment company S. D. Myers Inc. used the same NAFTA provision to sue the Canadian government for profits claimed lost during the national ban on export of PCB-contaminated waste between 1995 and 1997. Canada lifted the ban in 1997 after other US companies announced they would challenge it using NAFTA. Proceedings of the case, kept confidential under NAFTA rules, are ongoing. Council of Canadians, "Canada Slapped with NAFTA Lawsuit Against Another Environmental Law," <www.islandnet.com/ ~ncfs/maisite/fta-myer.htm>, Aug 24, 1998. A third claim against Canada was brought in January 1999 by Sun Belt, a US water importer,

but as of this writing details were not publicly available. Public Citizen Global Trade Watch, "NAFTA at Five: School of Real-Life Results," <www.citizen.org/pctrade/nafta/reports/5years.htm>, Jan 1, 1999, p. 22 *n*. 46.

80 The case is still being arbitrated, as are two similar lawsuits for the right to open hazardous waste disposal facilities, *Azinian et al.* v. *Mexico* and *Waste, Inc.* v. *Mexico.* Ibid., p. 22, *n*. 45.

81 Ibid., p. 22, *n*. 44.

82 Ibid., cf. Ahmed Rashid, *Taliban* (London: Pan Books, 2nd edn, 2001). Other players in the game are Turkey, Pakistan and Iran, who are also constructing communication links as the basis for future pipelines, and seeking to be "the preferred route of choice" for future ones, whether they head south or west or east. China also participates, desiring the energy necessary "to fuel its rapid economic growth" as well as political influence in one of its border regions.

83 Rashid, *Taliban*, p. 146.

84 Ted Rall, "The Great New Game: Oil Politics in Central Asia," *AlterNet*, Oct 11, 2001.

85 Ibid.

4 The war on the land, sea and other conditions of life

1 John Noble Wilford, "Ages-Old Icecap at North Pole is Now Liquid, Scientists Find," *New York Times*, Aug 19, 2000, p. 1, p. A12.

2 <http://www.turnpoint.org>.

3 The last twenty-five years have also seen a resurgence in other infectious diseases, which was not predicted. On the contrary: in 1975 prominent biologists and medics were claiming, with some justification, that infectious disease in the West had been effectively eliminated. The resurgence of TB in Britain is dramatic. In the US the incidence of TB "declining steadily since 1982, rose by 18 percent [in the 1990s]" (Harvard Working Group, "Globalization, Development, and the Spread of Disease," *The Case Against the Global Economy*, ed. Mander and Goldsmith (San Francisco, CA: Sierra Club Books, 1996), p.162). It is estimated that one-third of the world's population carries the infection. Certified cases of TB in England have also increased in the last ten years: from 4,960 cases in 1988 to 5,915 cases in 1998 (Communicable Disease Surveillance Center, <www.doh.gov.uk/HPSSS/TBL_A5.HTML>). Nevertheless, the Centre Européen pour la Santé declared that, between 1995 and 1997, the rate of TB cases decreased in Western Europe (except for Albania, the Czech Republic and Israel) and increased in the countries of the ex-Soviet Union by 7 percent. In total in the WHO region the rate increased by 4 percent. The highest rate of TB in Western Europe is in Portugal and Albania (50 or more cases per 100,000); in Spain (like Eastern Europe, 20–49 cases per 100,000); followed by the United Kingdom and Central Europe (Germany, France) with 10–19 cases out of 100,000); Italy, Denmark and the Netherlands have fewer than ten cases out of 100,000. (Euro TB, *Report on the Tubercolosis Cases Notified in 1997,*

September 1999, pp. 19–31.) The problem is not only the spreading of the disease but a growing inefficacy in the cure. "The *global spread* of drug resistant TB is occurring much more quickly than anticipated. In one year's time, drug resistant TB in Germany and Denmark recently increased by 50 percent." (WHO report 2000, p. 5: Statement by Dr. David L. Heymann, Executive Director for Communicable Diseases, WHO, before the Committee on International Relations, US House of Representatives, June 2000.) The World Health Organization now regards the disease as out of control, as "several strains of the bacterium now [resist...] all anti-TB drugs." (Ibid., p. 163.)

4 David W. Chen, "Lives That Were Changed Forever by the After-effects of a Mosquito Bite," *New York Times*, Aug 19, 2000, p. A13.

5 This response – pesticides – followed a pattern, which is in wide use in the South (see below). In many poor countries, DDT is still used to control the mosquitoes that carry malaria (a disease killing an estimated 2.7 million people each year), and DDT has its own toxic effects. Sheryl Gay Stolberg, "Effort to Ban DDT Faces a Fight Over its Use in Reducing Malaria," *New York Times*, Aug 29, 1999, pp. A1, A6. If the New York experience is any indication, the North will enter the same cycle, in which an increase in mosquito-borne diseases leads to more pesticides, and more of their negative effects on health, as all diseases carried by mosquitoes will be affected by climate change. Dr. Robert E. Shope of the Yale University School of Medicine quoted in Randolph E. Schmid, "Climate Changes Threaten to Spread Disease," *Associated Press*, Dec 5, 1989. "Temperature and precipitation changes may influence the geographic distribution and behavior of disease carrying vectors; this would influence the incidence of diseases spread by the vectors." In general the rate of development of parasites increases as the temperature increases and a rise in sea levels causes coastal flooding and hence more breeding areas. Despite the uncertainties, the general increase in mosquito transmission dynamics and prevalence is still evident. W. J. M. Martens, "Health Impacts of Climate Change and Ozone Depletion: An Ecoepidemiologic Modeling Approach," *Environmental Health Perspectives*, Vol. 106, Supp. 1 (1998).

6 Harvard Working Group, "Globalization, Development, and the Spread of Disease," p. 162.

7 Ibid. In most tropical countries, diseases such as malaria are the major cause of death. (It is currently estimated that 2,400 million people are at risk of contracting malaria, 1,800 million people are at risk for dengue and 600 million may contract schistomiasis. When global warming is taken into account the numbers increase by 720, 195, and 40 million people respectively.) In addition to malaria, cholera, salmonellosis, amoebiasis and various worm infestations are currently confined to tropical areas.

8 James Hansen *et al.*, "Global Warming in the Twenty-First Century: An Alternative Scenario," *Proceedings of the National Academy of Sciences USA*, Aug 29, 2000, p. 1.

9 Specifically, the emissions weighed 521,395 million metric tons in 1975. By 1995, they had increased to 931,781 million metric tons.

Similarly, in 1975 atmospheric CO_2 levels were 331.0 parts per million (ppm); in 1995 they were 360.9 ppm. World Resources Institute, "Atmosphere and Climate Data Tables," *World Resources: A Guide to the Global Environment, 1998–1999* (New York and Oxford: Oxford University Press, 1998), Data Table 16.3, p. 347.

10 Ibid., Data Table 16.4, p. 349.

11 Andrew C. Revkin, "Study Proposes New Strategy to Stem Global Warming," *New York Times*, Aug 19, 2000, p. A12. The strategy, proposed by NASA scientist James Hansen, is to cut back on other greenhouse gases, methane and nitrous oxide, which takes the heat off fossil-fuel production.

12 Ibid., quoting Dr. Robert T. Watson, chair of the UN Intergovernmental Panel on Climate Change.

13 Seth Dunn, "Carbon Emissions Fall Again," *Vital Signs 2000: The Environmental Trends that are Shaping our Future*, ed. Lester R. Brown, Michael Renner, and Brian Halweil (New York and London: W.W. Norton, 2000), pp. 60–7 (online version at <www.worldwatch. org>).

14 Dunn, "Carbon Emissions Fall Again," p. 159, *n*. 1. The text for this note reads: "Figure for 1999 is a preliminary Worldwatch estimate based on BP Amoco, *BP Amoco Statistical Review of World Energy 1999* (London: Group Media and Publications, June 1999), on US Department of Energy (DOE), Energy Information Administration (EIA), *Monthly Energy Review January 2000* (Washington DC, 2000), on DOE, EIA, *International Energy Outlook 1999* (Washington DC, March 1999), on PlanEcon, Inc., *PlanEcon Energy Outlook* (Washington DC, October 1999), on European Commission (EC), *Energy in Europe: 1999 Annual Energy Review*, Special Issue (Brussels, January 2000), on Eurogas, "Natural Gas Consumption in Western Europe Continued its Growth in 1999" (Brussels, February 2000), on International Monetary Fund (IMF), *World Economic Outlook* (Washington DC, October 1999) and on Jonathan E. Sinton and David G. Fridley, "What Goes Up: Recent Trends in China's Energy Consumption" (Berkeley, CA: Lawrence Berkeley National Laboratory, 9 December 1999); figures for 1950–98 are from emissions data (including gas flaring, but excluding cement production) from G. Marland *et al.*, "Global, Regional, and National Fossil Fuel CO_2 Emissions", in *Trends: A Compendium of Data on Global Change* (Oak Ridge, TN: Carbon Dioxide Information Analysis Center, Oak Ridge National Laboratory, DOE, March 1999)." It is difficult to see what, in any of the studies cited in the first part of the note, supports the notion that emissions shrank in 1999, as all of them (even BP Amoco) pertain to 1998! However, the 1999 figure is an *estimate* (although what it is based on is unclear). More egregious is the figure for 1998. The sole source cited for this is the highly reputable CDIAC's Marland *et al.* study. But, as I noted in the text, Marland *et al.*'s emissions figures go only to 1996. C. D. Keeling and his team at the California Scripps Oceanography Institution, recently honoured by (then Vice-President) Gore for forty years of work tracking CO_2 emissions, have found an increase in the 1998 and 1999 atmospheric levels, and found

moreover that 1998 has the highest concentrations of carbon dioxide so far. The fact is that there is no real evidence for a drop in emissions, and very real evidence for an increase in levels. The fact too is that the reliable record of emissions so far (to 1996) shows that they have increased dramatically in the last thirty years, and the atmospheric levels have increased accordingly. (<http://cdiac.esd.ornl.gov/ftp/ maunaloa.co2>. Figures for 1998 and 1999 from the main tabulator of emissions related to atmosphere and climate change, the Carbon Dioxide Information Analysis Center (CDIAC), are not yet available.)

15 EPA, "Protection of the Ozone Layer," *Environmental Indicators* (October 1995).

16

> Mobile air conditioning accounted for 56,500 metric tons of CFCs – 28 percent of the CFCs used for refrigeration in the United States, or about 13 per cent of total production. Thus, approximately 1 out of every 8 pounds of CFCs manufactured in the US is used, and emitted, by motor vehicles.
>
> (Jeremy Leggett (ed.), *Global Warming: The Greenpeace Report* (Oxford: Oxford University Press, 1990), p. 261)

17 Lynn Mortensen (ed.), *Global Change Education Resource Guide* (Washington, DC: National Oceanic and Atmospheric Administration, 1996).

18 Leggett, *Global Warming*, p. 269.

19 The direct relationship between ozone depletion and skin cancer is hard to elucidate because of the long incubation time exhibited by skin cancer. Sheila Hoar Zahm and Susan S. Devesa, "Childhood Cancer: Overview of Incidence Trends and Environmental Carcinogens," *Environmental Health Perspectives*, Vol. 103, Supp. 6, pp. 177–84.

20 Ultraviolet radiation on skin has an immunosuppressive effect. "It is possible that susceptibility to important skin infections such as leishmaniasis or leprosy might be increased by greater exposure to ultraviolet light because of the expression of these diseases depends on the cell-mediated immune response." Leggett, *Global Warming*, p. 156. Dr. Raymond Daynes of the University of Utah stated in an article from the *Associated Press*: "Ultraviolet radiation, already known to cause skin cancer, also has a major effect in reducing the response of the human immune system" (Dec 5, 1989).

21 Posters and ad campaigns telling us how to protect ourselves from dangerous radiation are prevalent. In addition, entirely new products are being marketed, for example, arm shields to cover the exposed left arm while one is driving.

22 Schmid, "Climate Changes Threaten to Spread Disease."

23 In 1994, the state of Florida did draw 90 percent of its water from underground sources, while sixty of its seventy-six tank farms were contaminating the ground water. Illinois, South Carolina, Texas, New Jersey, North Carolina, Michigan, Oklahoma, Arkansas, Indiana, Kentucky, Idaho, Nevada, California, South Dakota, Wyoming, Ohio, Pennsylvania and Virginia are only some of the US states where

documented instances of oil tank leakage have occurred. Jack Doyle, *Crude Awakening* (Washington, DC: Friends of the Earth, 1994).

24 In addition, despite efforts to regulate it, lead from diesel fuel remains a water pollutant currently affecting human health. While lead emissions have declined about 97 percent from 1975 (US Department of Transportation, Bureau of Transportation Statistics, *Transportation Statistics Annual Report 1998*, BTS98-S-01 (Washington, DC, 1998), p. 120, Figure 4–10), it is an element whose molecules lie heavy in water. Atmospheric deposition occurs when air pollutants settle, or are precipitated, on land or water. Any chemical emitted into the air (including PCBs, lead, lindane, dioxins and different forms of nitrogen) can potentially become part of the water-pollution problem. United States Environmental Protection Agency, <http://www.epa.gov/owow/oceans/airdep/air1.html>. Also in air, where about 96 percent is emitted by aircraft (US Department of Transportation, *Transportation Statistics*, p. 119). The EU has regulations limiting lead concentrations in water; however, the Medical Research Council has concluded that there is no evidence for a safe level of lead. S. Zinser, "So Do You Really Know What is in This: Good Health," *Daily Mail* Dec 14, 1999, p. 51). This indicates that, currently, there is a certain amount of lead in water and that, regardless of the level, this lead may pose a threat to health. Lead is recognized as a widespread toxicant causing impairment of brain development and function in infants and children, even at low levels. Hypertension has also been associated with elevated levels of lead in the human body. Committee of the Environmental and Occupational Health Assembly of the American Thoracic Society, *American Journal of Critical Care Medicine*, Vol. 153 (1996), p. 6.

25 David Younkman, "Prepared Testimony of David Younkman, Executive Director American Oceans Campaign." *Federal News Service*, Aug 6, 1998. In this case, there is no doubt that the cause is direct because of all the bacteria that live in the pig's excrement. They can also decimate the fish populations in the rivers, streams and other bodies of water they enter. The Sierra Club has accused big hog farms of polluting 35,000 miles of rivers and streams in 22 US states (K. Myers, *New York Times*, Aug 16, 1998). Pig farms can produce as much raw sewage as middle-sized cities, and lack water treatment plants. Premium Standard is the US's third largest pork producer, with 550,000 hogs kept in close quarters at a time, and producing 600 million gallons of hog manure a year. This enormous farm is governed by "forgiving" EPA rules that pertain to smaller farms; however, currently a plan is in place to enact stricter pollution limits similar to those regulating industrial factories. According to the EPA, two-thirds of the 6,600 largest hog-producing operations lack the permits governing pollution discharges. Yet, the majority of the permits that do exist are inadequate against the pollution produced when the manure is spread on land (the main strategy for its disposal).

26 D. Johnson, "Pork Producer Settles Suit as Pollution Rules Tighten," *New York Times*, Aug 16, 1999, p. A12. Human waste also threatens the

world's waterways. Cuidad Juarez, across the Rio Grande River from El Paso, produces 75 million gallons of raw sewage per year, and has no sewage treatment plant. The waste flows from irrigation ditches into the Rio Grande, which is the prime source of water for much of Mexico.

27 Theo Colborn, Diane Dumanoski, and John Peterson Myers, *Our Stolen Future: Are We Threatening Our Fertility, Intelligence, and Survival? A Scientific Detective Story* (New York: Plume, 1997), p. 168.

28 Zinser, "So Do You Really Know What is in This," p. 30.

29 Lester R. Brown, "A New Era Unfolds," *State of the World* (New York: W.W. Norton, 1993), p. 15.

30 Colborn *et al.*, *Our Stolen Future*, p. 204.

31 Extension Toxicology Network, *DDT: Pesticide Information Profile*, a pesticide information project of cooperative extension offices of Cornell University, Michigan State University, Oregon State University, and University of California at Davis, <http://pmep.cce.cornell.edu/profiles/extoxnet/carbaryl-dicrotophos/ddt-ext.html>.

32 World Wildlife Fund, "WWF's Efforts to Phase Out DDT," *Global Toxics: Program Areas*, 2000, <http://www.worldwildlife.org/toxics/progareas/pop/ddt.htm>.

33 Ninety-six tons of DDT were exported by the US in 1991, along with 454 tons of other pesticides no longer in use in that country. Colborn *et al.*, *Our Stolen Future*, p. 138). Bhutan, Bolivia, Ethiopia, Guinea, India, Japan, Kenya, Malaysia, Mauritania, Mexico, Nepal, the Philippines, Sri Lanka, Sudan, Switzerland, Tanzania, Thailand, Venezuela, and Vietnam all allow DDT to be imported, and an estimated 1.36 million tons of DDT is cumulatively produced worldwide. World Wildlife Fund, "WWF's Efforts to Phase Out DDT." In the European Union, DDT is allowed to be imported for uses other than plant protection, provided one has written authorization, in Belgium, Denmark, France, Italy, the Netherlands and Spain. Even though DDT is officially banned for agricultural use in most of the countries that import it, India allows it to be used "under special circumstances" for agriculture. As of September, 1999, in Japan, permission from the Minister of International Trade and Industry is required for uses *other* than agricultural chemical, but the sale for agricultural use is prohibited. Rotterdam Convention, *Prior Informed Consent: Procedure for Certain Hazardous Chemicals and Pesticides in International Trade*, <http://www.fao.org/pic/SubstanceDecisions.asp?CasNumreq=50293>. While it was banned in the US in 1992, that year US pesticide manufacturers reported shipping more than 300 tons of DDT to Peru. At the same time almost 2,000 tons of other pesticides banned for domestic use were exported to developing countries; by 1994 this number had increased by 467 percent. (Janet Raloff, "The Pesticide Shuffle," *Science News*, March 16, 1996.) Despite DDT's relatively early ban in the United States, it is still present in that country as well. Its effects are difficult to eradicate because DDT has a long life, and can travel great distances. For example, black-footed albatrosses on Midway Island (3,100 miles from Los Angeles and 2,400 miles from

Tokyo) carry DDT in their bodies, even though there are no known uses of the chemical on the island. Since its ban in 1972, concentrations of DDT in the US have decreased ovrall. However, the rate of decrease in the Great Lakes region has slowed because other countries still use DDT; deposition from rainfall and the connectedness of water tables all over the world spread it to regions where it is no longer used. In fact, in an analysis of tree bark from ninety locations worldwide, DDT was found in measurable amounts at every testing site. National Research Council, *Hormonally Active Agents in the Environment* (Washington, DC: National Academy Press, 1999), p. 59. Also at <http://www.nap.edu/openbook/0309064198/htm/56.html>.
34 Ibid.
35 E. Goldsmith, "Global Trade and the Environment," *The Case Against the Global Economy*, ed. Jerry Mander and Edward Goldsmith (San Francisco, CA: Sierra Club Books, 1996), p. 90. With trade agreements increasing and countries being sued for erecting or sustaining nontariff barriers to trade, the United States may have to lower its standards, or be penalized in the world market because of GATT illegality. "In the free-for-all of the Global Economy no country can strengthen environmental regulations that increase corporate costs without putting itself at a 'comparative disadvantage' vis-à-vis its competitors and running afoul of GATT." Ibid., p. 87.
36 Barbara Robson, "A Chemical Imbalance: Estrogen-mimicking Chemicals in the Environment are being Linked to Reproductive Failure, Breast Cancer and Damaged DNA," *Nature Canada*, Vol. 26, No. 1 (1997), pp. 29–33.
37 Organochlorines, such as DDT and PCB, may have the ability to mimic estrogen in the human body. This may be why the reproductive systems in birds were so effected by DDT. Mary S. Wolff and Ainsley Weston, "Breast Cancer Risk and Environmental Exposures," *Environmental Health Perspectives*, Vol. 105, Supp. 4 (1997), p. 893. Breast cancer rates have also increased with pesticide and PCB residues in human tissues since 1940. See Zillah Eisenstein, *Manmade Breast Cancer* (Ithaca, NY: Cornell University Press, 2001).
38 Colborn *et al.*, *Our Stolen Future*, p. 18.
39 William Bryce, "Review of Biological Processes", cited in A. L. Gittelman, *Beyond Probiotics* (New Canaan, CT: Keats Publishing Inc., 1998), p. 18.
40 Steve Kroll-Smith and H. Hugh Floyd, *Bodies in Protest: Environmental Illness and the Struggle over Medical Knowledge* (New York and London: New York University Press, 1997). Kroll-Smith and Floyd argue that the US economy, at least, is too dependent upon chemical use to put serious limits, not to mention halts, to such use out of concern for human health.
41 Jeremy Rifkin, *Entropy: A New World View* (New York: Viking Press, 1980).
42 HRH the Prince of Wales, "Seeds of Disaster," *Daily Telegraph*, June 8, 1998, p. 16.
43 Ibid.

44 Jeremy Rifkin, "New Technology and the End of Jobs," *The Case Against the Global Economy*, eds Jerry Mander and Edward Goldsmith (San Francisco, CA: Sierra Club Books, 1996), pp. 110–11.
45 Jeremy Rifkin, *The Biotech Century* (New York: Putnam, 1999), p. 16.
46 Colin Tudge, "Why We Don't Need GM Foods," *New Statesman*, Feb 19, 1999, pp. 9–10.
47 Approximately three-quarters of prescription drugs based on plants now in use "were derived from drugs used in indigenous medicine" (Rifkin, *The Biotech Century*, p. 49). There is an excellent discussion in Shiva of the pirating of indigenous knowledge, where the genes of plants long known for their healing (or sweetening) properties have been patented by First World biotech corporations. Vandana Shiva, *Biopiracy: The Plunder of Nature and Knowledge* (Boston, MA: South End Press, 1997). Rifkin adds that efforts to establish royalty arrangements reimbursing the Third World countries whose knowledge has been appropriated have been met with the claim that such arrangements "would undermine research efforts to increase world food production". Rifkin, *The Biotech Century*, p. 53.
48 Researchers in Nebraska found that people with a severe allergy to Brazil nuts are also allergic to soybeans engineered with Brazil-nut DNA.
49 Toxic substances have been observed in genetically modified yeast, bacteria, plants and animals. These toxins were unexpected consequences of the genetic alterations, and were not detected until a major health hazard arose. Quoting Michael Antoniou, <http://www.safe-food.org/-issue/scientists.html>. In 1989, a genetically engineered brand of dietary supplement killed thirty-seven Americans and disabled 5,000 other people. It is believed that the bacteria became contaminated during the recombination process. Ronnie Cummins, "Hazards of Genetically Engineered Foods and Crops," 1999, <http://www.organicconsumers.org> and <http://www.turnpoint.org>.
50 Laura Tangly, "How Safe is Genetically Modified Food," *U.S. News and World Report*, July 26, 1999, p. 40.
51 Mark Nichols, "Tampering with the Natural Order," *Maclean's*, May 17, 1999, pp. 59–60. Ecological threats do not only begin at the bottom of the food chain. When organisms are genetically engineered with traits that make them grow faster and larger, evolution will favor them over normal organisms competing for the same niche.
52 The extent of government support can be seen most clearly in government policy toward GM foods. The US Food and Drug Administration considers most GM foods safe, does not require extensive testing for long-term impacts in many cases, and does not require labeling of most GM foods.

> The FDA believes that the new techniques are extensions at the molecular level of traditional methods and will be used to achieve the same goals as pursued with traditional plant breeding. The agency is not aware of any information showing that foods derived by these new methods differ from other foods in any meaningful or uniform way, or that, as a class, foods developed by the new

techniques present any different or greater safety concern than foods developed by traditional plant breeding. For this reason, the agency does not believe that the method of development of a new plant variety (including the use of new techniques including recombinant DNA techniques) is normally material information within the meaning of [the law regulating such labeling] and would not usually be required to be disclosed in labeling for the food.

(US Food and Drug Administration, Department of Health and Human Services, "Statement of Policy: Foods Derived From New Plant Varieties," *Federal Register*, Notices, May 29, 1992, 57.104, p. 22991)

53 The assessment is Richard Lacey's. Lacey argues that there is no valid nutritional or public interest reason for the introduction of genetically engineered foods. <http://www.safe-food.org/-issue/scientists.html>.

54 Kenny Bruno, "Say it Ain't Soy, Monsanto," *Multinational Monitor*, Vol. 18, Nos. 1–2 (1997), p. 27.

55 The best-known example is the effect on monarch butterflies.

56 Joseph Cummings, <http://www.safe-food.org/-issue/scientists.html>.

57 George Wald, <http://www.safe-food.org/-issue/scientists.html>. There are currently four different types of tomatoes approved for sale that contain another species' genes resulting in delayed ripening. "The Gene Exchange," <http://www.purefood.org/ge/ucs98gefood.cmf>.

58 Edward Goldsmith, "Global Trade and the Environment," *The Case Against the Global Economy*, p. 87.

59 Colborn *et al.*, *Our Stolen Future*, p. 133.

60 <http://www.econ.ag.gov/Briefing/forces/>.

61 Hilary F. French, "Reconciling Trade and the Environment," *State of the World* (New York: W.W. Norton, 1993), p. 166.

62 Kristen Lyons, "Agro-Industrialization and Social Change within the Australian Context: A Case Study of the Fast Food Industry," *Globalization and Agri-Food Restructuring: Perspectives from the Australasia Region*, ed. David Burch *et al.* (Aldershot: Avebury, 1996), p. 245.

63 The number of farms is projected to reach 1.6 from 1.7 million by 2000. <http://www.econ.ag.gov/Briefing/forces/>.

64 Forces shaping US Agriculture, <http://www.econ.ag.gov/Briefing/forces/>.

65 Lyons, "Agro-Industrialization and Social Change," p. 241.

66 Karen Lehman and Al Krebs, "Control of the World's Food Supply," *The Case Against the Global Economy*, ed. Jerry Mander and Edward Goldsmith, p. 123.

67 Lyons, "Agro-Industrialization and Social Change," p. 244.

68 French, "Reconciling Trade and the Environment," p. 163.

69 Brown, "A New Era Unfolds," p. 11.

70 Ibid., p. 12.

71 Karl Marx, *Theories of Surplus Value*, *Capital*, Vol. 3. For more detail, see the theoretical discussion in Chapters 9 and 10.

72 Brown, "A New Era Unfolds," pp. 11–12.

73 Ibid., p. 5.

5 Health cuts and corporate wealth

1 Cancer is now regarded as a chronic as well as a potential terminal disease: cancer is increasingly something to be lived with over time, and therefore chronic. The difference between an illness and a disease is this:

> To have a disease is to be officially certified as unable to work at full capacity, or perhaps at all . . . Diseases, in one important sense, are a rhetoric of entitlement. [Its use] pressures people and organizations to relieve a person from some (if not all) social responsibilities.

Illness on the other hand is the term people tend to use for themselves. It "is not meant to signal a theory of etiology, pathophysiology, or treatment." Steve Kroll-Smith and H. Hugh Floyd, *Bodies in Protest: Environmental Illness and the Struggle over Medical Knowledge* (New York and London: New York University Press, 1997), pp. 55–6.

2 Canada, with a far more evolved welfare state than we find in the US, provides a recent illustration. Whether healthcare spending is increasing in real terms depends on two things: funding and the incidence of illness. The incidence is increasing, but there is not a proportional increase in the existing allocation. Indeed, funding appears to have been cut! See "PM Rejects Health-Care Pleas: Provinces Should be Spending More Instead of Cutting Taxes, Chrétien Says," *Globe and Mail*, April 1, 2000, p. A1 and p. A15. Ontario health minister Elizabeth Witmer's government has been publicly attacking Ottawa over cuts to healthcare funding.

3 The contrast between these cuts and third-way policy on free trade shows just how thoroughly the third way follows new right policies in serving a common multinational cause, one which is seeking ever more disciples in Europe.

4 For an excellent critique of dependency as a concept and its recent use, see Nancy Fraser and Linda Gordon, *Decoding "Dependency": Inscriptions of Power in a Keyword of the Welfare State* (Evanston, IL: Northwestern University Press, 1991).

5 I will be referring principally to: OECD, *Social and Health Policies in OECD Countries: A Survey of Current Programmes and Recent Developments* (Paris: OECD, Directorate for Education, Employment, Labour and Social Affairs, 1998).

6 "Womb to Tomb: Welfare State in Nordic Countries," *The Economist*, Nov 5, 1994, p. N11.

7 Bill Powell, "Days of Rage in Paris: Citizens Protest Austerity Measures Throughout Europe," *Newsweek*, Dec 11, 1995, p. 51.

8 In a paper for the International Labour Organization, Michael Cichon challenges the widely accepted view that most capitalist welfare states are simply not economically affordable and must scale back to a leaner version approximating the US model. Cichon argues that "there are good reasons to believe that high levels of social spending in Europe

are not only financially sustainable but might even be economically efficient since they help in sustaining high levels of productivity and thus reduce the number of hours that European populations have to work." Cichon compares the US model to the European model and finds that European workers are more productive and that their wages are higher. He finds no significant difference in the redistributive effect of the two models, except that Europe's model has been able to eradicate poverty to a much greater degree than that of the US. The question then becomes: why is the political perception so inconsistent with these realities? Why are so many people so convinced that the European model welfare state is not affordable? In part, the answer lies in the reduction in corporate taxation. Michael Cichon, "The European Welfare States at the Crossroads," Issues in Social Protection, Discussion Paper no. 3, Social Security Department, International Labour Office (Geneva: International Labour Office, 1997).

9 Greg M. Olsen, "Half Empty or Half Full? The Swedish Welfare State in Transition," *Canadian Review of Sociology and Anthropology*, Vol. 39, No. 2 (1999), pp. 241–67.

10 John Gray, *False Dawn: The Delusions of Global Capitalism* (New York: New Press, 1998); see also George Soros, *The Crisis of Global Capitalism* (New York: Public Affairs, 1998).

11 Most of our discussion of cuts in social expenditures is drawn from the OECD's report on the programs and recent changes in social and health policies in OECD countries. This report offers a very comprehensive look at social welfare spending in a large number of North American, Western and Eastern European, and Asian nations. OECD, *Social and Health Policies*, p. 83.

12 Ibid., p. 84. Moves toward universal coverage in OECD member countries generally involved assistance targeted toward a particular population which currently receives inadequate or no health coverage, or efforts to reduce the impacts of cost-cutting measures on the poorest members of the country. In Australia, programs were introduced to include Aborigines in health insurance programs, as well as to reach out to rural areas to increase access to healthcare. Canada has introduced a prenatal nutrition initiative for Aboriginal children, as well as a women's health initiative. Norway and Denmark have focused on providing better services for the mentally ill. The US in 1997 implemented a five-year program to try to increase coverage for children under Medicaid, as 10 million children in the US were uninsured. Hoping to minimize the impact of the many cost-cutting measures it was implementing in its health program, Germany in 1997 introduced a cap on the amount an individual can be asked to pay out in co-payments – 2 percent of gross income (1 percent of gross income for people with chronic diseases). Italy is working to guarantee access to prescription payment exemptions for the poorest populations and is considering altering government health coverage so that it pays more in benefits to the poorest individuals. Similarly, the UK is examining inequalities in the way its population is covered. But these targeted moves are not moves toward universal health coverage. In fact, *contra*

the OECD's universal claim, Switzerland seems to be the only Western
welfare state which is working toward what is traditionally understood
by "universal coverage." In 1996, it introduced a compulsory insurance
system, which both expands benefits and better ensures access to
benefits. OECD, *Social and Health Policies, Annex: Tables and Charts*,
pp. 142–3.

13 OECD, *Social and Health Policies*, pp. 83–4. Growing costs are
explained additionally as due to: "increased standard of living,
increased productivity, and increased expectations of the population,"
as well as doctors' "variable practice patterns." This claim, however, is
not backed up with any evidence of such a shift. "Higher standards and
expectations" could as well be described as a response to increased
stress and anxiety. "Variable practice patterns" refers to the difficulty
of knowing which resources doctors should and do use when treating
patients. In other words, doctors treat different health concerns
differently, and they may not treat them in the best or least wasteful
manner. Ibid., p. 84.

14 This is a significant question for future research. What percentage of
health spending on new technologies goes to subsidizing medical
corporations rather than to healthcare services? For that matter,
funding for university research is increasingly corporate-oriented:
universities rely more on corporate funding as education funding from
the state is reduced along with healthcare.

15 Catherine Hoffman, "Persons with Chronic Conditions: their
Prevalence and Costs," *Journal of the American Medical Association*,
Nov 13, 1996, pp. 1474 and 1476.

16 Ibid., 1476. The other 15 percent of noninstitutionalized persons with
chronic illnesses are persons aged nought to seventeen.

17 Kenneth G. Manton, Larry Corder, and Eric Stallard, "Chronic
Disability Trends in Elderly United States Populations: 1982–1994,"
*Proceedings of the National Academy of Sciences of the United States of
America*, vol. 94 (1997), p. 2594.

18 S. Jacobzone, E. Cambois, E. Chaplain, and J. M. Robine, *The Health
of Older Persons in OECD Countries: Is it Improving Fast Enough to
Compensate for Population Aging?* (Paris: OECD, 1998), pp. 16, 61–3.

19 Ibid., pp. 24–5 and 59–60.

20 Dean Baker and Mark Weisbrot, *Social Security: The Phony Crisis*
(Chicago and London: University of Chicago Press, 1999), Table 3.1,
p. 58.

21 Hoffman, "Persons with Chronic Conditions," p. 1477.

22 Ibid., p. 1478. Following up on data published in *JAMA* by Short and
Banthin which estimated that "29 million nonelderly people with private
health insurance are at risk of being underinsured, defined as a function of
a family's risk of incurring high out-of-pocket costs for medical
services relative to their family income," the researchers looked at the
costs incurred by people with chronic disease to estimate the likelihood of their being underinsured (by Short and Banthin's definition).

23 At this point we are unable to determine whether or not these facts are
replicated throughout the West and Japan, although the OECD is

currently undertaking a study on pharmaceutical costs across their member states.

24 They have also adopted the US language of "service" and "providers," language which replaces a vocabulary of professional care and commitment ("patients and practitioners") with one of exchange relations.

25 OECD, *Annex to Social and Health Policies*, pp. 111–18.

26 Ibid., p. 113.

27 This discriminatory move against residents in Australia without citizenship anticipated similar moves in the United States a year later.

28 OECD, *Annex to Social and Health Policies*, pp. 90, 111.

29 Ibid., pp. 111–18. The OECD report does not always provide dates for the various reforms it documents, though it is a report on recent developments and most of these reforms where implemented in the ten years before 1998. I include dates wherever the information is available from the OECD report.

30 As chronic illnesses such as heart disease, arteriosclerosis, hypertension, diabetes, cancer, arthritis, emphysema, gall bladder disease, rheumatism, heart attack and stroke become the most prevalent diseases and leading causes of death in the United States (at the very least), researchers have found a major shift toward reliance on prescription drugs for healthcare. They find the prescription drug expenditures "vary directly with chronic conditions." Elderly people with three or more chronic conditions spent 16 percent more on drugs than elderly people with no chronic conditions; for nonelderly people, the difference was 20 percent. Curt Mueller, Claudia Schur and Joan O'Connell, "Prescription Drug Spending: The Impact of Age and Chronic Disease Status," *American Journal of Public Health*, Vol. 87, No. 10 (1997), pp. 1626, 1628. This is to be expected in an economy which causes more chronic illness at the same time that it spends money on medical technology that prolongs life. But those whose lives are prolonged by technology cannot be those that suffer from chronic illnesses. Life-prolonging technology is most relevant to those between the ages of sixty to eighty years. As we have seen, 60 percent of chronic illnesses occur in working-age adults.

31 Sandra Coney, "New Zealand Dismantles its Health and Welfare System," *The Lancet*, Jan 12, 1991, p. 102.

32 Ibid. As Jane Kelsey has shown, New Zealand was transformed from a model welfare state to a neoliberal or monetarist state in a few years from 1984 to 1991. Labor or social democratic governments were once again the initiators of policies reversing human needs. Jane Kelsey, *Economic Fundamentalism* (London and Easthaven, CT: Pluto Press, 1995).

33 OECD, *Annex to Social and Health Policies*, p. 111.

34 OECD, *Social and Health Policies*, p. 93.

35 Ibid., p. 96.

36 Ibid.

37 Robert Pear, "Annual Spending on Medicare Dips for the First Time," *New York Times*, Nov 14, 1999, p. 1.

38 OECD, *Social and Health Policies*, p. 92.

39 Ibid., p. 91.
40 Gabrielle Fagan, "Winston Renews Attack Over Health Policy", *Press Association Newsfile*, Feb 2, 2000. Winston added: "our figures for cancer treatment are among the worst in Europe." Furthermore, in his interview with the *New Statesman*, Winston argued that NHS policies will make the UK "inferior on vital areas such as heart disease and cancer compared to our less well-off neighbours." Cardiovascular disease and cancers are two of the most prevalent chronic diseases in Western welfare states. Robert Winston, interview with Mary Riddell, *New Statesman*, Jan 17, 2000.
41 Ibid.
42 OECD, *New Directions in Health Care Policy*, Health Policy Studies No. 7, Paris, 1995 quoted in OECD, *Social and Health Policies*, p. 90.
43 OECD, *Social and Health Policies*, p. 91. Other countries working on decreased hospital stays include Austria, Hungary, Finland, Poland and Luxembourg.
44 Belgium, Hungary, Korea, Luxembourg, Poland and Turkey are the only exceptions to this trend within the OECD. OECD, *Annex to Social and Health Policies*, pp. 111–18.
45 Ibid., p. 118.
46 Figures from the OECD on spending as a percentage of GNP for recent years – 1999 and 2000 – are not yet available. It may very well be that health spending as a percentage of GDP declined in the US in 1999. The significant point is that spending was increasing apparently for OECD countries between 1985 and 1991 – but for a *total* increase of 1 percent on average. Between 1992 and 1995, healthcare expenditures as a share of GDP did not increase at all but stayed "stable" (when looking both at the G7 and at the overall OECD average).
47 Robert Samuelson, "We Cannot Be 'Reassured'," *Newsweek*, Oct 4, 1999, p. 59. Samuelson warns "that, by 2030, the projected ratio of workers to Social Security beneficiaries will drop from today's roughly 3–1 to about 2–1."
48 OECD, *Social and Health Policies*, p. 64.
49 Ibid., p. 75.
50 Ibid., p. 77.
51 OECD, *Annex to Social and Health Policies*, pp. 83–9.
52 Ibid., pp. 90–6. In many, but not all, cases the increases are the result of raising the pensionable age for women by bringing it up to the same age as men. When I say "will raise the pensionable age" I refer to legislation which sets a future date for the rise in the pensionable age.
53 I return to unemployment in the next chapter.
54 The following countries have all tightened eligibility requirements for disability benefits: Australia (1991), Canada (1994–5), Greece (1998), the Netherlands (1993), Norway (1990–1), the United Kingdom (1995–6) and the United States. New Zealand tightened eligibility requirements for sick pay in 1995–6. OECD, *Annex to Social and Health Policies*, pp. 35–9 and 41.
55 OECD, *Social and Health Policies*, p. 53.
56 Ibid., p. 57.

57 Ibid., p. 56.

58 Introducing the option of suicide makes it easier to ignore underlying, treatable conditions of depression or other options which *do* make it easier to live with terminal illnesses. See, for example, Wesley J. Smith, *Forced Exit: The Slippery Slope from Assisted Suicide to Legalized Murder* (New York: Times Books, 1997), pp. 224–52. In addition, "assisted suicide" is not as revolutionary as it looks. The Catholic church condemns the prolongation of life by "extraordinary or disproportionate means." National Conference of Catholic Bishops (USA), "Ethical and Religious Directives for Catholic Health Care Services, Part Five, Issues in Care for the Dying," National Conference of Catholic Bishops, November 1994, Directive 57.

59 Jennifer M. Scherer and Rita J. Simon, *Euthanasia and the Right to Die: A Comparative View* (Lanham, MD, Boulder, CO, New York and Oxford: Rowman & Littlefield Publishers, 1999), pp. 21–2. Smith, *Forced Exit*, pp. 147–58.

60 Surely we should be looking at the technology involved in extraordinary means in a lot more detail. A patient would need to be just as rational to request extraordinary means *not* to be used as he or she would need to be to request assisted suicide. But extraordinary means offer less potential for abuse. The significant exception, or complicating case, is having to live in pain, but medically the instances involving the prolongation of life in a way that involves the prolongation of pain are extremely rare.

61 Smith, *Forced Exit*.

6 Education and the cost of children

1 Figures for the countries above are for the following years: Australia (1975–94), Canada (1975–94), Denmark (1983–94), Finland (1986–95), Germany (1984–94), Italy (1984–93), Japan (1984–94) Norway (1986–95), Sweden (1975–95), United States (1974–95). OECD, *A Caring World: The New Social Policy Agenda* (Paris: OECD, 1999), Table 3.3, p. 72.

2 Peter T. Kilborn, "Charity for Poor Lags Behind Need," *New York Times*, Dec 12, 1999, p. 1.

3 OECD, *Information and Technology Outlook 1997* (Paris: OECD, 1997), p. 48.

4 Total employment in office and computing equipment declined in the US, Canada, Australia, Germany, Italy and Portugal between 1980 and 1993. Total employment in radio, TV and communication equipment declined in all but three OECD countries, while employment in communications services rose in most countries by between 0.2 and 1.6 percent during the same time period. Ibid.

5 OECD, *Social and Health Policies in OECD Countries: A Survey of Current Programmes and Recent Developments* (Paris: OECD, 1998), p. 45.

6 OECD, *Social and Health Policies in OECD Countries, Annex: Tables and Charts*, pp. 26–33.

7 OECD, *Social and Health Policies*, p. 50.
8 Ibid., p. 51.
9 Ibid., p. 49.
10 Ibid., p. 48.
11 Ibid., p. 49.
12 Virginia Ellis, *Los Angeles Times*, May 27, 1998, p. A1. This article reports on the findings of a comprehensive survey using social service agencies in California, where 40 percent of the nation's immigrants live. There have now been modifications to the legislation by restoring food stamps (whose withdrawal was the immediate cause of hunger) for some immigrant groups.
13 Jason DeParle, "As Welfare Rolls Shrink, Load on Relatives Grows," *New York Times*, Feb 21, 1999, pp. 1 and 20.
14 OECD, *Social and Health Policies*, pp. 39–40.
15 "Government Backs Off Work Plan for Beneficiaries," *Waikato Times*, July 23, 1998, p. 2.
16 A week after the budget was introduced, the Blair/Field Green Paper on welfare reform, entitled *New Ambitions for Our Country: A New Contract for Welfare*, was published (March 26, 1998). The Green Paper focused on encouraging welfare recipients to move off welfare and into paid work, on closer surveillance of welfare fraud, and on reliance on private pensions. These are now embodied in the new Act. Field resigned early in the process, protesting that the Welfare Reform and Pensions Bill was too stringent in relation to means-testing, something excluded from the Green Paper's orbit: UK Department of Social Security, *New Ambitions for Our Country: A New Contract for Welfare*, Green Paper, Foreword by Prime Minister Tony Blair, UK Department of Social Security, March 26, 1998.
17 There is of course the question of whether there is a "US welfare state." There are about ten different components of what purports to be one: Temporary Assistance to Needy Families, Supplemental Security Income (basically disability income), Social Security (senior citizens), Unemployment Benefits (six months' provision), Food Stamps, Medicaid, Low-Income Housing Assistance, Earned Income Tax Credit, Job Training Partnership Act, and Head Start (a pre-school program for the children of low-income families). In addition to cash assistance, families with dependent children in need received food stamps and public housing assistance. In any potential comparison between the US and similar legislation in the UK, it is important to note that in the US there has never been a category of the chronically unemployed separate from the category of families with dependent children. If you are an unemployed person without children your federal cash assistance is six months' unemployment benefits. This has been the case since the New Deal's Social Security Act of 1935 and remains unchanged. Continuing welfare entitlements have been the province of those with children, either those whose partners were also unemployed or subject to a means test so stringent as to make little difference, or those without partners. This is reflected in the fact that recent legislation has caused a 52.3 percent reduction in families on

welfare and a 56.4 percent reduction overall in recipients of welfare. "Percent Change in AFDC/TANF Families and Recipients, August 1996–September 2001," Feb 27, 2002, <http://www.acf.dhhs.gov/news/stats/afdc.htm>. Families, of course, means largely women and children.

18 US Congress, *HR3734: Personal Responsibility and Work Opportunity Reconciliation Act*, section 103. The five years need not be consecutive, but five years is all any one individual is allowed.

19 Clinton promised in his 1992 campaign to "end welfare as we know it." The phrase quickly became a slogan, and one that was open to positive interpretations by conservatives and social democrats alike. Before the Workfare Bill, families in need of assistance were provided for by legislation termed Aid to Families with Dependent Children (AFDC), enforced in varying forms since the New Deal. AFDC was established in 1935 to assist widows in raising their children. The program remained the same until the 1970s, when it began to undergo several reforms. The AFDC worked in terms of a matching payment to the states: states contributed to cash payments; the government matched the federal amount, and in some cases topped it up to a point approaching subsistence. Under the new legislation, entitled Temporary Assistance to Needy Families (TANF), the government continues to match state funds in the form of block grants. In the longer term, the amount given to the states, while it is currently commensurate with the pre-TANF monies, will be significantly reduced by 2002, after the completion of what appears to be a five-year plan. For those who are not familiar with the US federal system, and may misread this material on the states as meaning that things will only be bad in some states, note that the states do not have any choice in the matter of ending "welfare as we know it."

20 Wyoming has decreased its caseloads by 86 percent. US Department of Health and Human Services, Administration for Children and Families, "Change in Welfare Caseloads Since Enactment of the New Welfare Law," June 1999, <http://www.acf.dhhs.gov/news/stats/aug-sept.htm>. See also Jason DeParle, "As Welfare Rolls Shrink, Load on Relatives Grows."

21 National Conference of State Legislatures, *Tracking Recipients After They Leave Welfare: Summaries of State Follow-Up Studies (Welfare Reform Project)*, July 1999, <http://www.ncsl.org/statefed/welfare/leavers.htm>.

22 The Balanced Budget Act of 1997 (PL 105–33) restored some of the benefits which HR3734 had cut for legal immigrants (for instance, legal immigrants who become blind or disabled after entering the US will have some social welfare entitlement, and food stamps, the loss of which is the main source of hunger, have now been reinstated but benefit only 30 percent of the immigrant population). See Virginia Ellis, *Los Angeles Times*, May 27, 1998, p. A1. Despite these changes, HR3734 still holds for anyone who arrived or arrives after August 22, 1996. This means that most legal immigrants who arrived after the bill's passage are no longer entitled to cash assistance for the elderly or

food stamps, which means that they can work for capital, but at a reduced overall cost in terms of social expenditure. *Immigrant Policy News*, State LegisLine, Immigrant Policy Project, National Conference of State Legislatures, Washington, DC, Jan 9, 1998: cited in Handsnet, Inc., "Welfare Reform Watch: Welfare Reform & Immigrants – Supplemental Security Income," <http://www.igc.apc.org//handsnet2/welfare.reform/Articles/art.890152096.html>. The proposed Hunger Relief Act of 2000 (S1805/HR3192) would restore legal immigrants' eligibility for food stamps. "Food Stamp Benefit Restoration Proposed," *StateServ*, National Conference of State Legislatures, Nov 4, 1999. See <http://stateserv.hpts.org>.

23 In 1994, California passed Proposition 187, which eliminated social services for illegal immigrants. Beginning in 1996, President Clinton's second term in office, a number of anti-immigrant bills were passed at the federal level, e.g., the Anti-Terrorism and Effective Death Penalty Act of 1996, which made it easier for the US to deport legal immigrants. For one discussion of recent changes to immigration policy, see Elizabeth Martinez, "It's a Terrorist War on Immigrants," *Z Magazine*, July 1997. The situation has of course been exacerbated by September 11, 2001. As a non-citizen living in the US, I could now be imprisoned without charge, and executed by a military tribunal without ever once having a right to public trial.

24 The *New Republic* editorial encouraging Clinton to sign the Welfare Reform Bill is highly representative of much popular dialogue surrounding the bill:

> There is an epidemic – the metaphor of pathology is not inappropriate, for what is involved is the health of the black community – of single parent families, unmarried mothers, deserting fathers ... Today, the percentage of black children living in single parent homes is ... 69 percent.
>
> ("Sign It," *New Republic*, Aug 12, 1996)

25 Center for the Study of Social Policy, "World Without Work: Causes and Consequences of Black Male Joblessness," *The Black Family: Essays and Studies*, 6th edn, ed. Robert Staples (Belmont, CA: Wadsworth Publishing, 1999) p. 293.

26 US Department of Justice Office of Justice Programs, Bureau of Justice Statistics, *Correctional Populations in the United States, 1996* (US Department of Justice, 1999), Figure 1, p. 4.

27 The Sentencing Project, "Losing the Vote: The Impact of Felony Disenfranchisement Laws in the United States," (Washington, DC: The Sentencing Project, 1998); <http://www.sentencing project.org/policy/9080.htm>.

28 The US incarcerates at a rate of 600 per 100,000 people. This is about four times the rate of incarceration in Hong Kong and sixteen times that of Japan. It is six to seven times that of countries such as England, France, Germany and Italy and nine to ten times that of Scandinavian countries. The Sentencing Project, "International Rates of Incarcer-

ation, 1995," *Americans Behind Bars: US and International Use of Incarceration* (Washington, DC: The Sentencing Project, 1995), Table 1; <http://www.sentencingproject.org/policy/9030data.html>.

29 The federal and state prison population, for 1997, was 49.4 percent black, 47.9 percent white, 1.8 percent American Indian/Alaska native, 0.8 percent Asian/Pacific Islander. It was over 93 percent male. US Department of Justice Office of Justice Programs, Bureau of Justice Statistics Bulletin, *Prisoners in 1998* (US Department of Justice, 1999), p. 9.

30 Jail population statistics are from 1998 (the latest year available): ibid., p. 2. Parole and probation statistics are from 1996 (latest year available): US Department of Justice Office of Justice Programs, Bureau of Justice Statistics, *Correctional Populations in the United States, 1996*, p. 1.

31 Ibid., p. 6.

32 The number of women in prison as a percentage of the total prison population increased by 6.2 percent from 1996 to 1997 and by 6.5 percent from 1997 to 1998. US Department of Justice Office of Justice Programs, Bureau of Justice Statistics Bulletin, *Prisoners in 1998* and *Prisoners in 1997*.

33 Jason DeParle, "As Welfare Rolls Shrink, Load on Relatives Grows." DeParle's figures are based on the US Census Bureau's statistics.

34 UK Department of Social Security, *New Ambitions for Our Country*, p. 1.

35 Frank Field, "A Hand-Up or a Put-Down for the Poor?," *New Statesman*, Nov 27, 1998, p. 8.

36 Under Clinton's legislation, states are no longer required to use government funding explicitly for cash assistance; block grants can be used to fund other state programs that could be deemed assistance to the poor, such as, and this is critical, subsidies to companies for new production projects which will employ those previously on welfare. HR3734, section 103. The Blair/Field Green Paper, in addition to recommending more private pensions to supplement the state pensions, also promises £75 a week for six months to employers for each long-term welfare recipient they take on, and £60 a week for each young unemployed person. UK Department of Social Security, *New Ambitions for Our Country*, Chapter 3, pp. 3–4. Indeed, the "New Deal" implemented these payments to employers in 1998. "What Small Businesses Need to Know About the New Deal for Young People" and "What Employers Need to Know About the New Deal for People Aged 25 Plus," Fact Sheets, available at <http://www.thesite.org/newdeal/newdeal_info/factsheets.html>.

37 There are provisions to sanction families in which minor dependent children do not attend school, and where parents are not actively pursuing a secondary-school diploma if they have not already completed high school. Additionally, states are directed to deny or cut support to families who do not cooperate in establishing paternity and obtaining child support, and toward teenage parents who do not attend school or who are not living in an adult-supervised environment. In the

preamble to the legislation, out of wedlock births are held responsible for everything from low birthweight to illiteracy to street crime. All of these are also associated with families which are singly headed by women due to death, divorce or desertion, but these cases offer less purchase for a moral lean. (HR3734, sections 101, 103.) By contrast, the far more benign Blair/Field Green Paper stresses the importance of education in preventing teenage pregnancies. UK Department of Social Security, *New Ambitions for Our Country*, Chapter 7, p. 5.

38 Ibid., Chapter 1, p. 7.

39 The first section of the Workfare Bill (entitled "Congressional Findings") records with considerable disapproval that in 1991, 29.5 percent of all births were to unmarried women and that, by 2015, 50 percent of all births will be out of wedlock.

40 The conservative estimate is that 9 percent of married-couple families with children under eighteen years of age are below the poverty line, compared with 46 percent of families headed by single women: HR3734, section 101. The fact that these women have been on welfare, below the poverty line, reveals that women have already been reproducing the next generation of labor-power at a reduced overall social cost. Without welfare, they will reproduce labor-power at an even more reduced rate.

41 This is a modern instance of *paradiastole*, the rhetor's art revived in the Renaissance and recently analyzed by Quentin Skinner ("Thomas Hobbes: Rhetoric and the Construction of Morality," *Proceedings of the British Academy*, Vol. 76 (1991), pp. 1–61). You use paradiastole when you choose your words according to whether you like or dislike the action. Thus, say, "courageous" and "reckless" can be used to describe the same thing. For the deployment of paradiastole by the right in the US today, and an analysis of why postmodern theory leaves those on the left defenseless against linguistic manipulation, see my "Foreword" to Richard Feldstein, *Projecting Political Correctness* (Minneapolis, MN: University of Minnesota Press, 1997).

42 Samuel Brittan, "Foot on the Ladder," *Financial Times*, Dec 10, 1998, p. 19.

43 See Diane Coyle, *The Independent*, March 19, 1998, p. 21.

44 "Working Families' Tax Credit is a Badly Flawed Measure," *The Independent*, Sept 8, 1999, p. 3.

45 Richard Blundell and Howard Reed, *The Employment Effects of the Working Families' Tax Credit* (London: Institute for Fiscal Studies, 1999), p. 2. Andrew Dilnot and Julian McCrae, *Family Credit and the Working Families' Tax Credit* (London: The Institute for Fiscal Studies, 1999), pp. 7–12.

46 UK Department of Social Security, *New Ambitions for Our Country*.

47 The second reference paraphrases the Blair/Field Green Paper, Chapter 7, p. 2. The Green Paper of course talks of "lone parents" in preference to "women" and partners "with higher incomes" rather than "men." As many feminists have pointed out, neutral language masks economic and power disparities. The occasional exception does not justify the mask.

48 There may be exceptions. They do not constitute a rule, as Coyle points out (*The Independent*, March 19, 1998, p. 21). If there is to be a revision along these lines, that revision could only be equitable if it simultaneously mandated that men take real, equal (in terms of hands-on time) responsibility for the rearing of children. "Rights" would then rest on labor, rather than on a claim to property in children.

49 OECD, *Social and Health Policies*, p. 34. Robert Graham, "French Parliament Approves Means Test," *Financial Times*, Oct 31, 1997, p. 2. Robert Graham, "France to End Family Means Testing," *Financial Times*, June 16, 1998, p. 2.

50 OECD, *Social and Health Policies*, p. 120.

51 OECD, *Annex to Social and Health Policies*, pp. 210–13.

52 Gösta Esping-Anderson, *After the Golden Age: The Future of the Welfare State in the New Global Order*, Occasional Paper No. 7, World Summit for Social Development (United Nations Research Institute for Research and Development, 1994), p. 51.

53 Kathleen Lyons and Darryle Lynette Figueroa, "NEA Study Shows Public School Enrollment Growing While Education Spending Lags Behind," Press Release, National Education Association, Dec 13, 1999.

54 OECD, "Education: Expenditure, 1996," *OECD in Figures, 1999* (Paris: OECD, 1999), pp. 66–7. Data was not available through the OECD for Germany, Norway, Sweden, the US, Japan and many other OECD countries. There were much larger increases in Ireland (33 percent), Mexico (65 percent), and Spain (25 percent).

55 Jacques Steinberg, "Fair or Not, Rules Are Bent to Bankroll Public Schools," *New York Times*, Sept 24, 1997, p. A1; "Ecole: les parents veulent exister", *Le Figaro*, June 1, 2000, p. 1.

56 Heather-Jane Robertson, *No More Teachers, No More Books: the Commercialization of Canada's Schools* (Toronto: McClelland & Stewart, 1998) p. 731.

57 These calculations are based on numbers from the UN Population Division from 1998.

58 Irving H. Buchen, "Business Sees Profits in Education: Challenging Public Schools," *The Futurist*, Vol. 33, No. 5 (1999), p. 38.

59 Kevin Fedarko, "Starting from Scratch: Privately Owned and Managed School in Wichita, Kansas," *Time*, Oct 27, 1997, p. 82.

60 Peter Schrag, "'F' is for Fizzle: The Faltering School Privatization Movement," *American Prospect*, May–June 1996, p. 67, *n*. 26.

61 M. Bradford, "Diversification and Division in the English Education System: Towards a Post-Fordist Model?" *Environment and Planning A*, (1995), pp. 1595–612, at p. 1600. Bradford's study of these schools concluded that they "have contributed to the social stratification of society" (p. 1610).

62 Robertson, *No More Teachers*, p. 733.

63 EU, *White Paper on Education and Training: Teaching and Learning: Towards the Learning Society*, p. 13; <http://europa.eu.int/en/record/white/edu9511/index.htm>.

64 OECD, *OECD in Figures, 1999*, p. 66. Overall, OECD countries for

which the OECD has information show a 1 percent decline in per student spending on tertiary education between 1990 and 1996.

65 Sarah Lyall, "British Students Facing a New Test: Tuition," *New York Times*, July 24, 1997, p. A7.

66 Ibid.

67 Victor Dwyer, "Academia Inc.: Scrambling to Make Ends Meet, Universities are Turning Themselves into Sleek New Profit Machines," *Maclean's*, Nov 24, 1997, p. 66.

68 Burton Bollag, "Berlin's 3 Universities Are Hit With Drastic Budget Cuts After Years of Prosperity," *Chronicle of Higher Education*, Jan 23, 1998, p. A47.

69 Geoffrey Maslen, "Australian Academics and Students Protest Government Cuts in Higher-Education Funds," *Chronicle of Higher Education*, April 10, 1998, p. A57.

70 Jim Delahunty, "New Zealand: The Welfare State Ploughed Under," *Monthly Review*, Vol. 45, No. 6 (1993), p. 28.

71 Dwyer, "Academia Inc.," p. 66.

72 University of Saskatchewan President George Ivany, quoted in Dwyer, op. cit.

73 Marilyn Strathern, "The Tyranny of Transparency," *British Educational Research Journal*, Vol. 26, No. 3 (2000), pp. 309–21.

74 Asia-Pacific Economic Corporation, "Declaration of the APEC Education Ministerial 'Toward Education Standards for the 21st Century,'" APEC, August 6, 1992.

75 Republic of Korea, "The Provisional Themes for the 2nd APEC Human Resources Development Ministerial Meeting," 1997; <http://felix.ven.bc.ca/ed8resea/korean1.html>.

76 APEC Human Resource Development Ministers, "Joint Ministerial Statement," 2nd Meeting of APEC Human Resource Development Ministers, Seoul, Korea, Sept 26, 1997.

77 Esping-Anderson, *After the Golden Age*, p. 46.

78 Ibid., p. 50.

79 Ibid., p. 51.

7 The third way and the feminization of poverty

1 Jonathan Hoenig, *Greed is Good: The Capitalist Guide to Investing* (New York: Harperbusiness, 1999).

2 John Gray's project in *False Dawn* (New York: New Press, 1998) was to show this, as noted above.

3 Environmental accords make it possible for the North to sell their pollution rights to other countries.

> The . . . dynamics [of the GATT] have encouraged a flourishing trade in hazardous waste. Disposal costs in some developing countries are as low as $40 for wastes that would have cost as much as $250 to $300 to dispose of in the US. While efforts are presently under way to negotiate treaties that would curtail the export of hazardous waste, the measures that are being advanced through

GATT to weaken control on exports run counter to these initiatives.

> (Steven Shrybman, "International Trade and the Environment:
> An Environmental Assessment of the General Agreement on
> Tariffs and Trade," *The Ecologist*, Vol. 20, No. 1 (1990), p. 32)

4 See Chapter 3.
5 Everything small gets lost in globalization. Richard C. Longworth sums this up with the observation that

> efficiency [is] a word that is becoming more important every year, as global lenders and global markets demand ever higher profits, ever lower costs, ever greater efficiency. Machines often are more efficient than people. Big stores are more efficient than small stores. Mass production is more efficient than craftsmanship.
> (*Global Squeeze: The Coming Crisis for First World Nations* (Chicago, IL: Contemporary Books, 1998), p. 210)

Bill Quinn illustrates the same point in his study of Wal-Mart: the "biggest retailer in the world" puts an estimated number of 100 small businesses out of business for each individual Wal-Mart opened, adding up to approximately a quarter of a million stores and counting. In addition,

> for every job created by a Wal-Mart, at least 1.5 jobs are lost . . . The biggest reason for this is that Wal-Mart typically employs 65 to 70 people for every $10 million in sales; other small businesses employ 106 people for each $10 million in sales. So Wal-Mart can do more business and pay less for employee salaries – and it will.
> (*How Wal-Mart is Destroying America and the World and What You Can Do About it* (Berkeley, CA: Ten Speed Press, 2000), p. 5)

Wal-mart is now moving into the UK.
6 See Quinn on "predatory pricing" driving smaller scale competitors out of business. Ibid., p. 3.
7 Clinton first used the term "third way" in 1992, but it has since been largely identified with Blair's New Labour and Giddens's definition: Anthony Giddens, *The Third Way* (Cambridge: Polity, 1998). (See below for a discussion.)
8 Elaine Kamarck and William Galston, "The Politics of Evasion," quoted in Jonathan Chait, "The Slippery Center," *New Republic*, Nov 16, 1998.
9 Giddens, *The Third Way*, p. 26.
10 Tony Judt, "The Third Way Is No Route to Paradise," *New York Times*, Sept 27, 1998, p. 15.
11 Ibid.
12 Chait, "The Slippery Center," p. 18.
13 Giddens, *The Third Way*, p. 26.
14 "No one any longer has any alternatives to capitalism – the arguments

that remain concern how far, and in what ways, capitalism should be governed and regulated." Ibid., pp. 43–4.

15 Steven Charnovitz points specifically to NAFTA's use of environmental promises and its simultaneous disregard of these commitments. "Regional Trade Agreements," *Environment*, Vol. 37, No. 6 (1995), pp. 16–40, at p. 20 and p. 40.

16 Some critics

> argue that achieving the Third Way's stated objective of a fairer economy will demand new forms of global regulation, especially in the areas of environmental and labor standards, and new efforts to control the speculation in national currencies, which can quickly undermine prosperous economies.
>
> (E. J. Dionne Jr., "The Third Way in Politics,"
> *Seattle Times*, Aug 16, 1998)

On the other hand, as Scott Nova puts it: "globalization is being shaped and advanced by carefully planned legal and institutional changes embodied in a series of international agreements . . . [which] promote the unregulated flow of money and goods [and] strip elected governments of their regulatory authority." "M.I.A. Culpa," *The Nation*, Jan 13, 1997, pp. 5–6. For Soros, "the lack of adequate international supervisory and regulatory authority" contributed to the East Asian collapse and the consequent "global financial crisis." George Soros, *The Crisis of Global Capitalism* (New York: Public Affairs, 1998), p. 179. Simply put, regulation is in capital's interests.

17 See Chait, "The Slippery Center," p. 10.

18 Giddens, *The Third Way*, pp. 82–3.

19 Ibid., p. 148.

20 Ibid., p. 58.

21 See Tim Lang and Colin Hines, *The New Protectionism: Protecting the Future Against Free Trade* (New York: New Press, 1993), for a discussion of the concerted opposition to NAFTA in the US Congress, and how the clauses its opponents managed to insert in the name of environmental protection have been vitiated completely in the legal interpretations of the agreement.

22 Ibid. While Lang's and Hines's path was that of a careful analysis of trade figures, and my initial account was a logical extrapolation based on revising the first premise of value theory (published the same year), the common cause here is reassuring for those who think a good theory should bear some relation to the known facts.

23 Giddens, *The Third Way*, p. 125.

24 Here again we see how Giddens is caught between advocating policies which serve the present needs of capital, while holding on to some sense of social justice. But unlike pension rights financed by nation states, portable eductation standards, I predict, will do well. They enhance globalization. As we saw in Chapter 5, it is no accident that welfare reform and pension reduction through "public/private partnerships" go hand in hand. On the other hand, the capital power

accumulated in private pension funds is immense. See Robin Blackburn, "The European Left, Pension Reform and Complex Socialism" (unpublished paper).

25 I am not re-engaging here with the debate that the reproductive labor of women contributes indirectly to surplus-value, having argued already that the ideal situation for capital is one where women both contribute to surplus-value production directly and reproduce labor day-to-day at a reduced social cost ("Women and Work," *Journal of Australian Political Economy*, Vol. 1, No. 2 (1977), pp. 8–30). In this argument, which I developed in relation to migrant women, I concur with Jane Humphries ("Class Struggle and the Persistence of the Working Class Family," *Cambridge Journal of Economics*, Vol. 1, No. 3 (1977), pp. 10–37). The question that neither I nor Jane Humphries addressed is the specific cost of generational reproduction and its bearing on surplus-value production. While intertwined with day-to-day reproduction in nature and the "family wage" alike, generational reproduction is still a separate issue in that the unpaid female laborer's rejuvenation of the male laborer need not accompany her rearing of children. The welfare mother rears children without a man; she is outside of an economy where there is some return to her through the man's wages for her labor in childrearing. Who benefits? If the welfare mother is not employed, capital does not benefit directly, although it benefits indirectly through a reduced overall social cost of reproducing the next generation. But capital has never been one to care much for the long term. When the welfare mother is employed, capital acquires surplus-value directly, and also benefits from subsidized labor and subsidized childcare. When she is employed *and* reproducing cheaply, both capital's short-term interest and the interests of overall social reproduction are served. Meantime, the man who fathers but is not paying for children also benefits. His economic interests are directly aligned with capital's. The woman who is engaged in childcare and full-time work cannot compete with that unencumbered man in the marketplace; and so the existing discrepancy between male and female salaries is enhanced.

26 Fernand Braudel, *The Wheels of Commerce*, trans. Siân Reynolds, Vol. 2, *Civilization and Capitalism, 15th–18th century* (Berkeley, CA: University of California Press, 1992), p. 36. See also p. 31, on the disruption of Parisian traffic "on market days [by] several women and stallholders, from the fields as well as from the city."

27 See Lillian B. Rubin, *Worlds of Pain: Life in the Working-Class Family* (New York: Basic Books, 1976), p. 161.

28 The ubiquity of this drive to financial success is another question. Migrants in Western Europe from Turkey, for instance, adhere closely to their communities, going back regularly to wives and children.

29 The real issue – as I have attempted to foreshadow – is the difference between a formal contractual rights issue and a rights-based-in-labor issue. The rights to the product of one's labor is a right of the flesh, acknowledging that one has expended energy. It may or may not derive from natural law (one would need to write a reinterpretation of natural

law to make this case). Contractual rights are based in property. When Hobbes saw that the mother's rights (which extended even to infanticide) rested in her labor in bearing and rearing the child, he acknowledged a tie to the natural law his individualism helped overturn. At the level of political philosophy, we could see the history of the last three centuries as one wherein the formal, contractual rights of the individual to freedom and equality have increasingly eroded the natural rights of the flesh. Just as an interpretation of natural rights through labor differs from one based on the conventional (that is, not natural) rights of the individual, so is the conventional or contractual different from the symbolic realm: if the subordination of women is inscribed relentlessly in religion especially, we are led to deny the labor of women. This denial begins, as I have argued elsewhere (in *Exhausting Modernity*), with the appropriation of all creativity by the father in religion, an appropriation in which the mother's creative labor is invisible. In the immediate case, the denial of the mother's rights in natural law may be obscuring the significance of the rights of labor in natural law generally.

8   The source of profit

1   The justification for this, aside from the third-way speak about self-actualization and cosmopolitanism, rests on a mélange of mid-twentieth-century economic theories. As stressed before, third-way proselytizers believe somewhat or a lot in trickle-down economics. Clinton, attempting to persuade Congress to enable him to negotiate new global trade agreements, addressed the US with these words:

> Our economic strategy has worked to make the new economy work for all Americans. . . . Wages are rising in part because more American jobs are high-paying, export related jobs. And if exports keep expanding, that will help to keep wages rising. We must press forward with this economic strategy . . . By expanding trade, we expand opportunity for working families and give more and more of them a shot at the American Dream.

In this case, Clinton was attempting to win congressional approval of fast-track authority, which would have allowed him to negotiate more international trade agreements. William J. Clinton, "Radio Address of the President to the Nation," White House: Office of the Press Secretary, Nov 8, 1997.

2   Roy A. Lindberg, *Processes and Materials of Manufacture* (Boston, MA: Allyn & Bacon, 1964), p. 347.

3   In fact, wood, wind, water and fossil fuels are all stored solar energy in different forms. Energy extracted from the nuclei of atoms is energy from elemental hydrogen in more distant stars which later fused to create the sun and planets of our solar system. John Holdren and Philip Herrera, *Energy: A Crisis in Power* (San Francisco, CA and New York: Sierra Club Books, 1971), pp. 14–15.

4 See Chapter 4.
5 Brian Belcher and Geoffrey Hawtin, *A Patent on Life: Ownership of Plant and Animal Research* (Ontario: IDRC, 1991). Quoted in Jeremy Rifkin, *The Biotech Century* (New York: Putnam, 1999), p. 46.
6 Just as the effects of fossil fuels on the ozone layer were theoretically invisible a century ago, we do not yet understand electromagnetic pollution. See the discussion in Chapter 6.
7 Diana B. Henriques, "Investing: Less Thrill, More Chill in Day Trading," *New York Times*, July 18, 1999, Business Section, p. 1.
8 The aim of reparative technologies is to transform things which are not biodegradable into their opposite. It is to make them once more capable of reentering the cycles of generation, producing useful substance and harm-free energy. We are not without innovation in this field, especially in the realm of biotechnology. It is encouraging to hear (given that the cost of cleaning up existing toxic-waste sites globally is in excess of 5 trillion dollars, and that over 2 million tons of hazardous materials is generated annually in Europe and the US) that the Institute for Genomic Research "has successfully sequenced a microbe that can absorb large amounts of radioactivity" and that may be used to produce a means for "cleaning up radioactive dump sites." Jeremy Rifkin, *The Biotech Century*, p. 17. But we none of us wish to create the blob that munches all before it, which is why further research is mandatory. See also Gene Parkin, "Bioremediation: A Promising Technology," in Fredrick B. Rudolph and Larry V. McIntire (eds), *Biotechnology: Science, Engineering, and Ethical Challenges for the Twenty-First Century* (Washington, DC: Joseph Henry Press, 1996), p. 117, and the collection of brilliant ideas in Paul Hawken *et al.*, *Natural Capitalism* (London and New York: Little, Brown, 1999).
9 John Locke, *Two Treatises of Government*, ed. Peter Laslett (New York and Toronto: New American Library, 1965), II, 40, p. 338. Locke himself managed to work a logic of appropriation into his value theory.

> 'Tis taking any part of what is common, and removing it out of the state Nature leaves it in, which begins the Property . . . Thus the Grass my Horse has bit; the Turfs my Servant has cut; and the Ore I have digg'd in any place I have a right to them in common with others, become my Property, without the assignation of consent of any body. The labor that was mine, removing them out of that common state they were in, hath fixed my Property in them.
>
> (Ibid. II, 28, p. 330)

10 Karl Marx, *Capital*, vol. 1, trans. S. Moore and E. Aveling (Moscow: Progress Publishers, 1954), p. 53.
11 Ibid. (translation modified).
12 Ibid., p. 51.
13 Ibid., p. 207, *n*. 1.
14 These two views of abstract labor are meant to lie at the heart of most controversies in Marxist economics. On the one hand it seems as if Marx is insisting that what makes different labor-powers comparable

are their physiological aspects. On the other he is saying that "not an atom of matter enters into the objectivity of commodities as values." From this perspective, it has been argued that the "equalization of labour as abstract labour only occurs through the exchange of the products of that labour" (Tom Bottomore). Those who go for the "embodied labour view" (Lucio Colletti, *From Rousseau to Lenin: Studies in Ideology and Society*, trans. John Merrington and Judith White. London: NLB, 1972) – that abstract labor is about commensurable embodied labor – are meant to have a view of value which is not specific to capitalism, and thus to fall back to Ricardo's position (David Ricardo, *Principles of Political Economy and Taxation* [1821]. Amherst, NY: Prometheus Books, 1996). But this surely misses the point, which is that value is always produced by the fact labor gives more than it gets. In other words, the full significance of Marx's crucial distinction between labor and labor-power is not taken into account. The value of labor-power is set by the cost of its reproduction and hence, this value is dependent on the whole network of market exchange, which leads by tortuous paths to the satisfaction of human needs. On the other hand, labor's ability to give more than the cost of its reproduction depends on labor's physiological capacity. One could only conclude that arguments about embodied labor were precapitalist if one also concluded that the laborer has an unmediated relation to the commodity produced. When Colletti says that abstract labor is alienated labor, he is right, for only in the capitalist world, where one is alienated from the object of one's labor, is it possible to lose sight of how labor determines value: it is not labor that is paid for, but labor-power. Moreover, the idea that abstract labor, as the equalization of labor, only occurs through exchange is a tautological argument: the process of exchange determines what the value of labor is, but labor determines the value of commodities. To make any sense at all, the concept of "abstract labor-time" has to measure energy and time simultaneously.

15 Or perhaps they confuse the particular with the general, focusing on the difference between concrete and abstract labor solely in terms of Marx's distinction between particular use-values and general exchange-value. Here, of course, the fault is partly Marx's own. As we have seen, he focused on use-value in terms of the particular use-value of a particular commodity. But use-value also has a quantitative dimension, once the concept of biosphere is taken into account.

16 We will return to this question below, when discussing Marx's failure to reckon with the overall quantitative dimension to nature as the source of all use-value.

17 Neglect of the time in "abstract labor-time" has confused not only Marx's followers. His opponents have assumed that Marx himself neglected time. One cultural critic of Marx observed to me that his initial interest in Marx waned when he compared Marxist stipulations as to the source of profit with the realities of his own company. "The fact is," wrote Clive Smith (a founder of America On-Line), "we are far more interested in how fast we can get to market than we are in

what percentage goes on labor" (personal communication). For Marx, Clive Smith would be right to rush to market. Value must be produced within a given time. On the other hand, in rushing, and rushing means keeping abreast of the latest useful technologies, he might forget that labor-power is the one ingredient in production that should give more than it costs.

18 For an extended discussion, see my *Exhausting Modernity* (London: Routledge, 2000), Part 2, "Economy."

19 See Brennan, *Exhausting Modernity*, and Ted Benton, "Marxism and Natural Limits: An Ecological Critique and Reconstruction," *New Left Review*, Vol. 178 (Nov/Dec 1989), pp. 51–86. The crucial point here is that the energy involved is the basis of the *material* addition in production.

20 For Marx there were three departments of consumption, referring to luxury and subsistence goods (departments 1 and 2) and consumption for production (department 3).

21 Marx, *Capital*, vol. 1, p. 207, *n*. 1.

22 As we will see below, it is an accounting figured solely on the spatial axis, determined by the speed of acquisition.

23 Not only may it seem that I am veering toward supply and demand economics, it may even appear that I am claiming, with Quesnay (François Quesnay, *Physiocratie ou constitution naturelle du gouvernement le plus avantageux et genre humain*. Geneva: Slatkine Reprints, 1984), that nature is the source of all value. As we have seen, Marx himself insisted that nature is the source of all use-value, and thus ultimately of exchange-value. He insisted, too, that a commodity always has both use-value and exchange-value. What distinguishes my reworking of value theory from Quesnay and the physiocrats on the one hand, and, for that matter, the time-management analysis of present-day economics on the other (which treats nature and the generation of human energy as externalities), is that I retain Marx's stress on this twofold nature of the commodity.

24 It may be objected here that I have not reckoned with transformation, with the capacity to transform, as something unique to labor. Did not Marx say that what distinguished the worst of architects from the best of bees was the former's capacity to exercise his will in transformation, in the conception and execution of his design? Marx did of course say this, but he went on to show that it was exactly this capacity that was lost with real subsumption, with the division of mental and manual labor, a division which rendered labor-power a commodity that progressively lacked opportunities to exercise a will and design in production. Nonetheless, and this is a core contradiction in the labor theory of value, "productive labor", the labor which produces surplus-value, is precisely labor robbed of its mind and its will in the production process. There are endless debates on the productive value of mental labor, meaning the work of the designers and managers with clean hands. See Nikos Poulantzas, *Political Power and Social Classes* (London: New Left Books, 1973). But the point is that purely manual labor in particular is generally designated productive.

25 Alec Wilkinson, *Big Sugar: Seasons in the Cane Fields of Florida* (New York: Alfred A. Knopf, 1989) pp. 75–7.
26 Kate Bronfenbrenner, "We'll Close! Plant Closings, Plant-Closing Threats, Union Organizing and NAFTA," *Multinational Monitor*, March 1997, p. 8.
27 Rainforest Action Network, *Drilling to the Ends of the Earth: The Case Against New Fossil Fuel Exploration* (San Francisco, CA: Rainforest Action Network, 1999).
28 Harvey, however, is acutely aware of capital's role in this process. David Harvey, *The Condition of Postmodernity: An Enquiry into the Origins of Social Change* (Oxford: Blackwell, 1999).
29 Within the framework of the old value theory, the speed of acquisition would have been measured by the labor-power expended in fetching and carrying. And labor-power is the nodal point where this version of value theory and its progenitor come together: to date, the labor-power embodied in the speed of acquisition is irreplaceable because no other energy source is capable of moving to market of its own accord, or transporting other energy sources.
30 Paying below subsistence wages contributes directly to illness and death, because one is without the sustenance necessary to refurbish the energy given out.
31 B. Joseph Pine III, *Mass Customization* (Boston, MA: Harvard Business School Press, 1993), p. 21.
32 Ibid., p. 25.
33 *Loc. cit.*
34 Ibid., p. 16.
35 The speed of bringing materials to the place of production is costed in the same way as the speed of production itself, and is indeed a part of production. But these crucial transportation costs also offset profit, if the cost of bringing an energy source to market outweighs the value that source adds in production. The fact that labor, unlike other energy sources, covers its own transportation costs is a key variable in class positioning.

9 Price, inflation and energy

1 On definitions of short-term profit, see my *History After Lacan* (London and New York: Routledge, 1993).
2 George Soros, *The Crisis of Global Capitalism* (New York: Public Affairs, 1998), p. 113.
3 Or is price really something intangible? Is not energy-time being measured here? I have argued somewhere else that the binding of energy in the fixed forms of commodities (fixed forms which are incapable of reentering the time of natural reproduction, which cannot be recycled to keep pace with natural time) creates another time altogether, through the compression of living energy into a form in which it cannot reproduce itself: evidently this is so with industrial capital. By this argument this is also the case for financial capital, which measures speed and speed alone. The phenomenal form of the

speed of acquisition, then, is money. Money, as a measure of speed, is then tied to the existence of asymmetrical time, for this time in turn accelerates energetically with the construction of bound things – nonbiodegradeable commodities. As Alberti put it in the fifteenth century, money is time. But money is time because it is both the symptom and the symbol of the creation of the artificial space-time of production. Teresa Brennan, *Exhausting Modernity: Grounds for a New Economy* (New York and London: Routledge, 2000).

4 Fernand Braudel, *The Wheels of Commerce* (Berkeley, CA: University of California Press, 1992), p. 428.

5 The transformation of value into price in terms of distance is compounded not only by the rate of exploitation, but by the fact that commodities conveyed over any distance have to be packaged. In a Danish study, "the price per kilo paid by consumers for flour found that the farmer got 21 per cent, the flour mill 11 per cent and 46 per cent was spent on packaging, transport and retailing." Tim Lang and Colin Hines, *The New Protectionism* (New York: New Press, 1993), p. 62. Let us say that the farmer got just enough for comfortable subsistence, and the flour mill makes enough profit to turn over, as it were. In that case, the price of the commodity is still more or less doubled by the costs of transportation and delivery, although the profit is not doubled. Take another example: "Of the money the consumer pays for bottled water: the water is only 8 per cent, the bottle 24 per cent, advertising, shipping and retailing 50 per cent, tax 13 per cent, and manufacturer's profit only 5 per cent" (ibid.). Once more, shipping and delivery – or distribution and exchange – are the area where the cost of the commodity escalates. In this case the price of the bottle of water is clearly determined by the distance it has traveled. The speed of acquisition is inflating that price, and diminishing profit margins, although the water in this case has little to do with them. Only when the rate of production outstrips the resource does real value feature as such.

6 See Brennan, *Exhausting Modernity*, pp. 2–6.

7 The disdain for "trade" in eighteenth and nineteenth century litera-ture is snobbery, of course, but contains the remnants of something more than aristocratic prejudice.

8 Soros, *The Crisis of Global Capitalism*, p. 146.

9 Are items being exchanged, in line with the logic of inflation, that have a higher price but less use-value? Another question, what of those items which compensate for the distances imposed on daily life?

10 See the report by Ned Leonard, "The Internet Begins With Coal," <info@greeningearthsociety.org>. This report cites one in *Forbes Magazine*, May 31, 2000.

11 "The Internet Begins with Coal" suggests that this figure is as high as two-thirds. But the figure is contested by the US Department of Energy (DoE, 2001 online).

12 Marx, *Capital*, Vol. 3.

13 The answer to the childfree movement, which resents the tax breaks, is that those tax breaks are woefully insufficient given the social function

performed by unpaid labor in rearing the next generation. But more than this is at stake. If one defines oneself as a member of a society, bound by certain obligations to it as well as guaranteed certain rights, the continuity of that society is as much an obligation contingent on its membership as obeying its traffic rules (which also make that society cohere). A society without a future is a depressed one. A society lacks a future when it is lowering rather than increasing its civilized stock, by producing fewer well-educated people, and ones who are less healthy. It is denying to others the conditions it took for granted. Of course the same argument applies to the natural world, and to conditions such as seas fit for sailing, air for breathing. The question for political philosophy at this point concerns whether one can have a tacit social contract whch pits the present prosperity of the few against the future of the totality. How does one justify life today at the price of global immiseration, with all its deathly consequences, tomorrow? For these are the consequences of the present denial of long-term environmental consequences, together with the refusal to divert more funds to education, health and social provision for the young and the old and the incapacitated. The idea that labor was entitled to a funded old age was the basis of national insurance in Britain, which is proportional to the amount of tax paid.

14 Robin Blackburn, *The Making of New World Slavery: From the Baroque to the Modern* (New York and London: Verso, 1997), pp. 339–40.

15 Ibid., p. 429.

16 Lester R. Brown, "A New Era Unfolds," *State of the World* (New York: W. W. Norton, 1993), pp. 9–10.

10 The prime directive

1 Seymour Martin Lipset, "Extremism of the Centre," in *International Fascism: Theories, Causes and the New Consensus*, (ed.) Roger Griffin (New York: Oxford University Press, 1998), pp. 101–6.

2 In the Levelers' *Petition of September 11*, 1648, Clause 10 prays: "That you would have freed all Trade and Merchanidising from Monopolizing and Engrossing, by Companies and otherwise . . ."

3 Braudel, *op. cit.*; see the discussion in Chapter 7.

4 Gandhi, *Collected Works of Mahatma Gandhi* (New Delhi: Navajivan, 1958–84) (3 vols), Vol. 2, p. 3.

5 Frederick Engels, "Socialism: Utopian and Scientific," Karl Marx and Frederick Engels, *Selected Works* (Moscow: Progress Publishers, 1969) (3 vols), Vol. 3, pp. 95–151.

6 "The Eighteenth Brumaire of Louis Bonaparte," Karl Marx and Frederick Engels, *Selected Works* (Moscow: Progress Publishers, 1969) (3 vols), Vol. 1, pp. 398–487.

7 The antagonism between many small businesses and big capital has been sensed by the French rural populists and others who have used the term, "a third way," in this century. Some of these movements have or had an agricultural or small business basis. But they are usually, although not necessarily, nationalist or worse, likely to blame their ills

on different peoples, immigrants from other places. Pauline Hansen in Australia for instance appeals to a rural and small-business constituency that is indeed at risk. But instead of blaming globalization and the concentration of wealth in fewer hands, she blames the labour flows globalization gives rise to: this mistaken attribution of blame is abetted not only by the traditional conservatism of the agricultural constituency, but by the lack of an analysis that points to real causes, and a real third way. This lack leads to poorly based alliances, just as it pre-empts real alliances. The grain of truth in LePen's fascism lies here, and it is high time it was removed from that chaff and inserted in fertile ground. On the complex background to French regionalism, see Julian, "The Occultism of Regionalism in French History," unpublished dissertation, 2001.

8 This process for Gandhi violates Marx's principle, which Gandhi took up: "from each according to his ability, to each according to his need."

9 Superficially, we are moving to an economy in which property is secondary to control, and leasing becomes more of the norm (see Jeremy Rifkin, *The Age of Access*). This is the shifting of an increasing burden of labor onto the consumer, the last fixture in the chain of production and distribution. If consumers do the work of distribution and consumption, they are not paid for it (as in the automatic telephone work discussed in Chapter 9).

10 It also helps solves the problem of utopias and projection. That is to say, we cannot easily take actions without those actions having unintended consequences. But actions are less likely to do this when they have been done before.

11 Ralph Atkins, "Lafontaine says workers should benefit from Tax Co-ordination," *Financial Times*, Dec 9, 1998, p. 1.

12 Ad Hoc Working Group on the MAI, *The MAI – Democracy for Sale?*

13 Although there is doubt as to "Who gets the credit" in some cases. See Anne Marie Goetz and Rina Sen Gupta, "Who Takes the Credit? Gender, Power, and Control Over Loan Use in Rural Credit Programs in Bangladesh," *World Development* 1996, Vol. 24/1, pp. 45–63.

14 Their inherent antagonism to large-scale capitals could be made explicit if the ideological greed of their owners was challenged at the outset. One way that this could be done is to restrict holdings, so that no profit could be retained past a certain point. This suggestion may have a place in the current quest to find alternatives to a socialism based on large-scale industrialization: the dream that has most clearly failed (see Susan Buck-Morss, "Fashion in Ruins: History after the Cold War," *Radical Philosophy* 68, Autumn 94, pp. 10–17, *n.* 13). It is time to go to Plan B.

15 The arguments that one can "Go Green and Prosper" (*Financial Times*, June 1998 editorial, *op. cit.*) are comforting, and even plausible if read in isolation from capital's overall dynamics. But they take no account of the distinction between relative and absolute surplus-value.

16 The ostensible biblical condemnations of homosexuality are partly a matter of translation, and partly a matter of projection. Homosexuality is interdicted in Judaism for two reasons: one is the Bibilical

condemnation of sodomy, the other the condemnation of onanism (if masturbation is condemned, so is mutual masturbation). This idea that homosexuality is at issue here carries over to Christianity – and is reinforced by references in Corinthians, Timothy and Revelation – to perversion. Sodomites is translated commonly as homosexuals and/or homosexual perverts, but this is precisely not a literal translation. To call a man a sodomite because he is gay is already to read through certain lenses and certain assumptions. Among many gays, sodomy is often eschewed. Given the obvious hygienic concerns that underpin taboos, where a man is enjoined "not to lie with another man *as if with a woman*" (Leviticus 18:22, my emphasis) it seems clear that sodomy is being condemned, not homosexuality. A man is not enjoined "not to lie with another man" period. A similar misinterpretation – arising, I suggest, through the projection of a certain masculine shame into a biblical sentence – is evident in the understanding of Onanism. Onan's offence was that he "whenever he lay with his [dead] brother's wife, he spilled his semen on the ground lest he should give offspring to his [dead] brother." "What he did was wicked in the Lord's sight" (Genesis 38:9/10). Onan's offence was not that he spilled his seed as such. Rather, he denied that seed to his sister-in-law Tamar when it was his responsibility to give it to her, and he did so moreover having used her to arouse himself. What is more likely here, that a need to masturbate for relief is condemned unilaterally, or that there is a unilateral condemnation of suffering? The point surely is Onan's relation to the other, not his relation to his penis. Only a being whose primary relationship is with a non-detachable organ could conclude that its masturbation was of such concern to God. Certainly Onan broke laws one must not break when he pulled away from a woman he was making love to, who was expecting a consummation that might give her a child, who had responded to her lover on that basis, and then, perhaps, had to watch him spill his seed on the ground. But the laws he broke are called truth and love, while the sin he committed is called unkindness or cruelty or thoughtlessness. It is the affective state in which the other does not exist as an other, but as an object.

17 Andrew Bradstock and C. C. Rowland (eds) *Radical Christian Writings: A Reader* (Oxford: Blackwell, 2002).

18 Revelation 21:6, εγω [ειμι] το αλφα και το ω, η αρχη και το τελος. εγω τω διψωντι. δωσω εκ της πηγης του υδατος της ζωης δωρεαν. (*The Greek New Testament*, 3rd edn © 1975, *United Bible Societies*, London); "To anyone who is thirsty I will give the right to drink from the spring of the water of life without paying for it . . ." (*Newcomer Good News Bible Second Edition* (British and Foreign Bible Society, Glasgow: Caledonian International Book Manufacturing Ltd, 1994.) Again, the problem is seeing through the lens of metaphor. The water of life is the water without which there is no life. Thirsty people welcome it. At the moment, they have to pay for it more each day.

19 But the awareness of contingency has lost sight of other epistemological dimensions in reason and explanation. See Linda Alcoff, *Real Knowing* (Ithaca, NY: Cornell University Press, 1996).

20 Brennan, *Exhausting Modernity, op. cit.*
21 Teresa Brennan, "Child Abuse and the Church," unpublished paper.
22 It is difficult to read the following excerpts from Revelation without concluding that what is being condemned is profit made at the expense of witting or conscious damage to the environment.
23 On the use of sexual imagery in Revelation see also Christopher Rowland, *Epworth Commentaries for Preachers* (London: 1991) and *The New Interpreter's Bible Commentary* (Nashville, TN: Abingdon, 1998).
24 Robin Blackburn points out the organizational potential of pensioner's funds in his *Banking on Life or Counting on Death* (London: Verso, 2003).
25 When Orphan Annie's Roosevelt asks Daddy Republican Capitalist to head his "New Deal" program, he is demonstrating the wit, or skillful means, which would mark out a real third way among those "social democrats" committed to the integration of private and public sectors. To draw on the brilliant entrepreneurial and creative resources locked up in capitalism today at the individual level of appointment – with a program geared towards redistribution via encouragement of small businesses – is another way of realizing the prime directive from a particular standpoint.
26 In addition, the idea that social being determines social consciousness is conflated by Marx with the idea that the material determines the ideal. My social being can determine my consciousness if I become a wealthy landowner and therefore become less inclined to believe that wealth should be redistributed, and if I go that one step further into rationalization and say that redistribution is a bad thing in itself, losing track of my individual investment in reaching that conclusion. But this is not the same as materialism – rather than idealism – being determinate. By my account all ideas are material, subtle matters some of them, but matter nonetheless.

Index

Note: page numbers in bold refer to boxes

abortion 168
acceleration 3–4; of consumption 153–4;
    effect on human beings 25–6; of
    production 1, 19, 39, 151–2, 153–4
Afghanistan, and oil supplies xix, 4, 34,
    49–50
agribusiness 1, 63–4
air pollution 34, 35–8, 183–4nn, 189–90n;
    constituents of 36–7, 186–8nn; controls
    on 35, 38; European definition 185n;
    road-traffic 37, 42, 189n, 190n;
    transboundary 185n, see also fossil-fuel
    emissions
air transport 193nn; pollution from 22–3, 42
al-Qaeda xvi, 50
Alcoff, Linda 230n
allergies 37, 60, 71
Alternative Public Schools (US) 89
Anderson, Sarah 177n
animal waste, and water supplies 55–6
antiglobalization movement 2, 9, 50, 168;
    creative responses 165–6; as women's war
    32, 168
Antoniou, Michael 204n
anxiety and fear 10, 30, 171–2
apocalypse, texts of xix–xx
Arab countries, oil reserves xvii
Arab-Israeli conflict 173n
aristocracy: disdain for trade 227n; social
    consciousness 171–2
Asia 9; "casino capitalism" 135
Asia-Pacific Economic Corporation 93
aspirations, and consumer indebtedness 28
asthma 35, 37–8, 184–5nn, 189–90n; and air
    pollution 186–8n, 189–90n
Atkins, Ralph 229n
Australia: education spending 88, 91;
    healthcare 66, 70, 72–3, 207n, 209n;
    income inequality 78; pensions 75, 76;
    small businesses 229n; welfare reforms
    66, 81, 86, 96; welfare spending 207n
Austria: healthcare 73; welfare reforms 86
automation 19, 39, 133–4
Baker, Dean and Mark Weisbrot 208n

Bakunin, Mikhail and Sergei Nechayev 174n
Bates, David V. 186n, 188n
Belcher, Brian and Geoffrey Hawtin 223n
Belgium: healthcare 72; pensions 76
Benton, Ted 225n
benzene 36, 37; in air pollution 187–8n
Bevan, Aneurin 97
bioderegulation 19, 33–4, 43
biorhythms 13, 34, 151
biotechnology 204–5n
birthrate, illegitimate 216nn
Blackburn, Robin 221n, 228n, 231n
Blair, Tony, UK Prime Minister 81, 84, 101,
    182n, 212n, 215nn; and third way 98, 99,
    219n
Blake, William 178n
Blundell, Richard and Howard Reed 216n
Boadway, B. Ted (et al.) 184n, 186n, 187n,
    188n
Bollag, Burton 218n
Born, Matt 176n
Boston University 89
Bottomore, Tom 224n
boundaries, national **141**
Bradford, M. 217n
Bradstock, Andrew and C.C. Rowland 230n
Braidotti, Rosi 183n
Braudel, Fernand, history of capitalism 105,
    138, 179n, 221n, 227n
Brazil: economic crisis 134; rainforests 16
Brennan, Teresa 178n, 183n, 225n, 226–7n,
    231n
Bretton Woods system 180n
Brittan, Leon 196n
Brittan, Samuel 216n
Bronfenbrenner, Kate 226n
Brown, Lester R. 177n, 202n, 205n, 228n
Brown, Lester R., Michael Renner and Brian
    Halwell 199n
Bruno, Kenny 205n
Bryce, William 203n
Buchen, Irving H. 217n
Buck-Morss, Susan 173n, 183n, 229n
Burch, David 182n, 205n

Burns, Elizabeth K. 182*n*
Burns, Leland 181*n*
Bush, George W., US President: "axis of
  evil" declaration xvi, 173*n*; climate plan
  with Exxon xix; commitment to war 18;
  definition of terrorism 1; lowering of
  environmental standards 179*n*; refusal to
  ratify Kyoto xix, 179*n*
business *see* corporations; small businesses

California, electricity crisis 127, 139
Callinicos, Alex 177*n*
Canada: education spending 88, 91;
  healthcare 70, 71, 72, 73, 184*n*, 206*n*;
  income inequality 78; as member of
  NAFTA 48, 196*n*; pensions 75;
  unemployment benefits 80; welfare
  spending 207*n*
capital: constant 110, 115, 119, 120–1, 127;
  elements of 143; finance 134–5; Marx's
  analysis of 11–12, 109–10, 143; variable
  109–10, 115, 120–1
capitalism 135, 167–8; alternatives to global
  13–18, 108, 150; competitive 156, 229*n*;
  contradictions of 152–3, 179–80*n*;
  declining economic position of women
  107; and imperialism xvi; inclination to
  globalization 7–8; natural 4; origins of
  105–6; social democratic acceptance of
  99–100; stages of 137–8, 139–46, **141–2**,
  152, 156, *see also* globalization; localism
carbon dioxide 53–4, 198–9*n*
carbon monoxide 36, 37, 187*n*
carbonic anhydride xvii–xviii
Cardoso, Fernando Henrique, President of
  Brazil 13, 134–5, 178*n*; and third way 98,
  100
Carr, Caleb 174*n*
Carson, Rachel, *Silent Spring* 56
Caspian Sea, oil reserves 4, 49–50
Castle, Stephen 173*n*
Central Asia, "Great Game" 4, 49, 197*n*
Central Asia Gas (CentGas) 4
Central and Eastern Europe 27, 104
centralization 7, 172; of control 150; in
  Marxist theory 14; of production 44, 153;
  reversal of 169, *see also* localism
CFCs 200*n*; effect on ozone 53, 54–5
Chait, Jonathan 219*n*
Chakrabarty, Ananda, gene patent case 112
Charles, Prince of Wales 203*n*
Charnovitz, Steven 220*n*
chemicals: fertilizers 61, 62–3, 64–5;
  pesticides 56–9, 61–2; pollution 4, 201*n*
Chen, David W. 198*n*
child poverty 78, 87, 94
childcare 83, 84
children *see* education; parents; women
China, and oil pipelines 197*n*
choice: and globalization 97–8; and price
  113; in welfare rhetoric 85, 107
Chomsky, Noam and Edward Herman 175*n*
Christianity xx, 162–3, 167, 168; on homosexuality 230*n*; and war on terrorism xv

Cichon, Michael 206–7*n*
class: and inequality 27, 171–2; Marxist view
  of bourgeoisie 151; mobility 151; and
  public transport 24, *see also* middle
  classes
climate change xvii–xviii, 34, 51–4; pollution
  and 3, *see also* air pollution; global
  warming; pollution; water
Clinton, Bill, US President 219*n*, 222*n*; and
  third way 98, 99, 100; and trade
  agreements 195*n*; and universal
  healthcare 74; Workfare legislation 80–3,
  85, 213*n*, 214*n*
Colborn, Theo, Diane Dumanoski and John
  Peterson Myers 202*n*, 205*n*
Colletti, Lucio 224*n*
Collier, Robert 195*n*
colonialism **141**, *see also* imperialism
communications: expanding networks 150;
  as source of profit 129, *see also*
  computers; telecommunications;
  transportation; World Wide Web
community: breakdown of 28–9; importance
  of 8; and mobility 103
commuting 23, 24–5, 29; between countries
  25
computers, electricity consumption by 5–6,
  34, 112, 126, 144
Coney, Sandra 209*n*
conservatism 18
consumers, and distribution costs 133–4,
  143, 229*n*
consumption 225*n*; acceleration of 153–4,
  see also fossil-fuel consumption
control: centralization of 150, 165–6, 229*n*;
  revolutionaries need to 165
coral reefs 52
Cornell, Drucilla 183*n*
corporations: centralization of 44; and costs
  of welfare provision 68; employment
  costs 75, 76; increasing use of electricity
  39; investment by 68–9; and public
  education 89–90, 93; resentment of
  taxation 14, 94; tax reductions 10–11, 12,
  68, 94
cost-effectiveness, as criterion 74, 104
Coyle, Diane 216*n*, 217*n*
crime 81
Cross, Gary 181*n*
Cummings, Joseph 205*n*
Cummins, Ronnie 204*n*
Czech Republic, pensions 76

D'Alema, Massimo, Italian Prime Minister
  98
Dallari, R. 184*n*
Daria, Oliva 190*n*
Davis, Devra L. and Paulo H.N. Saldiva 192*n*
Daynes, Raymond 200*n*
DDT: continued use of 56, 57, 198*n*, 202*n*;
  effects of 57–8, 202–3*n*
decentralization 166
Delahunty, Jim 218*n*
democracy 9

Denmark: healthcare 72, 73; income inequality 78; pensions 75; welfare spending 207*n*
DeParle, Jason 212*n*, 213*n*, 215*n*
dependency theory xvi, 159
deregulation 20, 148, 180*n*; of biology 19; historical context 105–8; reversal of 159; and social policy 101–4; and theft of time 20–1
Dilnot, Andrew and Julian McCrae 216*n*
Dionne, E.J. 220*n*
disability benefits 76, 210*n*
diseases: antibiotic resistance 61; auto-immune 58, 66, 71; cancers (carcinomas) 55, 57, 58, 188*nn*, 206*n*; gastrointestinal 30; infectious 52, 197–8*n*; leprosy 55; mosquito-borne 52, 198*nn*; respiratory 35, 36, 37–8, 189–90*nn*; of skin 55, 200*n*; tropical 198*n*, *see also* asthma; health; illness
distribution: consumers' role in 133–4, 229*n*; costs 227*n*
Doyle, Jack 192*n*, 201*n*
drugs 57; plant-based 204*n*
Duffy, Andrew 184*n*
Dunn, Seth 199*n*
Dwyer, Victor 218*n*

Eakin, E. 190*n*
economic growth, and provision of healthcare 69–70
economic theory: classical 11; exclusion of externalities 144–5; of globalization 3, *see also* labor theory of value; trickle-down effect
Economist, The: on MAI 45, 46; on welfare provision 67–8
Edfors-Lubs, M.I. 190*n*
Edison Project (US) 89
education 7, 80, 87–93; corporate influence on 89–91, 93; curricula changes 90, 91–2, 93; spending cuts 87–8, 93; tertiary (university) 90–3
efficiency, emphasis on 92, 219*n*
Ehrenreich, Barbara 183*n*
Eisenstein, Zillah 203*n*
elderly: assisted suicide 77; chronic illness 76–7; healthcare spending on 70–1, *see also* pensions
electricity 38–40, 125–6; Californian crisis of 127, 139; computers' consumption of 5, 34, 112, 126–7, 144; fossil-fuels to generate 34, 38, 144, 191*n*; increased production 191*n*; increasing consumption of 39
electromagnetic pollution 38
Ellis, Virginia 212*n*, 213*n*
Elsom, Derke M. 192*n*
emissions: controls 35, 38; fossil-fuel 191*n*; monitoring 199–200*n*; technology to reduce 4, 192*n*, *see also* air pollution; fossil-fuel emissions; global warming
employment: costs 75, 76; in information technologies 79, 126, 211*n*; subsidies 215*n*, *see also* unemployment

Enclosure Acts 139
energy 122–4; costs of 130–2, 173–4*n*; human 20, 21, 111, 146–8; local sources of 160; natural sources of 20, 21, 111, 136, 146–7, 222*n*; as source of profit 111–12, 124–9, *see also* labor
Engels, Frederick 228*n*
entrepreneurship, dependence on energy 111
Environment Agency (UK) 35
environmental concerns 8; domestic legislation 96; in EU 47; "green-washing" 4, 176*n*; and human stewardship of nature 164; incompatible with globalization 101–2; in MAIs 46–7; and toxic waste disposal 17, 218–19*n*, *see also* Kyoto Protocols
Esping-Anderson, Gösta 75, 87, 217*n*, 218*n*
European Union 42, 44; asthma 184–5*n*; education 90; environmentalism 47; and Kyoto xviii–xix; and MAI 196*n*; potential for 158–9, 167; rail transport 193*n*; resurgence of TB 197–8*n*; and road transport crisis 25; trade disputes with US 45–6; transportation of goods 42; unemployment 27; use of chemical fertilizers 62; welfare spending 68–9, 206–7*n*
evil, nature of xvi
exchange: and distribution costs 133–4; point of 143
exchange-value 114, 117, 137, 224*n*; as abstract labor-time 118–19; from natural energies 21, 115; real 139
exploitation: imperialism as xvii; for profit 154; of the South 108–9
extension 154; globalization as process of 3, 9, 51, 140, 145
Exxon, climate plan xix

Fagan, Gabrielle 210*n*
families: parents as percentage of electorate 88–9; taxation of 31
Fedarko, Kevin 217*n*
Feldstein, Richard 216*n*
Fernando, H., F. Cardoso and E. Faletto 176*n*
fertility, human 31; effect of chemical pesticides on 56–7, 58
fertilizers, chemical 61, 62–3, 64–5, 148
Field, Frank 83, 215*nn*
finance capital, speed of 134–5
Finland 78; education spending 88; healthcare 72; pensions 75; public housing policy 86
Florence, Progressive Governance (1999 conference) 98–100
food: effect of pesticides on 56–9; genetically modified 59, 204–5*n*; prepackaged 28, 182*n*; shortages 59–60
food production 63–4, 98; crop productivity 61–2, 64–5; effect of global warming on xviii; "Green Revolution" 62–3
Ford, Henry 130

fossil-fuel consumption: in electricity generation 34, 38, 144; and law of substitution 125–6; and pollution 34; real costs of 145–6; and sources of energy 125–7, *see also* electricity; oil

fossil-fuel emissions xvii, xix, xxi, 3, 191*n*; effect on climate 51–2; from transport 3–4, 6–7, 34, 40, 51, 191–2*nn*; in war 5, *see also* air pollution; pollution

France: air pollution 187*n*, 189*n*; diet 36; education spending 88, 91; healthcare 70, 71, 72; small businesses 228*n*; welfare reforms 86

Frank, André Gunder 176*n*

Fraser, Nancy and Linda Gordon 206*n*

free trade 6–7, 34, 160, *see also* international trade agreements; MAI

free will, human 167

French, Hilary F. 177*n*, 193*n*, 196*n*, 205*n*

French Revolution 174*n*

Freud, Sigmund xx, 165

Friends of the Earth 13

Galbraith, J.K. 27

Gandhi, Mohandas Mahatma 13–14, 228*n*, 229*n*; advocacy of localism 152–6, 172

GATT (General Agreement on Tariffs and Trade) 44–5, 101; and national environmental legislation 49, 96; on transport 41, *see also* WTO

genes, patented 112

genetic engineering 59–61, 148, 164, 175*n*, 204–5*nn*; and antibiotic resistance 61; toxic effects of 60–1

Germany: asthma 185*n*; education spending 91; healthcare 70, 71; income inequality 78; pensions 75, 76; welfare reforms 76, 80, 81, 86; welfare spending 207*n*

Giddens, Anthony 9, 101, 103, 178*n*, 219*n*, 220*n*

Gittelman, A.L. 203*n*

global capitalism, alternatives to 13–18, 108, 150

global warming xvii–xviii, xix–xx, 33, 51–4; greenhouse effect 52, 53, 199*nn*

globalization xvii, 7–8, 101–2; dependence on transport 34; effect on food production 63–4, 98; effect on labor 98; effect on small businesses 98; effect on women 109–10; factor in World Trade Center attacks 2; facts and myths 5–6; as process of extension 3, 9, 51, 140, 145; theories 176*n*; "trickle-down" effect of 96–7, *see also* antiglobalization movement; trade

Goetz, Anne Marie and Rina Sen Gupta 229*n*

Goldberg, Gertrude and Eleanor Kremen 173*n*

Goldsmith, Edward 185*n*, 192*n*, 193*n*, 197*n*, 203*n*, 205*n*

Goody, Jack 175*n*

Graham, Robert 217*n*

Gray, John 9, 12, 19, 176*n*, 178*n*, 179*n*, 182*n*, 183*n*, 196*n*, 207*n*, 218*n*

Greece: healthcare 72; pensions 75, 76; welfare reforms 86

Greenpeace 13, 55

Hansen, James 198*n*, 199*n*

Hansen, Pauline 229*n*

Harvey, David 226*n*

Hawken, Paul (*et al.*) 178*n*, 223*n*

health: air pollution and 35–6, 186–8*n*; alternative practices 30; bodily regulation 29–30; effect of chemical pesticides on 57–9; effect of globalization on 7; effect of traffic on 180*n*; essential bacteria 58; physical exhaustion 29–31, 146, *see also* diseases; illness; stress

healthcare 7, 69–74; for chronic illness 71, 72, 73; co-insurance 71–2; costs of 207–8*n*; for elderly 70–1; as financial priority 66; medical technology 70, 76–7, 209*nn*, 211*n*; personal 183*n*; pharmaceuticals 72, 204*n*; private insurance for 208*n*; reductions in spending 9, 10, 66, 72–4; variable practice patterns 207–8*n*, *see also* illness

Henriques, Diana B. 223*n*

Heymann, David L. 198*n*

Highfield, Roger, Christine McGourty and Adrian Berry 183*n*

Hirst, Paul 176*n*

Hobbes, Thomas 85, 222*n*

Hochschild, Arlie 181*n*

Hoenig, Jonathan 218*n*

Hoffman, Catherine 208*n*

Holdren, John and Philip Herrera 222*n*

homelessness 81

homosexuality 162, 229–30*n*

hormones: mimicked by organochlorines 203*n*; mimicked by organophosphates 56, 58

household appliances, increased use of 28, 39, 191*n*

household production 105, 157; as alternative to capitalism 108, 150; economic status of women in 107–8

housing 23, 29; public 86

human beings: effect of increased pace on 21–2, 39–40; immiseration by exhaustion 146

human needs: defined 17, 35; as secondary concern 96–7

Humphries, Jane 182*n*, 221*n*

Hungary, pensions 76

hydroelectric power 38

ideology, as prescriptive 97

illiteracy 78

illness: assisted suicide 77; chronic 70, 71, 72, 76, 94, 183*n*, 206*n*, 209*n*; mental 2–3, 5, 10, 17, 29; physical 2, 5, 22, 146, *see also* diseases; stress

IMF (International Monetary Fund) 63, 142

immigrants 212*n*; and welfare benefits (US) 82, 213–14*nn*

immiseration 146–9; of middle classes 127–8, *see also* poverty
imperialism xvi–xvii, **141**
imprisonment 107; US rate of 27, 83, 214–15*nn*; of women 83, 215*n*
income: inequality 7, 27, 78; redistribution 171; wealth 8, 156, *see also* wages
indebtedness 28, 127
India 151; effect of agribusiness on farmers 1, 62–3; localism in 14, *see also* Gandhi
Indonesia 134–5, 142
industrialization 105, **141**, 152
industry, manufactured goods 6
inflation 113, 137–9; interest rates as remedy for 142–3
information technologies, new (NITS) 79, *see also* computers; telecommunications
Intergovernmental Panel on Climate Change (IPCC) 52
International Energy Outlook, 1999 report 40
International Labor Organization (ILO): report on world employment (1998-9) 26–7; on welfare spending 206–7*n*
international trade agreements 195*n*; advantages to modern states 102–3; disputes under 45–6, 47, 48, 196–7*n*; environmental promises 220*n*; and extraction of resources 49–50; precedence over state legislation 43–4, 45–6, 49, 98, 220*n*; resistance to 160, 168–9; and toxic waste disposal 218–19*n*, *see also* GATT; MAI; NAFTA; WTO
investment: deregulation of 101, *see also* MAI
Iran 49, 50, 197*n*
Iraq: oil supplies 34, 49; US threat of war against xv, 50
Ireland: education spending 91; pensions 75; welfare reforms 81, 86
Islam xx, 8, 173*n*; economics 167; and terrorism xv, 175–6*n*
isolation, personal 28–9
isolationism **142**, 169–70
Israel xvi, 173*n*
Italy: air pollution 184*n*, 189–90*n*; education spending 88, 91; healthcare 71, 72, 73; income inequality 78; public transport 23; welfare reforms 75, 86; welfare spending 207*n*
Ivany, George 218*n*

Jacobzone, S. (*et al.*) 208*n*
Japan 78; healthcare 70, 72; pensions 75, 76
Johnson, D. 201*n*
Jospin, Lionel, French Premier 13, 134–5, 178*n*; and third way 98, 99
Journal of the American Medical Association (*JAMA*) 70
Judaism xx, 162, 167; interdiction of homosexuality 230*n*
judgment 162–3
Judt, Tony 219*n*
just measure, concept of 164

Kamarck, Elaine and William Galston 219*n*
Karliner, Joshua 176*n*
Kazakhstan 49–50
Keeling, C.D. 199*n*
Kelsey, Jane 209*n*
Keynes, John Maynard 97
Khor, Michael 177*n*
Kilborn, Peter T. 211*n*
Korea, South 93; healthcare 73; pensions 75, 76
Koren, Hillel S. 186*n*
Kroll-Smith, Steve and H. Hugh Floyd 203*n*, 206*n*
Kropotkin, Peter 178*n*
Kyoto Protocols: emissions control 4; importance of xvii–xix, 161, 167; US rejection of xviii–xix, 34, *see also* environmental concerns

labor: abstract 116, 117–18, 229–30*nn*; cheap 104; concrete 117, 118, 224*n*; effect of globalization on 98; migrant (guest workers) 104; mobility **141**; reproduction costs 12, 103, 146; rights based in 221*n*; specialized division of 155; unskilled and semiskilled 6; as variable capital 109–10, 115, *see also* energy
labor costs: employers' 75; and inflation 142
labor, human 20–1, 123; cheaper than technology 125; speed of 133–4, 143
labor mobility 103–4, 148; historical context 105–8
labor standards 157; deregulation of 20; and international trade agreements 46–7
labor theory of value 12, 114–19, 229–31*nn*; reworking of 14, 120–1, 122–9
labor-power 105; distinct from labor 223–4*n*; as energy 120–1, 122–3, 136; and profit 119–20, 125–6; pushed to limits 146–7
labor-time: abstract 116, 118, 136, 138, 224–5*n*; socially necessary 118–19
Labour Party, traditional internationalism 102
Lacey, Richard 205*n*
Laclau, Ernesto 176*n*
Lafontaine, Oscar 158
land concentration 140, **141**
Landau, Gustav 178*n*
Lang, Tim and Colin Hines 191*n*, 192*n*, 193*n*, 220*n*, 227*n*
language: of prime directive 172; of third way 99–100, 216*n*
Latin America 9
Laurance, Jeremy 184*n*
lead, pollution 201*n*
Leggett, Jeremy 200*n*
Lehman, Karen and Al Krebs 193*n*, 205*n*
Lenin, V.I. xvi
Leonard, Ned 227*n*
leukemia 37; childhood 188*n*
Levelers movement (seventeenth century) 151
life: capitalism's attack on 167–8; enjoyment of 35; right to 168

life expectancy 147, 148
Lindberg, Roy A. 222*n*
Lipset, Seymour Martin 228*n*
localism: Gandhi's advocacy of 152–6; need to
    return to 13–15, 166; as real third way 158
Locke, John 223*n*; on labor 114–15
London: air pollution 189*n*; car travel in 25
Longworth, Richard C. 219*n*
Los Angeles, smog 37, 189*n*
Lutzenberger, Jose 17, 179*n*
Luxemburg, Rosa xvi
Lyall, Sarah 218*n*
Lyons, Kathleen and Darryle Lynette
    Figueroa 217*n*
Lyons, Kristin 182*n*, 205*n*

MAI (Multilateral Agreement on
    Investment) 45–7, 126, 158, 159,
    195–6*nn*; Most Favoured Nation status
    195*n*, 196*n*; performance requirements
    195*nn*; resistance to 160
Mander, Jerry and Edward Goldsmith 185*n*,
    192*n*, 193*n*, 197*n*, 205*n*
Mann, Eric 188*n*
Manton, Kenneth G., Larry Corder and Eric
    Stallard 208*n*
Marland, G. (*et al.*) 199*n*
Martens, W.J.M. 198*n*
Martinez, Elizabeth 214*n*
Marx, Karl 205*n*, 225*nn*, 228*n*, 231*n*; analysis
    of capital 11–12, 109–10, 143; labor
    theory of value 12, 114–19, 120–1, 224*n*;
    materialism 231*n*; profit 119–20;
    scientific socialism 152–3; and surplus-
    value 143–4, 145; value of labor-power
    223–4*n*; on value and price 135–6; view of
    labor-power 105, 119, 146, 178*n*
Marxism, centralization as solution 14
Maslen, Geoffrey 218*n*
materialism 118, 231*n*
mechanization 39, 130–1
Medina, S. (*et al.*) 187*n*
men: absent 106–7; family responsibilities
    217*n*; as migrants 105, 106
Metalclad Corporation 48
methyl parathion (pesticide) 58
Mexico: healthcare 72; hypothetical
    revolution 170, 171; and NAFTA 48, 100;
    pensions 75; water pollution 202*n*
microinvestment 101, 159
microwave ovens 191*n*
middle classes: American 27; burden of
    taxation 10–11, 68–9; immiseration of
    127–8; specialization by 155
migration: from countryside 25; as form of
    slavery 21; interstate (US) 82; by men
    105, 106; and personal isolation 28; to
    urban areas 192*n*
money: interest on (usury) 140, **141**, 167; as
    time 227*n*; value of 135, *see also* price;
    value
Monsanto corporation 175*n*
Morris, William 178*n*
Mortensen, Lynn 200*n*

Most Favoured Nation status 195*n*, 196*n*
Mueller, Curt (*et al.*) 209*n*
multinational corporations: and agriculture
    63; and international trade agreements 46
Mumford, Lewis 178*n*
Murray, Dick 180*n*
Myers, K. 201*n*

NAFTA (North American Free Trade
    Agreement) 44, 101, 196–7*n*;
    environmental promises 47–8, 220*n*;
    increased freight transport 42; powers of
    45, 47–8, 96; resistance to 160, 220*n*
NATO xv
"natural capitalism" 4
natural disasters 190*n*
nature: contribution to value 115, 225*n*;
    human stewardship of 164; and Marx's
    materialism 118; neglected in Marx's
    analysis 11, 115, 178*n*; rhythms of 151–2;
    as source of all energy 111–12, 121,
    122–4, *see also* resources, natural
Neas, Lucas M. (*et al.*) 186*n*
Negri, Antonio and Michael Hardt 176*n*,
    177*n*
Netanyahu, Benjamin 175*n*
Netherlands: education spending 88, 91;
    healthcare 72; welfare reforms 81, 86
neurotoxins (MMT) 48, 196*n*
New Labour (UK) 100
new right governments 98, 169
New Zealand: education spending 91;
    healthcare 66, 72; pensions 75, 76;
    sickness benefits 76; unemployment
    benefits 80; welfare reforms 66, 81, 86,
    96, 209*n*
Nichols, Mark 204*n*
Nigeria 6, 177*nn*
nitrogen dioxide 188*n*, 189*n*
nitrogen oxides 36, 37, 40, 53, 199*n*
Norway: healthcare 73; income inequality 78;
    pensions 75; welfare reforms 81, 86;
    welfare spending 207*n*
nostalgia 156, 165
Nova, Scott 220*n*
nuclear power 38
Nussbaum, Martha Craven 179*n*, 183*n*

OECD 163–4; *Social and Health Policies*
    1998 report 69, 71, 86, 207*n*, *see also* MAI
oil: from Arab countries xvii, xix; role in
    global economy 4, 7; storage and water
    pollution 55, 200–1*n*; for transportation
    40
oil pipelines, control of (Central Asia) 4, 34,
    49–50, 197*n*
Olsen, Greg M. 207*n*
Onanism 230*n*
organochlorines 203*n*
organophosphates 56
overwork 19, 22, 179*n*; effect on health
    29–31; by women 181–2*n*
ozone: depletion of high-level 54–5, 200*n*;
    ground-level 36, 185–6*n*

packaging 227*n*; styrofoam 54–5
Pakistan 4, 197*n*
Parkin, Gene 223*n*
particulate matter, in air pollution 36,
  186–7*n*
patriarchal values 109, 165
Patterson, Ian 180*n*
PCBs (polychlorinated biphenyls) 57–8,
  196*n*
Pear, Robert 209*n*
pensions: as economic "drag" 103, 104;
  private 75, 215*n*; raised retirement age
  75–6, 210*n*; state cuts 74–5
pesticides 56–9, 61–2, *see also* DDT
Petras, John and Henry Veltmeyer 176*n*
petroleum 55
pig farms, pollution of water supplies 55–6,
  201*n*
Pine, B. Joseph 226*n*
Plumwood, Val 183*n*
Pokrodsky, Vladimir 148
Poland 86
political economy, classical 11, 115
politics: pragmatic 170, *see also* new right;
  social democracy; third way
pollution 3, 94; of air 34, 35–8, 42; air
  transport 22–3, 42; chemical 4, 56, 201*n*;
  from electricity generation 191*n*;
  electromagnetic 38; and natural disasters
  190*n*; personal vehicles 22–3, 40; of water
  55–6, *see also* disease; fossil-fuel
  emissions; illness
population: aging 70; excess 59
"portability" 148; of education standards
  220*n*; of pension rights 103, 104
Portugal: healthcare 72; pensions 75, 76
postmodernism 165
Poulantzas, Nikos 225*n*
poverty 7, 35; child 78, 87, 94;
  impoverishment of women 18, 95, 106,
  109, 168; in OECD countries 78, *see also*
  immiseration
Powell, Bill 206*n*
preference, and price 113
price 226–7*nn*; determination of 112–13;
  relation to trade 138; relationship to
  money 135; and value 113, 142–3
prime directive 163–5; and incentives to
  change course 165–8; in practice 168–72;
  principle of 163, 166
Pritchard, Richard 91
production: acceleration of 1, 19, 39, 151–2,
  153–4; centralization of 44, 153; local
  152–6; mechanized 39, 130–1; point of
  144; regional 158–9; speed of 15, 17–18,
  129–32, 151, 168–9, *see also* food
  production; household production;
  reproduction
productivity: academic 92–3; of agriculture
  61–2, 64–5; demand for 25–6
profit 94, 111–12; and cost of energy 130–1;
  dependence on speed 21, 129–32; in
  Marx 119–20; point of 143; and sources
  of energy 124–9; as surplus-value 115,

126; from Web enterprises 112, *see also*
  surplus-value
progress, moral 152
protectionism 102, 128, **142**
public/private partnerships 84
Puga, D. 179*n*

Quesnay, François 225*n*
Quinn, Bill 219*n*

race: and inequality 27; and welfare reforms
  (US) 82, 214*n*
radiation 38, 55, 200*n*
radicalism 18
railways, for freight 42, 193*n*
Rall, Ted 197*n*
Raloff, Janet 202*n*
Raquet, Michel, Greenpeace xix
Rashid, Ahmed 176*n*, 197*n*
Raynor, Thomas P. 175*n*
reappropriation 171
reason: God and xx; and religiosity 161–3;
  role of xvii, xx, 167, 172
redistribution 231*nn*
refrigeration, use of CFCs 54
regionalism, as real third way 158–9
regulation: need for 159, 163, 168, 178*n*, *see
  also* deregulation
religion: fundamentalist xvi, 9; resurgence of
  161–3; role in prime directive 167–8, 172;
  and universalism xv, xvi, 166, *see also*
  Christianity; Islam; Judaism
reproduction: cost of 116, 127, 128–9; costs
  of natural 121, 123–4, 125, 129; as
  economic "drag" 103–4, 148; human
  31–2, 87, 221*n*; of human labor 8, 12,
  103–4, 109–10, 146; of nature and natural
  resources 12, 154; prime directive
  principles for 164–5; real time of 151;
  social costs of 148–9; spatial/speed axis of
  129–30, 151; time allowed for 15–16, 125,
  136, 137, 151, 159
resources, natural: for biotechnology 204*n*;
  and environmental degradation 65;
  exported by South 177*n*; extraction rates
  5, 49–50, 128, 154; and global trade 5–6,
  46; local 43, 154, 159, 160; replenishment
  of 160; small businesses dependent on
  150; usage rates 176*n*, *see also* energy;
  nature; reproduction
Revelation, Book of 230–1*nn*; apocalyptic
  prophesies xix–xx, xxi, 161, 162–3, 174*n*
Revkin, Andrew C. 199*n*
Ricardo, David 11, 115, 224*n*
Riddell, Mary 210*n*
Rifkin, Jeremy 178*n*, 179*n*, 203*n*, 204*nn*,
  223*n*, 229*n*
Rifkin, Jeremy and Ted Howard 178*n*
rights, contractual 222*n*
Rio Grande River, pollution 202*n*
Robertson, Heather-Jane 88, 217*n*
Robson, Barbara 203*n*
Roosevelt, F.D. 97
Rosecrance, Richard 177*n*

Rowland, Christopher 163, 231*n*
Rubin, Lillian B. 221*n*
Rudolph, Fredrick B. and Larry V. McIntire 223*n*
Russell, Cheryl 181*n*
Russia, life expectancy 148

Samet, J. and M.J. Utell 188*n*
Samuelson, Robert 210*n*
Sapolsky, Robert 183*n*
Sassen, Saskia 181*n*
Saudi Arabia 50
scale, economies of 44
Scherer, Jennifer M. and Rita J. Simon 211*n*
Schmid, Randolph 198*n*, 200*n*
Schor, Juliet B. 19, 25, 179*n*, 181*n*, 183*n*
Schrag, Peter 217*n*
Schröder, Gerhard, German Chancellor 98
Schumacher, E.F. 14, 178*n*
Schwartz, Joel 186*n*
seas: effect of global warming on xviii, 52; pollution of 193*n*
Seattle, WTO demonstrations 2, 98, 166
seeds, high-yield 62
self-interest 87
Sen, Amartya and Martha Craven Nussbaum 179*n*
sewage, and water pollution 201–2*n*
sexuality, religious fundamentalist views on xvi, 162
Sherwin, Russell P. 188–9*n*
shipping 193*n*; decline in 40, 42, 43, 194*n*
Shiva, Vanda 177*n*, 204*n*
Shope, Robert E. 198*n*
sickness benefits 76
Skinner, Quentin 216*n*
slave labor 147
sleep, lack of 29
small businesses 101, 150–1, 155–6, 171; compared with big business 150, 155; effect of globalization on 98; in France 228*n*; potential for 159, 160, 229*n*; resentment of taxation 14, *see also* corporations
Smith, Adam 11, 115
Smith, Clive 224–5*n*
Smith, Wesley J. 211*n*
smog, Los Angeles 37
social consciousness 231*n*
social democracy: fosters globalization 8; and third way 96–7, 98, 99
social justice 16, 228*n*
social regulation, tacit 19
socialism: failure of 9, 14; scientific 152–3
society, obligations of 228*n*
soil, degradation of 62, 64–5
Soros, George 10, 12, 135, 178*n*, 207*n*, 220*n*, 226*n*
South Africa, Truth and Reconciliation Commission 166
South, the: air pollution in 193*n*; continued use of DDT 202*n*; exploitation of 108–9; and globalization 1, 7; impact of "Green Revolution" on 62–3; increased vehicle

use 40, 41; industry 177*n*; and international trade agreements 46, 48–50; and Islam xv, xvi; low wages 26; potential for sustainable economies 168–9
space: and time 11–13, 108–10, **141–2**; victory of (over time) 142–3, **142**
Spain 72, 76
specialization 139–40, **141**, 152, 154; by middlemen 155
species extinction 175*n*
speed: of acquisition 225*n*, 226*n*; of finance capital 134–5; of human labor 133–4; of production 15, 17–18, 130–2, 151, 168–9, 226*n*; as source of profit 21, 101, 129–30, 225*nn*; of trade 12–13, 134–5, *see also* acceleration
spiritual authority, need for 166–7
Staples, Robert 214*n*
Star Trek 163
states: domestic legislation over-ruled by international treaties 43–4, 45–6, 49, 96, 102–3; welfare provision 10, 12, 68, 96
Steinberg, Jacques 217*n*
Stolberg, Sheryl Gay 198*n*
Stone, Glenn Davis 175*n*
Strathern, Marilyn 92, 218*n*
stress 13, 22, 29; and commuting 24; effect on physical health 29–30, 146
subsidies 169; employment 215*n*
substitution, law of 121, 125–8
suburbanization 23–4
suicide, assisted 77, 211*nn*
sulfur dioxide 36, 188*n*, 189*n*
Summers, Lawrence H. 16–17, 179*n*
supply and demand 124–5, 136
surplus-value: absolute 144, 145–6; as measure of price 135–6; relative 144–5, 146; sources of 123, 125, *see also* profit
Sweden: business investment 68; healthcare 70, 71, 72; income inequality 78; pensions 75
Switzerland 76; air pollution 190*n*; education spending 88, 91; welfare spending 208*n*
synthesis 16
Syria 49

Tajikistan 49
Taliban 4, 31
Tangly, Laura 204*n*
taxation: burden shifted to middle classes 10–11, 68–9; to enforce localism 14, 169; to fund pensions 74; to fund welfare states 10, 12, 68; reforms 178*n*; tax credits 84–5
technology: as constant capital 120, 127; costs of 94, 119–20, 128; and energy 111–12, 123; irreversible 156–7; and labor-time 116–17, 119; medical 70, 76–7, 209*nn*, 211*n*; and profit 124, 128–9; reparative 4, 113–14, 223*n*; unnecessary 157
telecommunications: automated 133; employment in 79, 126, 211*n*; use of electricity 34, *see also* computers

terrorism: definitions of 1, 174–5*n*; Islamic 175–6*n*; threat against West 7, 50

terrorism, war on xv–xvi; and control of oil pipelines 4, 34

third way 96–7, 98–101; emphasis on productivity and efficiency 92, 219*n*; policy innovations 100; real 156–60; view of globalization 5, 9; withdrawal of welfare support 27, 79, 206*n*

Third World *see* South, the

time: abstract labor 116, 118–19; allowed for reproduction 15–16, 129–30, 148–9; as constraint on business 15; critical to profit 119, 128; human 9; natural 128, 129, 139–40, 168; sacrificed for space 9–10, 125–6, 128; and space 11–13, 108–10, **141–2**; and speed of trade 12–13, 140–1; work time 21, 25–6

tobacco 36

Tocqueville, Alexis de 25, 181*n*

Tolstoy, Leo 178*n*

toxic waste: pollution of water 55; reparative technology 223*n*

toxic waste disposal 17, 48, 218–19*n*

trade: aristocratic disdain for 227*n*; deregulation 101, 148; international 41–4, 194*n*; manufactured goods 6; nontariff barriers 203*n*; over distance **141**, 152, 227*n*; in primary products 5; and profit 138; relation to price 139; and reproduction time 159; speed of 12–13, 134–5; and transportation 177*n*, *see also* free trade; GATT; international trade agreements; NAFTA; WTO

training 80

transformation, in labor theory of value 225*n*, 227*n*

transport: commercial 40–1, 42–4; commercial vehicles 191*nn*; personal vehicles 22–3, 40, 41, 180*n*, 191*n*; public 23, 24–5; rapid xix, 3–4; road accidents 181*n*; use of fossil fuels 3–4, 6–7, 34, 51

transportation: expanding networks of 140, 150, 152; and international trade 41–4, 191–2*n*; as source of profit 129, 177*n*

travel: commuting 23, 24–5; increased time spent in 21; individual 22–3

"trickle-down" effect 8, 68–9, 96–7; of global economics 97–8, 222*n*

tuberculosis, resurgence of 197–8*n*

Tudge, Colin 204*n*

Turkey 72, 197*n*

Turkmenistan 4, 49

Uchitelle, Louis 181*n*

UK: air quality 35; All Work Test for sickness benefits 76; asthma 184–5*n*; education spending 88, 89, 91; healthcare 66, 67, 70, 73; National Health Service 73, 210*n*; pensions 75, 76; public housing 86; resurgence of TB 197*n*; unemployment benefits 80, 83; Welfare Reform and Pensions Act (1998) 81,

83–4, 212*n*; welfare spending 207*n*; Working Families' Tax Credit (WFTC) 84–5

ultraviolet radiation 55, 200*n*

unemployment 27, 79, 80; and assumption of mobility 107; and training and education 80; US 27, 82–3, 107

unemployment insurance 79–80, 83

Unger, Umberto and Cornel West 179*n*

United Nations: ban on DDT 57; Center for International Trade Law (UNCITRAL) 48; Codex Alimentarius 57; Research Institute for Social Development 75; role in regulation 178*n*; UNCTED as alternative to WTO 101

universities 90–2; research audits 92–3

Unocal project 4, 176*n*

urbanization 35, 140

US xxi, 2, 212–13*n*; air quality 35; Balanced Budget Act (1997) 213*n*; child-free movement 31, 227–8*n*; chronic illness in 70; Democratic Leadership Council (DLC) 99, 100; deregulation in 20, 30; and energy costs 173–4*n*; fossil-fuel emissions xvii, xviii, xxi, 23; GM crops in 60; healthcare 71, 73, 74; immigrants 213–14*nn*; imprisonment rate 214–15*nn*; income inequality 27, 78; increased incidence of stress 30; isolationism 169–70; moralism towards women 82, 83, 84, 215–16*n*; National Education Association 88; need for spiritual authority 166–7; New Deal (1935) 81, 97, 212*n*, 231*n*; pensions 75, 76; Personal Responsibility and Work Opportunity Reconciliation Act (1996) (Workfare) 80–3, 85, 213*n*; rejection of Kyoto Protocol xviii–xix, 34; Temporary Assistance to Needy Families 213*n*; unemployment 27, 80, 82–3; and war against Iraq xv, xix, 18; water pollution 55; welfare spending cuts 66, 80, 86, 93–4, 207*n*; women in workforce 25–6, *see also* Bush; Clinton; NAFTA

US Department of Energy, Carbon Dioxide Information Analysis Center (CDIAC) 53

US Environmental Protection Agency (EPA) 57, 58

US Food and Drug Administration (FDA) 57, 204–5*n*

use-value 117–18, 123–5, 137, 224*n*

usury 140, **141**, 167

Uzbekistan 49

value: dependent on natural energy 111, 125; labor as source of 114; Locke's theory 223*n*; of money 135; and price 113, 142–3, 226–7*n*; of reparative technology 113–14, *see also* exchange-value; labor theory of value; surplus-value; use-value

Verhovek, S. 196*n*

Vinocur, John 178*n*

wages: fall in real 26–7, 146; family 147, 182*n*; reduced to pay for technology 120
Wal-Mart 219*n*
Wald, George 205*n*
Wallace, Lance 188*n*
war 9, 18; increased fossil-fuel emissions 5; US threat against Iraq xv, xix, 18, 50
water: increasing demand for 56; pollution 55–6, 200–1*nn*
water transport 42, 43
Watson, Robert T. 199*n*
wealth, distribution of 8, 156
welfare 7; individual responsibility for 67; reductions in 27, 66–7, 68–9, 93–4, 96; safety net 27, 83–4; social costs of 9, 67–8, 87, 94, 148, *see also* healthcare; pensions; taxation; unemployment
welfare reform 66–9, 78–9, 80–7, 109, 207–8*nn*; means-testing 86, 212*n*; moralist assumptions 85; public/private partnerships 84; in third way policies 100, 206*n*
welfare state 97, **142**, 146; cost inefficiency 104; and economic productivity 206–7*n*
WHO (World Health Organization) 35; and air pollution 187*n*; and use of DDT 57
Wilford, John Noble 197*n*
Wilkinson, Alec 226*n*
Williams, Deborah 180*n*
Wilson, William Julius 24, 180*n*
Winston, Robert, Lord 73, 210*n*
Witmer, Elizabeth 206*n*
Wolff, Mary S. and Ainsley Weston 203*n*
women: childcare by grandmothers 83, 84; domestic (unpaid) work 147, 181–2*nn*; as economic actors (historical) 105–6, 160; impoverishment 106, 109, 168, 183*n*; lower earnings 26, 32; moralist

assumptions about 83, 84, 85, 106–7; patriarchal relationship 109, 165; in prison 83, 215*n*; religious fundamentalist views on xvi, 8; reproductive role 221*n*; in workforce 181*n*, 182*n*; workforce participation 25–6, 27–8, *see also* women as mothers; women as single mothers
women as mothers 173*n*, 221*nn*; economic position of xvii, 31, 107–8, 109; impoverishment of 18, 95; potential of 157, 160; rights in natural law 222*n*
women as single mothers 82, 107, 108, 216*nn*; as economic "drag" 104, 148; rights to childcare 85; welfare for 27, 67, 79, 94–5
women's movements: feminism 32; right-wing 31–2
work: increased time in 21, 25–6, 181–2*n*; overwork 19, 22, 29–31, 179*n*
World Bank, research on asthma 37
World Resources Institute 53, 193*n*
World Trade Center attacks 1–2
World Wide Web, profits from 112, 113
WTO (World Trade Organization) 44, 45–6, 101; Seattle demonstrations 2, 98, 166; state-to-state dispute settlement 196*n*, *see also* General Agreement on Tariffs and Trade (GATT)

Yang, C.Y. (*et al.*) 188*n*
Yemen, life expectancy 147
Yin, Song-Nain (*et al.*) 188*n*
Younkman, David 201*n*

Zahm, Sheila Hoar and Susan S. Devesa 188*n*, 200*n*
Zinser, S. 201*n*, 202*n*
Zionism xx